EVANSTON PUBLIC LIBRARY

P9-BZS-674

EVANSTON
PUBLIC LIBRARY
IN MEMORY OF
ELEANOR ELLIS PERKINS
1969

398.45 Brigg.K

Briggs, Katharine Mary.

The fairies in English
tradition and
[1967]

SEP 1 4 1978

OCT 1 1980

JUL 23 1979

MAR 1 4 1981

MAR 28 '81

APR 1 1982

JUN 22 1983

SEP 27 1983

DATE DUE

APR 9 - 2002	
JAN 9 - 2003	
JAN 0 4 2004	
APR 0 5 2007	

DEMCO, INC. 38-2931

SEP 14 1918

THE FAIRIES IN ENGLISH TRADITION
AND LITERATURE

1 William Blake's illustration to Milton's L'Allegro.
We have here the drudging goblin, the woman pinched
and pulled by fairies and the Will o' the Wisp

THE FAIRIES

IN ENGLISH TRADITION
AND LITERATURE

K. M. BRIGGS

EVANSTON PUBLIC LIBRARY
1703 ORRINGTON AVENUE
EVANSTON, ILLINOIS 60201

The University of Chicago Press

Library of Congress Catalog Card Number 67–24298
The University of Chicago Press, Chicago
Routledge and Kegan Paul Ltd, London
Published 1967
© K. M. Briggs 1967

Printed in Great Britain

CONTENTS

v

CONTENTS

ILLUSTRATIONS

ACKNOWLEDGEMENTS

I HAVE to thank a great many people for their kind advice, help and co-operation in the production of this book. From some collectors and percipients I have received first-hand and hitherto unpublished accounts of fairy appearances. R. L. Tongue has contributed many from her collection, Miss Alice Stuart of Edinburgh has given me unpublished anecdotes and stories from Barra, Mrs Mona Smith has allowed me to use the tale of her father's vision of fairies in Skye, Mrs Robertson, the folk singer, has told me the story of her grandmother's fairy. Others who did not wish to be mentioned by name have told me of fairy experiences. T. F. G. Paterson of Armagh County Museum gave me free use of his material, so did Mr Michael Murphy, Sam Hanna Bell of the Belfast BBC, and Mrs Harris and other officials of the Ulster Folk Museum. I have very specially to thank Mr Megaw and all his team at the School of Scottish Studies. All of their materials have been made available to me, and I have particular cause of gratitude to Dr Hamish Henderson for allowing me the run of all his magnificent wealth of recordings. The School of Scottish Studies has been a home from home to me. I have received equal hospitality and kindness from the Irish Folk Commission in Dublin, and have specially to thank Professor O'Duilearga, Mr Sean O'Suilleabhain and Dr Thomas Wall for their help. Mr Cubbon and other members of the staff of the Manx Museum were most helpful to me when I was exploring Manx fairylore, and so were Miss Mona Douglas and Miss Dora Broome. The late W. W. Gill made his wealth of material available to me, and I have to thank his executors of Lloyd's Bank in Liverpool for permission to avail myself of his kindness. Mrs Hélène Leather has allowed me to make lavish use of E. M. Leather's excellent book, *Herefordshire Folklore*; Mr Alban Atkins has showed me and allowed me to reproduce 'The Fairies are Out', by his grandfather James Nasmyth. I am grateful to Mr John Adlard and Dr Gert Schiff for giving me offprints of their works and allowing me to make use of them. As usual I am much indebted to Miss Cynthia Borough of the Bodleian Library for her diligence in hunting out books for me. I have to thank Mrs Nash-Williams for her help with proof-reading.

I must also make the following acknowledgements for leave to publish quotations:

Mr Brian Branston for permission to quote from *The Lost Gods of England*; Messrs Jonathan Cape, for quotations from Laurence Housman's *Moonshine and Clover*; the Clarendon Press, Oxford, for permission to quote *Celtic Folk-Lore* by John Rhys; Messrs Eyre and Spottiswoode, for a quotation from *The Little Grey Men* by B.B.; Messrs John Farquarson Ltd for quotations from *Nine Unlikely Tales for Children* by E. Nesbit; The editor of *Folk-Lore* for quotations from that Journal; Messrs Macmillan and Mrs Bambridge for permission to use a quotation from *Puck of Pook's Hill* by Rudyard Kipling, as also to Messrs Doubleday and Co. for extending that permission to the U.S.A.; the Trustees of the National Gallery of Scotland for the reproduction of Paton's two pictures, 'The Quarrel of Oberon and Titania' and 'The Reconciliation of Oberon and Titania'; the David Higham Associates for quotations from *The Little Bookroom* by Eleanor Farjeon; Mr E. M. Teare for permission to quote from the works of Sophia Morrison; the Pierrepoint Morgan Library for the reproduction of 'The Goblih' by William Blake; the Theosophical Publishing Company Ltd for leave to quote from *Fairies at Work and Play* by Geoffrey Hodson: the Literary Trustees of Walter de la Mare for the use of quotations from *Broomsticks*; and Professor Tolkien for the use of a quotation from *The Hobbit*.

PREFACE

THIS book is a continuation of *The Anatomy of Puck*, which dealt with the fairy beliefs used by Shakespeare, his contemporaries and his immediate successors. In the course of working on it I found so many accounts of the fairies that belonged to later times that it seemed to me worth pursuing the subject and examining the survival of fairy beliefs and the various fashions in the literary treatment of fairies, from Shakespeare's time to the present day.

Literary fashions change, but on the whole the fairy beliefs have remained pretty constant. As in my earlier books, I have had no special axe to grind. This is not an attempt to prove that fairies are real. My intention has been to report objectively what people believed themselves to have seen. My standard has been truth to tradition rather than truth to fact, and I have discussed the fairy standards and practices seriously, as one discusses characters in a good book; my credence has been given rather to aesthetic truth than to fact. As far as my personal belief goes the most I can say is that I am agnostic on the subject. For the sake of fairness, however, I have included in the Appendix an account of the Cottingley Fairies, whose photographs have never been proved to be fraudulent, though they fail to command aesthetic credence.

K. M. BRIGGS

Part One

THE FAIRY PEOPLES

One

HISTORIC SURVEY

THE famous pronouncement of Friar Bacon's Brazen Head—
'Time is, Time was, Time is past'—might well be taken to
apply to English fairy beliefs, which from Chaucer's time onwards have been supposed to belong to the last generation and
to be lost to the present one. The strange thing is that rare,
tenuous and fragile as it is, the tradition is still there, and lingers
on from generation to generation substantially unchanged.
Every now and then poets and writers draw on the tradition,
and make out of it something suitable to the spirit of their age.
Sometimes this passes back into tradition, and perhaps alters it
a little, it may be less than the critics and folklorists contend.
For instance, there is a school of thought that believes that we
owe the race of tiny English fairies to the literary fancies of
Shakespeare and his contemporaries. This is not so, for some of
our earliest fairies, the Portunes, are said by Gervase of Tilbury
to be only half an inch in height. The mentions of fairies in
medieval manuscripts are, indeed, sparse, but they cover most
of the types that we shall come across later. We have the child-
sized fairies whose kingdom Elidor visited, the fairy bride of
human size and more than human beauty, the wild hunt, the
miraculous passage of time in Fairyland, the fairy who needs
a human midwife and is invisible except by the help of a magic
ointment, the changeling, the misleading night fairy, the bogey-
beast and the Love-Talker or Incubus. And we have giants
and dragons as well. Even down to the last generation, before the

3

First World War, all of these types were still to be found, and I have little doubt that most of them could be found now if the secrecy which the fairies enjoin did not still bind the tongues of the scattered and obscure people who believe in them.

And yet all this talk of the residual nature of the fairy beliefs is true enough, though the flourishing time of fairy belief must be pushed back to the earliest historic times on these Islands, almost to the verge of pre-history.

Kipling's Puck calls the lost heathen gods who took their place among the fairy people 'the old things', and there is little doubt that they can claim their part in the building of the fairy tradition as well as the half-deified spirits of the dead and the spirits of woods and wells and vegetation.

The earliest written mentions of fairies of any kind in England occur in the Anglo-Saxon charms against elf-shot, but the fairy ladies of the medieval romances of the thirteenth, fourteenth and fifteenth centuries may well have an origin as old. Morgan le Fay or Fata Morgana and her kind probably show a mingling of Celtic and classical tradition, or perhaps stem from beliefs older than either. In the later Romances it is clear that most of the fairy ladies belong to the human race, and owe their great powers to their knowledge of magic. Nimue, the Lady of the Lake, in *Lancelot du Lac*, the thirteenth-century Prose Romance, lived in a wooded country covered by a magical cloud which gave it the appearance of a lake. The unknown author of this romance was a determined euhemeriser. When he introduces the Lake he calls it The Lake of Diana, and explains: 'Now Diana was queen of Sicily, and she reigned in the time of Virgil, the great author, and the foolish heathen folk held her for a goddess. And there was no lady in the world that more loved woodland pleasures, and every day she went to the chase, and the foolish heathen folk called her the goddess of the woods.'[1]

The fairies are treated to a similar rationalization.

Now the story saith that the Damsel that carried Lancelot into the Lake was a fay. In those days all maidens that knew enchantments or charms were called fays, and there were many of them at this time, and more in Great Britain than in other lands.

[1] *Sir Lancelot of the Lake*. A French Prose Romance of the Thirteenth Century. Translated by Lucy Allen Paton (London, 1929), p. 66.

4

They knew, as the story saith, the virtue of herbs and of stones and of charms, whereby they might be kept in plenty and in the great wealth that they possessed. . . . The Lady that nourished him abided only in woods and in forests that were vast and dense, and the lake whereinto she sprang with the child was naught but enchantment, and it was in the plain at the foot of a hill that was lower than that whereon King Ban had died. In the part where the lake seemed widest and deepest the Lady had many fair and noble dwellings, and in the plain below there flowed a little stream, that abounded in fish. And her abode was so hidden that none might find it, for the semblance of the lake covered it so that it might not be seen.[1]

This was the line taken in the later romances, but in *Lanzelet*, the German translation of the twelfth-century poem, there is no doubt at all that Lancelot was brought up in Fairyland.

A lady bore the child away, a wise fairy of the sea, a queen better than any in all the world to-day. In her realm she had ten thousand maidens, whereof none knew man or man's array. They wore shifts and kirtles of samite and of silk. I will not deny it, but I say not that it is sooth, the Lady's land bloomed throughout the year as it were mid-May, and her domain was fair and broad and long, and full of joy were its borders. The mountain whereon the mighty castle stood was of crystal, round as a ball. No stranger guest and no king's host was feared therein. All round about it lay the sea and a wall so strong that never a man might be bold enough to deem that he could avail aught against it, and albeit there was a gate, it was of hardest adamant. There within they bided, knowing no fear. He that wrought the castle adorned it cunningly. Without and within it was of gold, like a star. Within its moat naught grew old, or even after a hundred years was less fair.[2]

The same view of the fairies is taken by the twelfth- and thirteenth-century chroniclers. Walter Map (born about 1140) is one of the earliest. His story of *Wild Edric*, whose ghostly train was to be seen even to the nineteenth century, is one of the best-known of his tales, in which the fairy wife, who still survives in modern Welsh folklore, is described in detail.[3] The

---

[1] *Sir Lancelot of the Lake*, pp. 72–3.
[2] Ibid., *Lanzelet*, pp. 7–8.
[3] Walter Map, *De Nugis Curialium*. Translated by F. Tupper and M. B. Ogle (London, 1924), pp. 94–5.

Fairy Wife of Brecknock Mere is still closer to modern tradition.[1] Map has a Melusine tale of a demon wife, and one of a wife rescued from the troop of the dead, which is very like later rescues from Fairyland.[2] It is from Walter Map too that we hear of the Herlething, the Band of Herla seen on the borders of Hereford and Wales in the first year of the reign of King Henry II.[3] Map was a Hereford man, but a Norman, and some of his tales come from Brittany or Normandy, as, for instance, that of Henno cum Dentibus of Normandy who married a demon wife.[4]

Map's friend, Geoffrey of Monmouth, gave us the first romantic version of the Arthurian legend, for Arthur had been little more than a name in the earlier chronicles. Giraldus Cambrensis, another contemporary, introduces us to a subterranean fairyland, without sun, moon or stars, inhabited by small people, fair-haired and beautiful, with horses and greyhounds in the same proportion. They ate neither fish nor flesh but milk-sops flavoured with saffron. They were good people, though without any ordinances of religion, very honourable and truthful. The child Elidor, who had been led into this fairyland, came and went freely among them, and would have continued to do so, but that, urged by his mother, he stole a golden ball from the King's son. On the way home with it he was tripped up by two of the little fairies and the ball taken from him. He could never again find his way into their realm.[5] The tale of *Gitto Bach* is a later, somewhat similar tale of a child's visits to Fairyland.[6] In the seventeenth century we have Bovet's *Fairy Boy of Leith*, and at about the same time the Kirk Session in Borgue records the questioning of the Boy of Borgue, who claimed intercourse with the fairies. Giraldus Cambrensis has also two poltergeist or boggart stories.

Gervase of Tilbury, who flourished about 1211, set down a remarkable amount of folklore material in Part III of *Otia Imperialia*.[7] As Chancellor of the Holy Roman Empire he was a

---

[1] Walter Map, ed. cit., p. 91.
[2] Ibid., p. 97.   [3] Ibid., p. 223.   [4] Ibid., pp. 218–20.
[5] Giraldus Cambrensis, *The Itinerary through Wales* (Bohn's Antiquarian Library), pp. 390–1.
[6] T. Keightley, *Fairy Mythology* (London, 1900, 1st edition 1850), pp. 416–17.
[7] *Gervase of Tilbury, MS Cotton Vespasian E IV*, ed. by F. Liebrecht (Hanover, 1826).

6

travelled man, and his tales came from various sources. He tells us several things about the Dracae, water spirits of the Rhone Valley, fairies who used to entice women away by floating in the form of golden cups down the streams where they were washing.[1] The first fairy midwife story, complete with the ointment, is told of them,[2] and also the earliest version of the Migratory Legends 4050, 'The Hour Has Come but not the Man', is told of the Dracae.[3] The Grant is an English Goblin, who changes his shape like a Picktree Brag or a Hedley Kow.[4] The Portunes—called Portunes in England but Neptunes in France—were very early tiny fairies, who, like the later ones, visited houses at night and did their cooking at human hearths.[5] The Portunes, rather prosaically, ate frogs. The legend of the drinking horn stolen from the fairies, which is used in the sixteenth century play, *The Wisdom of Dr. Dodypol*, and of which a version is told by Aubrey, is also told by Gervase of Tilbury.[6]

Some interesting matter, too, is to be found in the thirteenth-century chronicle of Ralph of Coggeshall. He tells us about a merman—Walter Map also gives an account of Nicholas Pipe, a merman[7]—but his two most interesting tales are those of the fantastic spirit of Malekin and of the Green Children.

Malekin claimed to be a human changeling stolen from her mother in the cornfield, but she had been invested with the fairy nature, for she was invisible except when she chose to show herself; then she appeared like a tiny child wearing a white tunic. She consumed food left out for her like a Brownie, and talked to the servants in broad Suffolk but to the chaplain in Latin. The end of her seven years of captivity was approaching, and at the end of another seven years she would have an opportunity to regain her human form. It is unusual to find tales of female changelings, and it is interesting to have this early account of the changeling traffic from the fairy point of view.[8]

The other tale, that of the Green Children, is more unusual still, and has a curiously convincing and detailed air. It is an account of two children who were captured near Wolfpits in

---

[1] *Gervase of Tilbury*, ed. cit., p. 38.
[2] Ibid., p. 39.   [3] Ibid., p. 39.   [4] Ibid., p. 30.   [5] Ibid., p. 29.
[6] Ibid., pp. 28–9.   [7] Walter Map, ed. cit., p. 232.
[8] *Ralph of Coggeshall*, Rolls Series 66, ed. by Joseph Stephenson, pp. 120–1.

Suffolk. They were of a pale greenish colour, they seemed stupefied and frightened and did not understand what was said to them. They refused all food at first, and finally ate broad beans with great eagerness. They gradually learnt to eat mortal food; the boy pined and died, but the girl survived, lost her green colour and learnt to talk. According to her account they lived in an underground country, where there was neither sun nor moon but a soft light like twilight. One day they entered a cavern and heard a soft sound like distant bells, which they followed until they emerged into the full light of day. The sunlight so stupefied them that they fell to the ground and were caught. Both children were baptized, and the girl grew up and married a local man, but she was always rather free and wanton in her behaviour.[1] William of Newburgh confirms the account, and adds to it that the girl called the country St. Martin's Land, and said that the people in it were Christians.[2] It is perhaps only a coincidence, but beans are traditionally the food of the dead, and the witches' imps were often called Martins or Martinets.

A fairy mound and the theft of a fairy drinking horn are to be found in William of Newburgh's Chronicle as well as in Gervase of Tilbury, but here the theft is justified, for the cup was a poisoned one.[3] Variants of this tale go down to modern times, but sometimes the poisoned cup is offered by a witch.

As I have said, these fairy references in the early chronicles contain many beliefs that crop up in oral tradition through the centuries. After their time the witch scare began to overcloud Europe and it is possible that it is under its influence, and also because of the growing practice of magic and alchemy, that the supernatural people became human enchantresses. Keightley suggests that the Korrigans of Brittany may have derived from that priesthood of women on an Island in the Seine which is mentioned by Pomponius Mela; and that the fairy ladies in their turn may derive from the Korrigans.[4] At any rate it is rather paradoxical that the word 'fairy' now generally used to describe non-human and non-angelic

[1] *Ralph of Coggeshall*, ed. cit., pp. 66, 120–1.
[2] *Guilielmi Neubrigensis Historia* (Oxon., 1719), Lib. I, c. 27, pp. 90–3.
[3] Ibid., Bk. I, cap 28, pp. 95–6.
[4] T. Keightley, ed. cit., p. 431.

creatures, should have been first used about the illusions con-
jured up by these human enchantresses.

In some of the romances there are glimpses of other meanings.
In the delightful fifteenth-century *Orfeo*,[1] for instance, Fairyland
is the Kingdom of the dead. Marie de France's thirteenth-
century *Sir Lanval* is a true fairy story, dressed as a romance.
The fairy lady forbids Lanval, in the real fairy style, to speak
of her. When he does so all his fairy wealth vanishes and he is
left helpless under Queen Guinevere's accusation. But in the end
the fairy relents and carries him to Avalon, from which he can
come one day in every year to joust with a challenger.[2] The
prohibition and the vanishing bride is recurrent in folk tradition. The fifteenth-century romance of Thomas of Ercildoune,
though inferior to the ballad, is interesting in its conception of
Fairyland, with the Fairy Queen who loses her beauty when a
human man has intercourse with her, though she regains it
later, and with the teind to Hell which the fairies must pay
and which plays such a part in the later Scottish folk tradition.
Two traditions seem to mingle in this poem—the first of
Fairyland as the country of the dead, and the second of the
fairies as fallen angels, not quite devils and yet subject to
Satan.[3]

The fifteenth-century *Huon of Bordeaux* is principally remarkable as an early introduction to Oberon, the Fairy King.
He is the size of a three-year-old child, but in the romance this
is supposed to be not his natural size but the consequence of a
fairy curse.[4] In fact the malevolent fairy of Motif F316 makes
an early appearance here. Even more interesting is the dual and
conflicting morality of the tale. Sir Huon is told by a hermit
that he must by no means answer if he is accosted by King
Oberon; yet when he breaks the prohibition Oberon proves
friendly and good comes of it. In the end, Sir Huon, a mortal
man, is promoted to the throne of Fairyland. There seems to be
no anti-clerical bias in this; the author has that double attitude

---

[1] W. C. Hazlitt. *The Romance of King Orfeo. Fairy Tales, Legends and Romances
Illustrating Shakespeare* (London, 1875), pp. 82–100.

[2] *Lanval, Poësies de Marie de France*, ed. by B. de Roquefort (Paris, 1920), I, pp.
200–50.

[3] W. Carew Hazlitt, ed. cit., pp. 101–22.

[4] *The Boke of Duke Huon of Bordeux, done into English by Sir John Bourchier, Lord
Berners* (Early English Text Society, 1883–7), Vol. I, p. 73.

9

towards Christianity and the fairy world that is still to be found among the peasantry of Ireland.

At the Reformation, when the ordinary man was as much occupied by theology as the specialist, the fairies and devils drew closer together. This fusion has been helped by the identification made by the Early Christian Fathers of the pagan gods with devils, of which Milton makes such effective use in *Paradise Lost*. The great gods of the heathens were generally regarded as devils rather than as fumbling attempts to find God. Where the lesser deities, nymphs, fauns, satyrs and so on, had descended into being fairies they would naturally also be considered devils. If some of them, however, were supposed to derive from ancestral spirits or ghosts the attitude towards them would differ with the faith of the believer. The Protestant theologians, anxious to repudiate the notion of Purgatory, laid it down as a fundamental truth that the dead could not walk. The good were in Heaven and the bad in Hell, and there was no return from either. An illustration of this can be seen in the English translation of Pierre de Loyer's *A Treatise of Spectres or Straunge Sights, Visions and Apparitions appearing sensibly unto Men* (1605). On page 7 we find:

> Now these *Lares* were domestical or household gods; because (as Seruius said) in olde times the dead bodies were usually enterred and buried in their houses: and therefore those *Lares* (that is to say) the soules of the dead, were adored and worshipped euery one particularly in that house, where their bodies were enterred.

De Loyer, however, describes these spirits as devils, for, later in the same passage, speaking of the reasons suggested by Plutarch for the Lares' dog-skins, he says:

> But hee might have added this rather (if hee had beene a Christian) That as Dogges are naturally enuious: So these *Lares* or Diuels of this kinde, do beare enuy and malice to mankinde. Notwithstanding *Festus* (whome we do gladly alledge) seemeth to affirme; That these *Lares* are sometime good: for he names them sometime *Praestites* because they were thought to make all things safe, and to keepe and preserue all thinges carefully: and sometimes *Hostilios*: for that they were supposed to driue away enemies. But howsoeuer it bee, certaine it is they were no other then verie Diuels; who if they seemed sometimes to ayde and helpe men, and

10

to doe them some good: yet the same was to the intent they might afterwardes worke them the more and greater harme and damage, as well inwardly in their Soules and consciences as outwardly in their bodies and goods.

This tendency was strong among the Puritan writers in England in the sixteenth and seventeenth centuries. For instance, the Brownie or Hobgoblin was a spirit very like the Roman Lar. Like the Lar he was almost invariably singular, devoted to the service of the house, hairy or clad in rags and ready to receive offerings of meal or milk. Occasionally one is described as a shining boy. In several stories—such as *The Cauld Lad of Hilton* and Patrick Kennedy's *Pooka of Kildare*[1]— they are said to be ghosts of servants who worked in the house. In Puritan times, however, hobgoblins, imps and devils are all lumped together. Rowland called Robin Goodfellow 'A good fellow devill, So called in kindnes, cause he did no evill',[2] and Warner in his *Albion's England*[3] denies that he did any good at all, and says that he got the housewives up in their sleep to do the work for which he got the credit.

Even among the Puritans, however, a strand of belief persisted in the fairies as beings of a middle order between men and angels, or as 'spiritual animals'. This controversy, and the general fairy beliefs among Shakespeare's contemporaries I have discussed in an earlier book, *The Anatomy of Puck*. In this present book I am trying to trace the traditional fairy beliefs in these Islands down to the present day, and to touch on the literary use and abuse of them. The fairy tradition was a good deal neglected in England in the eighteenth century; but Ireland, the Highlands and Wales continued to pour in material, and few literatures are as strong in fairy lore as English literature.

[1] Patrick Kennedy, *Legendary Fictions of the Irish Celts* (London, 1891, 1st ed. 1866), pp. 114–17.

[2] Samuel Rowland, *The Knave of Spades*, Hunterian Club no. 22 (1874), Booke 14, p. 40.

[3] W. Warner, *Albion's England* (1602), Chapter 21, p. 368.

11

Two

THE FAIRY REALMS

THE fairies of these Islands are of different sizes, habits, dispositions and kinds and they have their habitations in different places, but, great or small, benevolent or wicked, they most commonly lived underground. The Green Children of Ralph of Coggeshall came from St. Martin's Land, the twilight, subterranean land without great heat or cold. The Daoine ò Sidhe of Ireland, who are held to be the diminished gods of one of the earliest races of the Irish, live for the most part in the hollow hills. Evans Wentz, collecting fairy beliefs in Wales at the beginning of this century, found a tale of the parentage of Taliessin with a complete description of an underground Celtic fairyland.[1] The Highland fairies are to be seen at certain phases of the moon inside their hills, which are raised on pillars for the short time that their habitation is visible. According to Aubrey, a Wiltshire shepherd going on Hack Pen was led under it, and saw revelry and heard various kinds of music. The Oxfordshire fairies were last seen going into a hole near the King Stone of the Rollright Stones. Even when the fairies hold their revels outside and under the moon they are often supposed to come up from their permanent home underground.

Sometimes, however, the fairy palaces are out in the open, visible to those to whom the fairies wish to show them, though apt to vanish at any moment and to leave the guest exposed to

[1] Evans Wentz, *Fairy Faith in Celtic Countries* (Oxford, 1911),' Einion and Olwen', pp. 161–3.

12

the windy night. There was such a palace on the top of Glastonbury Tor, visited on one occasion by St. Collen, who held
wholeheartedly to the belief that fairies are devils. This is how
the story went.

St. Collen was a Celtic saint, who made himself a hermitage
at the foot of Glastonbury Tor. One day he heard two men
talking of the King of the Fairies, who had his palace near by.
St. Collen looked out of his cell and told them to be quiet, for
they were talking of devils. The men were greatly frightened,
and warned him that the King of the Fairies would not forgive
such an insult, and would surely send for him. And, sure enough,
a few days later a stranger came to the cell and begged St.
Collen to come with him to meet the King.

Three times St. Collen refused; but at last he consented to
come; but he took a flask of holy water with him, hidden under
his cloak.

The fairy palace stood at the top of the Tor, full of lights and
splendour and sweet music, and the King was seated at a rich
banquet, waited on by pages in scarlet and blue. He made much
of the saint, and begged him to partake of the food.

'I do not eat the leaves of a tree,' said St. Collen. A shudder
ran round the table; but the King said: 'And how do you like
my fair liveries of scarlet and blue?'

'Blue is for the eternal cold, and red is for the flames of
Hell whence you came,' said St. Collen, and he threw the holy
water over their heads. The lights and the music died; there
was no King, no Court, no Castle, nothing but the green turf on
top of Glastonbury Tor. This austere tale contradicts the
traditional belief in the value of politeness in dealing with
fairy people.[1]

In Man too the high hill-tops are thought of as suitable to the
fairies. W. W. Gill in *A Second Manx Scrapbook* gives this
description:

> The fairies were most frequently to be seen, heard and smelt
> ('a stale, sour smell') in the lonely upper parts of glens, where the
> bright slender rivers tumble swiftly and musically from pool to
> pool and only a narrow strip of sky shines down between the high
> green banks; but they dwelt also on bare, dry hill-tops where

---

[1] S. Baring Gould, *Lives of the Saints* (London, 1914), 16 vols., Vol. 16, p. 224.

dancing could be enjoyed, and in places where green burial-mounds swell from the level sward so delightful for dancing.[1]

He further quotes an account given him by Miss Mona Douglas of a fairy palace very much after the style of St. Collen's.

> Johnny Callow, an old grave-digger in Lezarye, used to tell me when I was small about a man who was crossing Skyhill one night, and was 'took' and lost his way. At last he saw a great house before him, bigger than Ballakillingan, all lighted up and the door open, and ones going in and out. He never thought where he was or what it would be, but went on towards it, and inside there were scores of grand ladies and gentlemen in silks and satins and velvet, and all the tables and chairs and dishes were of gold and silver, shining fit to blind you, and there was mortal grand food and drink all set out ready. He walked right in, but none of the ones that was there seemed to see him, so he thought he would take shelter and watch them for a bit, and he did, sitting all quiet in a corner. But he was tired coming in off the mountains after his day's work, and before long he went to sleep, and when he woke up in the morning house and people and all was gone, and he was lying in the fern up on the top of (?)Skyhill. I don't remember whether Johnny said he had eaten of their food or not.[2]

The Legend of Innis Sark given by Lady Wilde suggests a similar conception of Fairyland, not perhaps a subterranean one but one made by the working of glamour, for it is about a young man who fell asleep under a haystack on November Eve and woke in the same place next morning. After some nightmare experiences in the fairy kitchen he found himself at a royal banquet. He had seen an old hag chopped up and boiled to serve the guests, but at the banquet he saw 'fruit and chickens and turkeys and butter, and cakes fresh from the oven, and crystal cups of bright red wine'.

> 'Now sit down and eat,' said the prince, who sat at the top on a throne, with a red sash round his waist, and a gold band on his head. 'Sit down with this pleasant company and eat with us; you are welcome.'
>
> And there were many beautiful ladies seated round, and grand noblemen, with red caps and sashes; and they all smiled at him and bade him eat.

[1] W. W. Gill, *A Second Manx Scrapbook* (London, 1932), pp. 229–30.
[2] Ibid., pp. 235–6.

14

'No,' said the young man; 'I cannot eat with you, for I see no priest to bless the food. Let me go in peace.'

'Not at least till you taste our wine,' said the prince with a friendly smile.

And one of the beautiful ladies rose up and filled a crystal cup with bright red wine, and gave it him. And when he saw it, the sight of it tempted him, and he could not help himself, but drank it all off without stopping; for it seemed to him the most delicious draught he ever had in his whole life.

But no sooner had he laid down the glass, than a noise like thunder shook the building, and all the lights went out; and he found himself alone in the dark night lying under the very same hay-rick where he had cast himself down to sleep, tired after his work.[1]

The effect of the fairy draught was fatal to him, and he pined away and soon died.

The supernatural beings in this story seem to be regarded purely as fairies, though the two kinds of fairies, good and bad, are mentioned at the beginning of the tale. But in others very like it the fairies are plainly identified with the dead. In one, *November Eve*, a young man who had stayed out imprudently on Hallow e'en was swept into a band of fairies going to a fair. He met Finvarra the Fairy King and Oonagh his Queen; they gave him fairy gold and wine and were full of merriment, but for all that they were the company of the dead. When he looked steadily at any one of them he found him to be a neighbour who had died—perhaps many years before. When he recognized them they came around him, shrieking with laughter, and tried to force him into the dance. He resisted them until he fell senseless, and when he woke next morning he was lying in a stone circle, and his arms were black and blue with the marks of fairy fingers.[2]

The Cornish tale of *The Fairy Dwelling on Selena Moor* is something similar to this one, though the fairies are homelier people without a king or queen. Their habitation was an old ruined barn surrounded by bogland, but it appeared by glamour to be a house set in a beautiful garden and orchard, with all kinds of fruit growing in it. Perhaps such a house had once

---

[1] F. S. Wilde. *Ancient Legends of Ireland* (London, 1887), 2 vols., Vol. I, p. 138.
[2] Ibid., Vol. I, pp. 145–8.

stood there, and the fairies were inhabiting the past. The tale is about a Mr. Noy, a well-liked farmer, who lived near Selena Moor and who went out to the neighbouring inn one night to order drink for the Harvest Home next day. He left the inn, but never arrived home. They searched for him for three days, and at last, passing within half a mile of his home, they heard dogs howling and a horse neighing. They went over the treacherous bogland of the moor, and found a great thicket, where Mr. Noy's horse was tethered, with the dogs beside it. The horse had fed well on the rich grass, but the dogs were very thin. The horse led them to a ruined bowjey (or barn) and there they found Mr. Noy sound asleep. He was surprised to see that it was morning already, and was very dazed and bewildered, but at last they got his story from him. He had made a short-cut through the moor, but had lost his way and had wandered, he thought, many miles over country unknown to him, until he saw lights in the distance and heard music. He hurried towards it, thinking that he had come at last to a farmhouse, where they were perhaps holding a Harvest Home supper. His horse and dogs shrank back and would not come with him, so he tied his horse to a thorn, and went on through a most beautiful orchard towards a house, outside which he saw hundreds of people either dancing or sitting drinking at tables. They were all richly dressed, but they looked to him very small, and their benches and tables and cups were small too. Quite close to him stood a girl in white, taller than the rest, and playing a kind of tambourine. The tunes were lively, and the dancers were the nimblest he had ever seen. Soon the girl gave the tambourine to an old fellow near, and went into the house to fetch out a black-jack of ale for the company. Mr. Noy, who loved dancing and would have been glad of a drink, drew near to the corner of the house, but the girl met his eyes, and signed to him to keep back. She spoke a few words to the old fellow with the tambourine, and then came towards him.

'Follow me into the orchard,' she said.

She went before him to a sheltered place, and there in the quiet starlight, away from the dazzle of the candles, he recognized her as Grace Hutchens, who had been his sweetheart for a long time, but had died, or was thought to have died, three or four years before.

16

'Thank the stars, dear William,' she said, 'that I was on the look-out to stop ye, or ye would this minute be changed into the small people's state, like I am, woe is me!'

He would have kissed her, but she warned him anxiously against touching her, and against eating a fruit or plucking a flower if he wished ever to reach his home again.

'For eating a tempting plum in this enchanted orchard was my undoing,' she said. 'You may think it strange, but it was all through my love for you that I am come to this. People believed, and so it seemed, that I was found on the moor dead; what was buried for me, however, was only a changeling or a sham body, never mine, I should think, for it seems to me that I feel much the same still as when I lived to be your sweetheart.'

As she said this several little voices squeaked, 'Grace, Grace, bring us more beer and cider, be quick, be quick!'

'Follow me into the garden, and remain there behind the house; be sure you keep out of sight, and don't for your life touch fruit or flower.'

Mr. Noy begged her to bring him a drink of cider too, but she said she would not on his life; and she soon returned, and led him into a bowery walk, where all kinds of flowers were blooming, and told him how she came there. One evening about dusk she was out on Selena Moor looking for a stray sheep, when she heard Mr. Noy hallooing to his dogs, so she took a short cut towards him, and got lost in a place where the ferns were above her head, and so wandered on for hours until she came to an orchard where music was sounding, but though the music was sometimes quite near she could not get out of the orchard, but wandered round as if she was pixy-led. At length, worn out with hunger and thirst, she plucked a beautiful golden plum from one of the trees, and began to eat it. It dissolved into bitter water in her mouth, and she fell to the ground in a faint. When she revived she found herself surrounded by a crowd of little people, who laughed and rejoiced at getting a neat girl to bake and brew for them and to look after their mortal babies, who were not so strong, they said, as they used to be in the old days.

She said their lives seemed unnatural and a sham. 'They have little sense or feeling; what serves them in a way as such, is merely the remembrance of whatever pleased them when they lived as mortals—may be thousands of years ago. What

17

appear like ruddy apples and other delicious fruit, are only sloes, hoggins (haws) and blackberries.'

Mr. Noy asked her if any fairy babies were born, and she answered that just occasionally a fairy child was born, and then there was great rejoicing—every little fairy man, however old and wizened, was proud to be thought its father. 'For you must remember that they are not of our religion,' she said in answer to his surprised look, 'but star-worshippers. They don't always live together like Christians and turtle-doves; considering their long existence such constancy would be tiresome for them; anyhow the small tribe seem to think so.'

She told him also that she was now more content with her condition, since she was able to take the form of a small bird and fly about near him.

When she was called away again Mr. Noy thought he might find a way to rescue them both; so he took his hedging gloves out of his pocket, turned them inside out and threw them among the fairies. Immediately all vanished, Grace and all, and he found himself standing alone in the ruined bowjey. Something seemed to hit him on the head and he fell to the ground.

> Those to whom Mr. Noy related this story, said that he had learnt nothing new from Grace, for old folks always believed of the fair people such things as she told him, and they disliked to be seen, above all by day-light, because they then looked aged and grim. It was said, too, that those who take animal forms get smaller and smaller with every change, till they are finally lost in the earth as muryans (ants), and that they passed winter, for the most part, in underground habitations, entered from cleves or carns. And it is held that many persons who appear to have died entranced, are not really dead, but changed into the fairy state.
>
> The recovered gentleman further informed them that he had remarked among the small folks, many who bore a sort of family-likeness to people he knew, and he had no doubt but some of them were changelings of recent date, and others their forefathers who had died in days of yore, when they were not good enow to be admitted into heaven, nor so wicked as to be doomed to the worst of all places. Over a while, it is supposed, they cease to exist as living beings, for which reason fewer of them are now beheld than were seen in old times.[1]

[1] W. Bottrell, *Traditions and Hearthside Stories of West Cornwall* (Penzance, 1870–80), 3 vols, Vol. II, pp. 95–102.

Like many other visitors to Fairyland Mr. Noy pined and lost all interest in life after this adventure.

The theory of the origin of the fairies which this story exemplifies restricts them to the dead of a certain class, in this case to the heathen dead, and their modern recruits are those who died of a stroke, catalepsy or any trance-like illness. Sometime the fairies are said to be the ghosts of the old druids.

Bottrell gives a summary of a very similar tale about a farmer named Richard Vingoe who was pisky-led in Treville Cliffs. This fairyland, a pleasant underground country, was reached by a cavern. The fairies were hurling with a silver ball. Hurling is a favourite pastime of the Irish fairies.

The Sluagh Sidhe of Ireland are the People of the Hills, and they live as a rule under natural hillocks, not in barrows. They come up from these hills to revel, and their lights have been recorded in living tradition. They move in procession from hill to hill, and it is reputed to be very unlucky to build across their regular paths or to set any obstacle across them.[1] The same tradition is recorded by Mr. T. G. F. Paterson of the Armagh County Museum. This was about the fairy lights on Edenappa townland.

> I was only a chile—I was not much then, but many a time I remember hearing about the wee people on Slieve Gullion. Many a night there was light on the top an' the wee people cud be seen as plain as ye like disportin' themselves aroun' the bonfires. There'd be scores of fires an' hundreds of wee people. An' some of them was mounted an' wud ride their horses through the flames. Lots of the oul ones saw them. I saw the fires once but didn't see the horsemen.

Presumably this was on May Eve, and the fairy people, like the humans, were driving their cattle through the Beltane fires.

A tale of the fairies dancing round a bonfire in the Isle of Skye was sent to me in 1958 by a friend from Mona Smith, the wife of an Edinburgh minister. I include it as she wrote it.

> In the darkening of an Autumn evening over eighty years ago a little boy in the Isle of Skye was awaiting the return of his mother from a visit to an ailing neighbour.

[1] D. A. McManus, *The Middle Kingdom* (London, 1959), p. 22 and pp. 105-12.

19

He and an elder sister had been left with their grandmother while their mother was on her errand of mercy. Another little boy had joined them, and all three had played happily during the afternoon. Their own home was some distance from their grandmother's—just too far for little ones unaccompanied. Presently there came to call on the grandmother an elderly woman from the village, one whom the children knew well and whom they liked. Probably by this time they were becoming a little tired and cross, and their old friend was trying to amuse them. Suddenly she said, 'Come with me, I want to show you something.'

They all took hands and went out into the gloaming, and down the path by the side of the burn. Then the old lady stopped, and said: 'Look, do you see them?' And there, on the hill-side, all dressed in green, were fairies dancing in a ring round a fire.

The children were simply enchanted by what they saw, and one can imagine their excitement, and the wonderful story they had to tell their mother on her return.

Next morning they rushed out to look for the ashes of the fairy fire, but there was nothing to be seen.

That little boy was my father, and as children my brother and sisters and I were never tired of hearing this story. My aunt too, when she came to visit us, would corroborate the tale. And I have passed it on to mine, and have shown them the green, grassy mound 'where Papa saw the fairies.'

Two years ago, and for the first time, I met the third child, now an old man, and he could recall, as vividly and clearly as if it were yesterday, all the details of that wonderful evening. For those who might like to try and explain this experience, I must tell them that the old lady was credited with the second sight.

Here, though the first picture given is of the fairies dancing on the hillside by a burn, it is later described as a green, grassy mound. So it is probable that the fairies danced on top of it.

In Cornwall, too, there are tales of Fairy Hills, and revels upon them. The best known is that of the *Fairy Revels on the Gump of St. Just* told in Hunt's *Popular Romances of the West of England*. This is on the common folklore theme of greed punished (Motif F361.2). It is of an old miser, who, hearing of the rich plenishings of the fairies who used to revel on the Gump, determined to get some for himself. He set out in the full of the Harvest Moon—Lammas-tide—and as he climbed the Gump he heard fairy music. It was so compelling that he was forced to dance to it, and it seemed to be in the air all around, but at length he concluded that it was under his feet, and he was right, for presently the hill burst open and thousands of fairies poured out, while every plant on the hillside was hung with coloured lights. Then a regiment of Spriggans marched out, and passed behind the miser, encircling the hill. He was rather alarmed by this; but as the tallest of them did not reach his shoe-string he thought he could trample them down if necessary. In any case, he was diverted by the sight in front of him. Troops of musicians came out, and bands of soldiers, and then servants carrying all kinds of dainties on gold and silver dishes, and then the lords and ladies of the Court came out and ranged themselves in their places, and after them came a band of fairy children in gauzy clothes, who scattered flowers that rooted themselves as they fell; and finally came the King and Queen, who moved up to the high table, glittering with gold, silver and jewels. It was this that drew the miser's greedy eye. The whole exquisite minia-ture could be covered by his hat, and he went down on his knees and crawled up behind the table. The music, feasting and laughter went on undisturbed till he raised his hat over his head, and then suddenly every eye among those thousands was upon him. He brought down the hat, and at once a whistle sounded, the lights went out and he felt himself jerked over by a thousand cords. Before he knew what had happened he was lying on the hillside, his mouth gagged and every finger fastened to the ground, so that he could move neither hand nor foot. He felt himself pinched, pricked, kicked and thumped. The largest Spriggan danced on his nose. He lay all night immovable, but when the sun rose he broke the cobwebs that fastened him and tottered feebly down the Gump. It was some time before he had the courage to tell anyone of what had happened to him.[1]

There may be some prettification here—the fairy children in gauzy dresses scattering flowers that rooted themselves seem a little touched up—but, unless the story is completely falsified, it tells of royal fairy revels in a magnificent style, though per-formed by minute actors, since the whole royal table could be imprisoned under the miser's hat. There are several interesting points in this story. One is that the Spriggans, a kind of grotesque

[1] R. Hunt, *Popular Romances of the West of England* (London, 1930, 1st ed. 1881), 'The Fairy Revels on the Gump', pp. 98–101.

hobgoblin of Cornwall, are conceived of as a bodyguard to the Royal Court when they might well have been quite independent creatures, another is that the miser was bound down by cobwebs as Gulliver was by the Lilliputian cords. There may have been literary borrowing here, for the Gulliver story was condensed in an early chapbook which may well have been sold by pedlars in the West Country. On the other hand, Swift may have followed a folk tradition. The story of Fergus O'Conla's visit to the tiny fairies might have been known to him, and may have been the germ of *Gulliver's Travels*. Cobwebs are always supposed to be magical things, and he may have known and used a tale of fairy binding. A third point of interest is that the music heard by the miser sounded first underground. This is true to Celtic folk tradition, both in Ireland and the Highlands. T. F. G. Paterson reports an oral account from Cashel which might well be part of the miser's experiences.

> An' I remember me mother tellin' me—she's the one that had all the ould stories—but it's seldom I listened for I used to think the oul' people wur crazy—of someone crossing the Relig one evenin'. An' the music was so good he cudn't keep from steppin' till it. An' he jigged till it long an' well till he foun' it right under his feet. An' then he got the fear upon him an' he hooked as fast he cud. It wus well he wus able.

In Campbell's *Popular Tales of the Western Highlands* there are many anecdotes of the hill-dwelling fairies, rather more prosaically conceived than the Irish O' Sidhe. The tale of the smith's rescue of his son from the fairy hill is one of them. In this tale the fairies coveted the smith's only son, a handsome, merry boy, and left a wizened changeling in his place. The father took advice from a wise man, and discovered the imposture by the usual expedient of using eggshells instead of buckets; but though he got rid of the changeling, his own son was not returned to him, and he had to fetch him back from fairyland himself. A dirk, a Bible and a cock were necessary for the rescue, and he entered the fairy knowe at full moon, when it was raised upon pillars. He found his son among a group of mortal prisoners who were working at a forge in one corner, and succeeded in getting him safe away. It is curious that in this story the fairies bestowed skill in metal work upon their pupil, and

22

yet they were defeated by cold iron, the dirk stuck into the hillside.[1]

A more matter-of-fact tale is that of the pan borrowed by the Hill Woman from a mortal neighbour. This reads like a confirmation of MacRitchie's theory, that the fairies were a conquered people who had taken to the hills; the prosaic reward of meat and bones left in the pot, the fairy dogs which were loosed to chase the woman and were driven back by the human dogs when they came near to the steading, all sound like the intercourse of two alien tribes. There is even a hint that the human woman was as magical to the fairies as they were to her.[2] These hill-dwellers seem more mortal than dead.

In the Lowlands of Scotland and the North of England the fairy hills are also known. It was from the Eildon Hills that True Thomas was led into Fairyland, and they went down and down, crossing subterranean streams and reaching an enchanted orchard. Isobel Gowdie, the self-confessed witch, went under the hills to meet the fairies, and so did the Boy of Leith. A man accused of witchcraft in the seventeenth century excused himself by saying that he was given a white powder from a fairy hill. All through these islands people were liable to disappear into the hollow hills and to hear fairy music, as Aubrey's shepherd did under Hack Pen.

The underwater habitations of the fairies and the fairy islands are less widespread, and belong mainly to the Celtic parts of the country, except for individual spirits of rivers and wells like Jenny Greenteeth and Peg Powler. In the Bristol Channel area of Somerset there is a tradition of a fairy island that is occasionally to be seen, though not usually visible to human eyes, The Green Land of Enchantment it is called in a fragmentary folk-song collected by R. L. Tongue. This sounds rather like The Green Spots of the Floods mentioned by Southey and discussed by John Rhys in *Celtic Folklore*.[3] Rhys tells other stories of invisible islands along the Welsh coast. Sometimes a real island is supposed to be a fairy place, like the Isle of Man, the ancient home of the God Manannon, where the frequent

[1] J. F. Campbell, *Popular Tales of the Western Highlands* (London, 1890, 1st ed. 1860), 4 vols. 'The Smith and the Fairies', Vol. II, pp. 157–60.

[2] Ibid., Vol. II, pp. 52–4.

[3] John Rhys, *Celtic Folklore* (Oxford, 1901), 2 vols., Vol. I, pp. 20–1 and pp. 169–72.

mists were thought to be raised by enchantment. The most widespread of the Welsh fairy stories which still remains in oral tradition, the Fairy Wife, is generally told about a lake fairy. In many forms of it a father appears out of the lake to ratify the union and give a dowry of water cattle. The water cattle of the Highlands presumably belong to underwater fairies. Niam of the Golden Hair who loved Ossian lived in a fairy-island beyond the sea, not unlike the Hy-Brasail of Irish legend. There are lake fairies in Ireland, however, as well as in Wales. Lady Wilde has some passages about the fairies of Lough Neagh.

> Down deep, under the waters of Lough Neagh, can still be seen, by those who have the gift of fairy vision, the columns and walls of the beautiful palaces once inhabited by the fairy race when they were the gods of the earth; and this tradition of a buried town beneath the waves has been prevalent for centuries amongst the people.
>
> Giraldus Cambrensis states that in his time the tops of the towers 'built after the fashion of the country', were distinctly visible in calm, clear weather, under the surface of the lake; and still the fairies haunt the ruins of their former splendour, and hold festivals beneath the waters when the full moon is shining; for the boatmen, coming home late at night, have often heard sweet music rising up from beneath the waves and the sound of laughter, and seen glimmering lights far down under the water, where the ancient fairy palaces are supposed to be.[1]

[1] F. S. Wilde, ed. cit., Vol. II, pp. 189–90.

Three

TUTELARY SPIRITS

THE Fairies who take an interest in human destiny and work for human friends may be divided into two main types—the ancestral fairy who is attached to a family, and who most commonly bewails coming tragedy or occasionally gives advice or even luck-bringing gifts, and the Brownie or hobgoblin who performs tasks, and attaches itself sometimes to a family and sometimes to a place. The last kind is much commoner and more widespread. There is some over-lapping between them, of course, as there is in all folk tradition, but the main distinction is clear.

The chief of the ancestral fairies is the Banshee of Ireland; almost invariably attached to a family, and it must be to one of the old families. Lady Wilde gives a good description of it in *Ancient Legends of Ireland*.

But only certain families of historic lineage, or persons gifted with music and song, are attended by this spirit; for music and poetry are fairy gifts, and the possessors of them show kinship to the spirit race—therefore they are watched over by the spirit of life, which is prophecy and inspiration; and by the spirit of doom, which is the revealer of the secrets of death.

Sometimes the Banshee assumes the form of some sweet singing virgin of the family who died young, and has been given the mission by the invisible powers to become the harbinger of coming doom to her mortal kindred. Or she may be seen as a shrouded woman, crouched beneath the trees, lamenting with veiled face; or flying past in the moonlight, crying bitterly: and the cry of this spirit is mournful beyond all other sounds on earth, and betokens certain death to some member of the family whenever it is heard in the silence of the night.[1]

Lady Wilde goes on to say that the Banshee can even follow its family abroad, and gives an example of how the Banshee wailed before the death of two of the O'Gradys who had settled in Canada.

The Highland Banshee, the Little Washer at the Ford, is perhaps rather more general in her attentions. She washes the clothes of those about to die in battle; but since the clans are regionally dispersed in the Highlands this is not incompatible with devotion to a family. In the Highlands there are fairies who advise and help their families rather than merely lamenting them. The fairy of the Macleods of Dunvegan, who rocked the cradle of the infant heir and bestowed the fairy flag upon the family, is perhaps the best-known of these tutelary fairies. Like many fairy gifts the flag has its dangers and exacts its penalty. The Macleods seem to be specially favoured by the fairies, for in recent tradition the Green Lady of Hellasay will show herself only to Macleod.[2] The Grants also have fairy connections; they can be shot only through the green square of their tartans, and in the seventeenth century the family spirit, Meg Moulach, would stand beside the laird when he played chess to show him the winning moves.[3] There is a fairly widespread tradition of ghosts who appear only to the members of their own family, and this, though not exclusively Celtic, is very close to the Banshee tradition, for it is likely that the Banshee was originally an ancestral ghost. In England as well as in Scotland many families are credited with death tokens, such as the pigeon of the Oxenhams, but it is not very clear what these are supposed to be. The Billy Blind in some of the Border Ballads seems somewhere between the Banshee and the Brownie types. His office is more advisory than domestic. In the ballad of *Young Bekie* it is the Billy Blind who warns Burd Isbel of Young Bekie's inconstancy.

[1] F. S. Wilde, *Ancient Legends of Ireland*, Vol. I, pp. 259–60.

[2] An account of the Green Lady of Hellasay was given to Miss A. V. Stuart of Edinburgh by John MacPherson of Barra, some of whose tales have been published in *Tales of the Coddie* (Edinburgh, 1960.)

[3] John Aubrey, *Miscellanies*, Fifth edition (London, 1890), pp. 191 and 192.

O it fell once upon a day
  Burd Isbel fell asleep,
An up it starts the Belly Blin,
  An stood at her bed-feet.

'O waken, waken, Burd Isbel,
  How can you sleep so soun,
Whan this is Bekie's wedding day,
  An the marriage gain on?'[1]

The Billy Blind not only tells her this, but advises her what to do next and provides a magic ship which he himself steers to take her to young Bekie's land. The ballad of Young Bekie is a fairy-tale version of the legend of Gilbert à Becket, Thomas à Becket's father. The Billy Blind, however, was probably attached to it in the Border Country. Another Billy Blind occurs in the ballad of *Willie's Lady*, where he gives excellent advice, but no practical help. Another intermediate fairy was the Silkie of Denton Hall in Northumberland. This was a female spirit, wearing grey silk, one of the white ladies which seem halfway between ghosts and fairies. According to Henderson she was attached to the place rather than to the people, but some later experiences seem to suggest that she had strong family affections.

A lady who now lives in Oxfordshire was brought up at Lemington Hall, five miles from Newcastle, and as a girl Marjorie Sowerby, as she then was, used often to visit the last remaining Hoyles of Denton, two old ladies who were quite willing to speak to intimate friends about Silkie's kindness to them. The house was too big for them, and they really did not know how they would manage without her. She used to clean out the hearth and lay fires, and there was something too about bunches of flowers left on the staircase. In 1902 or so Marjorie Sowerby left the neighbourhood, and did not make any long stay in it until the Second World War. By that time the old ladies were long dead, and the house was occupied by another old acquaintance of hers. He was not the kind of person to get on with fairies and there was no talk of Silkie's kindness now; in fact, the new tenant was so much disturbed by banging and noises and poltergeist jokes that he was finally obliged to leave

---

[1] F. J. Child, *The English and Scottish Popular Ballads* (New York, 1957, 1st ed. 1882), 5 vols, Vol. I, p. 466.

the house. The Brownie had turned into a Boggart, as has often happened before.

The name Brownie is an English word, and the industrious and helpful household spirit is commoner in England and in the Lowlands of Scotland than in the Celtic area. In Cornwall the help of the Brownie appears to be invoked in the cry, 'Browney! Browney!' which is raised when the bees swarm; but this may be a name for the bees themselves, like the Scots 'Burnie, Burnie Bee'. In the West Country Pixies sometimes do the Brownies' work, and, like the Brownies, are laid by a gift of clothes. In Ireland, Kennedy's story of the *Pooka of Kildare* is a complete Brownie story; though the Pooka is generally more like a hobgoblin or bogey-beast. In Lady Wilde's tale the Pooka is also a friendly and helpful spirit, who does all the grinding in a mill for a young man who speaks him fair and throws a cloak over him.[1] Like other Brownies he is laid by a gift of clothes, but in this case he is pleased with the gift, and though he goes he bestows lasting good fortune upon the family. A tale of Pixies who, though they were laid by clothes, were not displeased by them and remained on friendly terms with the family, was collected by R. L. Tongue in Somerset.

The farmer of Knighton was very friendly with the pixies. He used to leave a floorful of corn when he was short-handed, and the pixies would thrash it for him. They did an immense amount of work for him, until one night his wife peeped through the keyhole and saw them hard at it. She wasn't afraid of their squinny eyes and hairy bodies, but she thought it a crying shame they should go naked and cold.

She set to work and made some warm clothes for them and left them on the threshing floor, and after that there was no more help from the pixies. They did not forget the farmer, however, for one day, after Withypool church bells were hung, the pixy father met him on an upland field.

'Wilt gie us the lend of thy plough and tackle?' (That is packhorses and crooks) he said.

The farmer was cautious—he'd heard how the pixies used horses.

'What vor do 'ee want 'n?' he asked.

'I d' want to take my good wife and littlings out of the noise of they ding-dongs.'

[1] F. S. Wilde, ed. cit., Vol. I, pp. 87–90.

28

The farmer trusted the pixies, and they moved, lock, stock, and barrel, over to Winsford Hill; and when the old packhorses trotted home they looked like beautiful two-year-olds.[1]

A Brownie on the Celtic fringe, on the edge of the Gaelic-speaking country in Perthshire, haunted Altmor Burn, not far from Pitlochry. He used to be heard paddling and splashing in the burn, then he would go up with wet feet to the farm near, and if everything had been left untidy he would tidy it, but if it was left neat he would throw everything about. It was counted unlucky to meet him, and the road was avoided at night. He was laid, not by a gift of clothes, but by a nickname. A man returning very merry from the market one dark night heard him splashing about in the burn, and cried out jovially, 'Well, Puddlefoot, how is it with you the night?' The Brownie was horrified. 'Oh! Oh!' he cried, 'I've gotten a name! 'Tis Puddlefoot they call me!' And he vanished, never to haunt the place again.[2]

It is very possible that this Brownie was a ghost, like the Brownie of Balquam, also called the Ghost of Brandey Dhu. The well-known Brownie story of the fetching of the midwife was told of him. He took a special interest in the Goodwife of Furmenton, and was laid by her son.[3]

Some sinister Brownies were supposed to haunt Fincastle Mill in Perthshire, a rare instance of Brownies appearing in numbers. Two tales of them were recorded by Hamish Henderson, and are in the archives of the School of Scottish Studies. One is of especial interest, for Maggie Moulach appears in it again. It is a 'Nemo' story. A young bride, going to grind meal in the haunted mill at Fincastle, at midnight, was molested by a Brownie, and told him that her name was 'Me Myself'. He became so troublesome to her that she threw boiling broth over him, and he stumbled out to die, telling his mother, Maggie Moulach, that he was scalded by Me Myself. So the bride escaped vengeance for a time; but after her marriage she was at a Ceilidh at some distance from Fincastle, where she told the tale of how she had got the better of the Brownies. Unfortunately

[1] R. L. Tongue, *Somerset Folklore* (F.L.S., 1965), p. 117.
[2] K. M. Briggs, *The Personnel of Fairyland* (Oxford, 1953), p. 127.
[3] Andrew Jervise, *The Land of the Lindseys* (1882), pp. 252–8.

Maggie Moulach had moved into the district too, and was invisibly listening to the tales. When the bride had finished, there was a cry of rage, a stool hurtled through the air, and the girl fell dead. So far Maggie Moulach deserves to be described as a goblin rather than a Brownie; but at the same time, she did Brownie work on a neighbouring farm. This tale well illustrates the ambivalent nature of the Brownies.

In Wales the Bwbach and the Bwca take the place of the Brownies. In *Celtic Folklore* by John Rhys there is a long and full story of a Bwca who, like the Silkie of Denton Hall, was useful and obliging as long as he was well treated, but behaved like a Boggart when he was disobliged. In his first home, a Monmouthshire farm, he got on very well for some time with the servant girl, who was suspected of having fairy blood in her. She left cream at the bottom of the stairs for him every night, and in return he did a great deal of work for her. At last the silly girl played a rude prank on him by filling his bowl with the stale urine that was used as a mordant in dyeing. He attacked her furiously, so that she had to scream for help, and then ran off to work at a neighbouring farm called Hafod y Ynys. The girl there fed him very well, but unfortunately she was curious and wanted to know his name, which he refused to tell her. One evening all the men were out, and the Bwca was hard at work doing the girl's spinning. She pretended to go out too, but she crept to the foot of the stairs and heard him singing in Welsh:

'How she would laugh, did she know
That Gwarwyn-a-throt is my name!'

She called out in triumph that she knew his name now, and he left Hafod y Ynys at once and moved to a neighbouring farmhouse, where he became great friends with Moses, the manservant. But Moses went off to fight against Richard Crookback and was killed at Bosworth Field. After that poor Gwarwyn-a-throt went completely to the bad, and at length a local wise man was summoned to lay him, and succeeded in sending him to the Red Sea.[1] The connection here with the Suffolk spinning fairy Tom Tit Tot and the Scottish Habetrot

[1] John Rhys, ed. cit., Vol. II, pp. 593–6.

and the Welsh Trwtyn-Tratyn is interesting, and many features of the tale occur in various Brownie stories. Wirt Sikes in his account of the Bwbach describes a creature almost exactly like the English Brownie, or domestic Hobgoblin.

> The Bwbach, or Boobach, is the good-natured goblin which does good turns for the tidy Welsh maid who wins its favour by a certain course of behaviour recommended by long tradition. The maid having swept the kitchen, makes a good fire the last thing at night, and having put the churn, filled with cream, on the whitened hearth, with a basin of fresh cream for the Bwbach on the hob, goes to bed to await the event. In the morning she finds (if she is in luck) that the Bwbach has emptied the basin of cream, and plied the churn-dasher so well that the maid has but to give a thump or two to bring the butter in a great lump.[1]

Later in the same passage Sikes speaks of the goblinish habits of the Bwbach.

'The same confusion in outlines,' he says, 'which exists regarding our own Bogie and Hobgoblin gives the Bwbach a double character, as a household fairy and a terrifying phantom. In both aspects it is ludicrous, but in the latter it has dangerous practices. To get into its clutches under certain circumstances is no trifling matter, for it has the power of whisking people off through the air. Its services are brought into requisition for this purpose by troubled ghosts who cannot sleep on account of hidden treasure they want removed; and if they cannot succeed in getting a mortal to help in removing the treasure, they employ the Bwbach to transport the mortal through the air.' This sounds as if the Bwbach was even more like the Irish Pooka than the English Brownie.

The Manx Brownie is the *fenodyree*, a hairy spirit of great strength, able to thrash a barnful of corn in a night. He is not very clever, for he once undertook to round up a flock of sheep at Snaefell, and had more trouble with the little grey one without horns than with all the rest. This turned out to be a hare. The same story is told of a Lancashire Brownie. The farmer of Ballochrink was so grateful for all that the Fenodyree had done that he laid out a complete set of clothes for him. The Fenodyree was much offended by the gifts, and

---

[1] Wirt Sikes, *British Goblins* (London, 1880) pp. 30 and 31.

31

lifted up the items one by one, mentioning the illness that each one would bring with it. Then he went off to the solitude of Glen Rushen.[1] It is curious that his Lincolnshire counterpart had complacently accepted the present of a linen shirt every year, and only when the farmer meanly gave him a hempen one did he take exception to it.

> 'Harden, harden, harden hemp!
> I will neither grind nor stamp!
> Had you given me linen gear,
> I would have served you many a year!'

So he said, and made off, never to return.[2]

These are some of the outlying peoples of the Brownie nature; their central position, as I have said, is in the English-speaking parts of England and Scotland. They are thickest on the ground in the Border Country. Their various traits and habits can be collected from a number of anecdotes. The common method of laying by a gift of clothes is shown in a story of the old Fortalice of Dolphinton in *The New Statistical Account of Scotland* under 'Coenam'.

A tradition is still current that a fairy, or brownie, assisted the people there in thrashing their corn in olden times, and that, in token of their gratitude for his services, an article of dress was placed for his acceptance in the scene of his nocturnal labours; but he, hurt and offended at the very offer of remuneration of any sort, quitted the place for ever, and in doing so is said to have uttered his regret in these lines:

> 'Sin' ye've gien me a harden ramp,
> Nae mair of your corn I will tramp.'[3]

A harden ramp is a shirt made of very coarse linen, and it is just possible that the Brownie may have resented the poverty of the gift in the same way as the Lincolnshire one did. His rhyme is reminiscent of the well-known one given by Reginald Scot:

> Since thou layest me, hempen, hempen,
> Here I'll no longer tread nor stampen,

[1] J. Rhys, ed. cit., Vol. I, p. 286.
[2] Ibid., Vol. I, p. 324, quoting notes by M. Peacock in *F.L.*, Vol. II, 1891, pp. 509–13.
[3] R. Chambers, *The Popular Rhymes of Scotland* quoting *The New Statistical Account of Scotland* (1845).

and here, too, a coarse shirt seems to have been given. The same is not true of the Cauld Lad of Hilton, who evidently, like the Pooka of Kildare, was anxious to be laid. He was a naked boy, said to be the ghost of a stable-boy killed by one of the Lords of Hilton in a passion. He haunted Hilton Castle in Northumberland, and, like the Brownie of Altmor, he threw everything about that was tidy, and set everything to rights that was left scattered. He used to be heard working at night and singing sadly:

> 'Wae's me! Wae's me!
> The acorn is not yet
> Fallen from the tree,
> That's to grow to the wood,
> That's to make the cradle,
> That's to rock the bairn,
> That's to grow to a man,
> That's to lay me.'

Things happened beyond his hopes, however, for the servants laid out a fine green mantle and hood for him. He put them on joyfully, and left his work forever, singing,

> 'Here's a cloak, and here's a hood!
> The Cauld Lad of Hilton will do no more good!'[1]

Another Brownie who seemed to desire a reward was the Brownie of Jedburgh, who, when the servant was dilatory, fetched the midwife to the mistress of the house at top speed. He had been heard by the servants to say, 'Wae's me for a green sark!' and the grateful laird had the clothes made and put out for him. He took them and vanished for ever, it was thought to Fairyland.[2] More usually, however, the Brownies seem to have been offended by the gift, like the Brownie of Glendevon, who departed in dudgeon, saying:

> 'Gie brounie coat, gie brounie sark,
> Ye'll get nae mair o' brounie's wark.'[3]

---

[1] T. Keightley, ed. cit., p. 296, quoting M. A. Richardson, *The Local Historian's Table Book* (1846), Vol. III, p. 239.

[2] Walter Scott, *Minstrelsy of the Scottish Border* (Edinburgh, 1932, 1st ed. 1801), 4 vols, Vol. I, p. 149, footnote i.

[3] R. Chambers, *Popular Rhymes of Scotland* (Edinburgh, 1870, 1st ed. 1841), p. 325.

To the same effect Henderson quotes a letter from a lady of Scottish extraction:

It is curious what dislike Brownies have to clothing. There was one in the old peelhouse where I was born. The servants, out of gratitude for his assistance, gave him what they deemed an indispensable portion of man's attire. Unfortunately it was part of a suit of livery, and he vanished, crying—

'Red breeks and a ruffled sark!
Ye'll no' get me to do yer wark!'

The story dates from my great grandfather's time; but the old dark closet where Brownie dwelt still exists, though dark no longer.[1]

There were other ways in which Brownies could be driven away, such as an attempt to baptize them; or they would go if they took offence at anything. They were generally considered to have a right to a bowl of the best cream, but the Brownie of Bodsbeck, near Moffat, was sensitive even about that. He generally liked to pick up his fare for himself, but one busy harvest-time the goodman put out a special bowl of cream for him, and called out to tell him where it was to be found. This was enough for the touchy Brownie, and he was heard crying,

'Ca', brounie, ca'
A' the luck of Bodsbeck awa'
to Leithenha'.'

After that his services, and the luck they brought with them, were transferred to the neighbouring farm of Leithenhall. Sir Walter Scott, however, suggests that money may have been left with the bowl.[2]

A word of thanks would sometimes drive away fairy help, but a word of criticism was equally resented. The Brownie of Cranshaws in Berwickshire did good work in mowing and thrashing for several years, until someone incautiously remarked that the corn was not well mowed or stacked. All next night the Brownie laboured, carrying the corn up to Raven's

[1] W. Henderson, *Folk-Lore of the Northern Counties* (F.L.S., 1879), p. 249.
[2] Walter Scott, ed. cit., Vol. I, p. 149, footnote i.
Chambers, ed. cit., pp. 325–6.

Crag, two miles away, and throwing it over. As he went to and fro he muttered:

> 'It's no' weel mow'd! It's no' weel mow'd!—
> Then it's ne'er be mow'd by me again;
> I'll scatter it owre the RAVEN STANE
> And they'll hae some wark ere it's mow'd again!'[1]

The Brownie was sometimes less popular with the servants than with his master and mistress, for he generally sided with authority. Chambers has a Peebleshire story of two maids who did not think themselves properly fed, so they stole a bowl of milk and a bannock, and sat down to take it together. But the invisible Brownie sat between them, and whichever tried to drink, it was the Brownie got both milk and cake. At last, when the maids began to quarrel and accuse each other of taking an unfair share, the Brownie burst out laughing and exclaimed,

> 'Ha, ha, ha,
> Brownie has't a'!'[2]

Wag-at-the-Wa' was a Scottish name for a Brownie-like creature whose favourite seat was the empty pot-hook hanging over the fire. To swing the pot-hook was to invite a visit from Wag-at-the-Wa'. He plagued idle servants, but he was fond of children, and his laugh would be heard among the rest when the household was merry. He was described as a grotesque old man, with short legs and a long tail, wearing a red coat and blue breeches and sometimes a grey cloak, with an old 'pirniecap', or nightcap, on his head, and a bandage tied round his face because he was very much plagued with toothache. He disliked the family drinking anything stronger than home-brewed ale. Like other fairies he was banished by the sign of the cross.[3]

In England the Herefordshire Brownie also used the pot-hook as a seat. In E. M. Leather's *Folk-lore of Herefordshire*, she says, 'The "sway", the iron bar over the fire on which pots and kettles were hung, was formerly made with a crook in it. At Crasswell this was said to be the seat of the Brownie; an old

---

[1] George Henderson, *Popular Rhymes of Berwickshire* (Newcastle, 1856), pp. 65–6.
[2] Chambers, ed. cit., p. 327.
[3] W. Henderson, ed. cit., pp. 256–7.

lady still living there in 1908 remembered the "Brownie sway" in her old home at Cusop dingle. If there were no curve in the sway, she said, people would hang a horse-shoe on it, upside down, that Brownie should have something to sit upon.'[1] In Hereford, as elsewhere, the Brownie was tricksy and easily offended, for E. M. Leather continues, 'But Brownie sometimes took offence at what he considered slights to himself, and his favourite and chief form of revenge was to hide the household keys; there was only one way in which they could be brought back. The members of the household sat in a circle round the hearth, after placing a little cake upon the hob, as a peace-offering to the Brownie. The party sat in absolute silence with closed eyes, when the keys would be flung violently at the wall at the back of the sitters. This was done at the Portway Inn, Staunton-on-Wye, seventy years ago.'[2]

A Somerset inn is said to be haunted by a spirit of the same mischievous and harmless kind, who seems also to be a hearth spirit. R. L. Tongue wrote the following account of it in the spring of 1964, immediately after hearing the story.

> Charlie is a Hob, who is still about at the Holman Clavel Inn on the Blackdowns. This year I met someone who lived next door to the Holman Clavel, and the moment Charlie was mentioned, she was delighted and chuckled loudly. She said he was very amusing, and never did anything very bad. Everybody knew about him in the locality. Across the Holman Clavel front room is a very large beam called the Cob Wheel. The house itself is very old, and it is made of cob (packed clay), and the Clavvy or Clavey, which is a beam above the fireplace is of course of holly— the Holman—It is here that Charlie has his usual seat.
>
> Once, when she was about, she was asked to help get a dinner for a local farmer, and they spread it all out. They got out the silver and the linen, and they made a very good show of it. And then one of the maids said, 'Oh! Charlie don't like 'ee!'
>
> Well, there was nothing they could do about it. There was the table beautifully laid; they were rather proud of it. All they could do about it was to shut the door and hope for the best. Well, before the guests arrived they went in again, to make sure that everything was all right. The doors had been kept closed, but when they looked in, the table was quite bare. All the tankards

---

[1] E. M. Leather, *The Folk-Lore of Herefordshire* (Hereford, 1912), p. 48.
[2] Ibid.

were hanging up again on their hooks; the silver had been put neatly in its place. Charlie certainly didn't like him.

In Yorkshire and Lancashire the more generalized name of Hob is often given to the Brownie. The Hob-Hole Hob of Runswick Bay was not domesticated, but lived in a natural cavern, the Hob-Hole. He was a benevolent creature, and his particular feat was to cure whooping-cough. Parents would bring their children to the cave, and murmur:

> 'Hobthrush Hob,
> My bairn's gotten t' kink cough,
> Tak't off! Tak't off!'[1]

Henderson found two Hobs laid, like Brownies, by a gift of clothing, one near Danby; who, like the Lincolnshire Brownie, seems to have taken exception to the quality of the gift, for his rhyme ran:

> Gin Hob mun hae nowght but Harding hamp
> He'll come nae mair to berry nor stamp!

The Yorkshire Hobthrust of Starfit Hall, Reath, on the other hand, seems to have been driven away by the reward, for his rhyme went:

> Ha! A cap and a hood!
> Hob'll never do mair good![2]

A few domestic spirits haunt special places and do special work, such as the cellar ghost, which guards the wine from thieving butlers and servants, Lazy Lawrence, who protects orchards, Awd Goggie, who frightens children away from un-ripe gooseberries, and Melch Dick, the guardian of nut thickets. According to the Wilkie Manuscript Killmoulis is the mill spirit in the Scottish Lowlands. He is a grotesque creature, with an enormous nose and no mouth, though he is said to be very fond of pork. He bewails any misfortune coming to the mill, but for all that he is fond of mischievous pranks, and can only be controlled by direct invocation from the miller. Occasion-ally in an emergency he will leave his corner to thrash grain or to fetch a midwife, but as a rule he is more of a nuisance than a help.[3]

---

[1] W. Henderson, ed. cit., p. 264.   [2] Ibid., p. 264   [3] Ibid., pp. 252–3.

It will be seen that the Brownies and the closely allied Hob-goblins, Hobs and Lobs, have all very similar characteristics. It is perhaps worth describing them in more detail. The earlier Brownies were often of human or more than human size, as was probably Milton's 'Lubbar Fend'; but in later times one would generally describe Brownies as small, wizened and shaggy, clad in rags or naked. Occasionally, like the Phooka, they took animal form. They are generally grotesque to look at. According to an Aberdeenshire tradition, known and used by George Macdonald, they have no separate toes nor fingers; the Lowland Brownies have no noses, only nostrils. The Boggarts have long, sharp noses, and Killmoulis has a huge nose and no mouth. Occasionally their appearance is that of a small child, naked or wearing a white tunic. As a rule they seem to have the power of invisibility, but are so expert in hiding and lurking that they hardly need to exercise it. They are ready to do any of the work about a house or farm; sweeping, churning, spin-ning, weaving, mowing, thrashing and herding are perhaps the chief. They are moved by personal friendships and fancies, and under the influence of these they will sometimes do extra work, such as fetching the midwife. They will take up their abode in a farmhouse or manor, but they often have a particular pool, stream, rock or cave as their permanent habitation. Tradition often connects them with the dead. They are almost always solitary, except that certain trooping fairies, like the Pixies, sometimes perform the Brownie tasks. A non-domestic task that the Brownie sometimes performed in old days was that of guarding treasure. Occasionally a Brownie was not available and a Dobie had to be put in his place. This was unsatisfactory, for the Dobies were simpletons and very easily outwitted.

It will be seen that the Brownie is very near to the classical Lar, who is sometimes supposed to have been either an ances-tral ghost or the ghost of a primitive hearth sacrifice. Where Brownies differ from Lares is that they are mobile, and will readily change from one place to another if they are dissatisfied. There is even a case of a Brownie who left with the servants when the miserly housewife dismissed them because the Brownie was doing all the work, and would not return until they were all reinstated.

The dual nature of the Brownie is apparent in most of the

tales. In some he is merely tricksy, touchy and easily driven away, in others he turns to active mischief, and can be really dangerous. His relationship with Puck and the Hobgoblins, with the Brag, the Brash and the Bogey-beast, is very apparent. The well-known story of the Lancashire Boggart—'Aye, George, we're flitting!' is evidently a tale of a Brownie who has got into bad ways. He is choosing, however, to follow the family rather than to remain in the house. This fluidity and freewill is characteristic both of the Banshee and the Brownie. They are not bound, like many ghosts, to a locality. A good case may be made out for both of them as ghosts, and yet there is about the Brownie at least an adaptability, individuality and homely tang which forbids one to think of him as merely a lingering and reminiscent image.

Four

FORGOTTEN GODS AND NATURE SPIRITS

T HE nature spirits are the rarest of all the fairies in these islands, and yet traces of them can be found in many places. The Cailleach Bheur, the Blue Hag of the Highlands, appears to be the personified spirit of Winter. She herds the deer, and fights Spring with her staff, with which she freezes the ground. When at length Spring comes, she throws her staff under a holly tree, under which green grass never grows.[1] It is the Cally Berry in Ulster who is in perpetual conflict with Fionn and his followers. Black Annis of the Dane Hills of Leicestershire is a hag-like creature of the same kind. Her name is said to be derived from Anu or Danu, the Celtic goddess, mother of the Tuatha de Danu.[2] In the Lowlands it is 'Gentle Annie' who brings the storms. In Wales The Old Woman of the Mountains leads travellers astray. She is one of the Gwyllion, the hill fairies of Wales. They are friends of the goats, as the Cailleach Bheur is of the deer. Occasionally they come down from the mountains and enter human houses, where they must be hospitably entertained.[3] A gentler and more benevolent mountain spirit is the Ghille Dubh of the Gairloch district. He was seen in the second half of the eighteenth century round Loch a Dring. He was black-haired and dressed in leaves and

[1] D. A. Mackenzie, *Scottish Folk-Lore and Folk-Life* (London, 1935), pp. 137–41.
[2] C. J. Billson, *County Folk-Lore 3. Leicestershire and Rutland* (F.L.S., 1895), pp. 4–9.
[3] Wirt Sikes, ed. cit., pp. 49–51.

moss. He looked after lost children and led them home. In spite of his kindness five lairds of the Mackenzies set out to shoot him. Fortunately they found no trace of him. A more excusable attempt was that to poison the Each Uisge, who lived in Loch na Beiste in the Gairloch district, by putting hot lime into the water. In this they did not seem to succeed as he was seen again in 1884.[1]

In Somerset there are occasional rumours of The Woman of the Mist. A description of her was given to R. L. Tongue at Bicknoller in 1962. 'The Woman of the Mist is seen in the Autumn and Winter along the hill-top road near Loxey Thorn. She sometimes looks like an old crone gathering sticks. She was seen face to face in 1920, and again in the 1950s. She just becomes part of the mist.'

In Somerset there are also tree spirits, some of them very sinister. Coppices which spring from the trunks of felled oaks are supposed to be haunted by the angry spirits of the trees, and local people avoid them after sundown. Willows are said to walk after people in the darkness, muttering. Birch trees are even more dangerous, for they are the tree of death. 'The One with the White Hand', a Somerset moorland spirit, was supposed to spring from a birch coppice. The boys at Taunton School had a tale of one who haunted the moors near Taunton. She would rise out of a scrub of birch and oak at twilight, and drift after benighted travellers so fast that they could not escape. Her clothes rustled as she moved like dead leaves, she was as pale as a corpse, and her long, white, skinny hand was like a blasted branch. If she touched a man's head with it he went mad, but if she laid her hand over his heart he died, and the mark of a white hand was found over his heart. A brave man laid her in the end with a handful of salt.

Water spirits of all kinds are the commonest of the Nature Spirits. The Mermaid, in spite of her name, is not confined to the sea, but comes as far inland as the salmon, and is even to be found in lakes and ponds. The water bull (*taroo ushtey*) and the water horse (*each uisgey*) of the Highlands generally come out of the sea, but the kelpies haunt rivers and lochs. The Irish lakes are infested with many kinds of monsters, such as the

[1] Osgood Mackenzie, *A Hundred Years in the Highlands* (London, 1949, 1st ed. 1921), pp. 196–7.

Ollphiast of County Meath and the 'Irish Crocodile' from the bottom of Lough Mask.[1] The English rivers have their water spirits, like Peg Powler of the Tees, who has long green hair and an insatiable desire for human lives. The froth on the upper reaches of the Tees is called 'Peg Powler's suds'.[2] Peg o' Nell, the spirit of the Ribble, is not primarily described as a water spirit. Like Sabrina, the spirit of the Severn, she is supposed to be a ghost, but Peg is the ghost, not of a princess, but of a servant girl at Waddow Hall, who was drowned in the Ribble; but since, like other river spirits, she claims a death every seven years it seems likely that she was originally the river spirit itself.[3] Often it is the river itself that is personified, like the Somerset Parrot or Dart. The Dart invocation is addressed directly to the river:

> Dart, here's a man
> To chill
> Or to kill.
> Now let me over
> To go where I will.[4]

In the well-known argument between Tweed and Till it is the rivers themselves who speak.

There are, however, plenty of inhabitants of water places known to folk tradition. The mermaids are perhaps of the most ambivalent character. The very sight of them at sea is death to sailors and it is their habit to decoy people under water, but at times they are benevolent, like the mermaid of Cury, who rewarded her rescuer with medical skill, and that in the Lowlands of Scotland, who rose in the water when a young girl's funeral was passing and lamented,

> 'If they wad drink nettles in March
> And eat muggons in May
> Sae mony braw maidens
> Wadna gang to the clay.'[5]

---

[1] W. G. Wood-Martin, *Traces of the Elder Faith of Ireland* (New York, 1902), 2 vols., Vol. I, p. 379.

[2] W. Henderson, ed. cit., p. 265.

[3] T. Parkinson, *Yorkshire Legends and Traditions* (London, 1889), 2 vols., Vol. I, pp. 108-9.

[4] R. L. Tongue, *Somerset Folklore*, p. 21.

[5] R. Chambers, ed. cit., p. 331. 'Muggons is southernwood.'

There is also a Shetland tale of a gentle mermaid who gave her life for a seal.[1]

The Irish Merrows are good-humoured enough, if we can believe Crofton Croker's tale of Coomara, but the gentlest of all are the seal people, who are reluctant to avenge even the greatest injuries. *The Seal Fisher's Adventure* shows them at their noblest.[2] Even the seals, however, can be rather alarming. In Edinburgh in March 1959, I was told by a Miss Bartholemew of an experience of her sister's on one of the Scottish Islands. She thought, one fine summer night, that she would go out to bathe in the sea and watch the seals. Her way ran past a freshwater loch, and she had been warned by the local people not to take that way at night. However, she went, and saw nothing, but heard a quick pattering like little footsteps all around her, which frightened her a little, so that she ran, and then the footsteps quickened and ran along with her. When she got to the seashore, she could see nothing of the seals; but she was still determined to bathe, so she took off her coat and shoes. As soon as she went into the sea the seals slipped into the water from the rocks on every side. A big dog seal came up and puffed in her face, and the others pressed themselves so close against her that she had to make quickly for the shore, or she would have been pressed to death. Her feeling, though perhaps not her express belief, was that the seals and the fairies who came pattering beside her were the same people.

The seal maidens are among the commonest of the fairy brides, and sometimes, as in the Orcadian tale of *The Great Silkie of Sule Skerry*, a mortal woman is wedded by a seal husband.[3] The Ben Varrey, the mermaid of the Isle of Man, is gentler than most mermaids, but sometimes she sets her love on one of the fishermen, and lays a spell on him.[4]

The Fuath (Foo-a) of the Highlands are malignant spirits of rather varied types; shellycoat, the Urisk, Each Uisge, are all Fuath. After giving some stories about them Campbell says: 'From all these it appears that the Fuath in Sutherland is a water

[1] G. F. Black, *County Folk-Lore, Orkney and Shetland*, Ishmule, pp. 185–7, quoting the Edmonston *Sketches*, 1856, pp. 79–82.

[2] George Douglas, *Scottish Fairy and Folk Tales* (London, n.d.), pp. 155–8.

[3] F. J. Child, ed. cit., Vol. II, p. 494.

[4] Dora Broome, *Fairy Tales from the Isle of Man* (Puffin Book, 1951), pp. 27–37.

spirit; that there are males and females; that they have web-feet, yellow hair, green dresses, tails, manes and no noses; that they marry men, are killed by light, and hurt with steel weapons; and that in crossing a stream they become restless.'[1] This last point seems curious in water spirits, but some of the Fuath, such as Nuckelavee, come from the sea and cannot cross fresh running water.

Very different from these evil and ugly creatures are the Gwragedd Annwn of Wales. They are the nearest thing we have to the classical water nymph, and are lake-dwellers, often gained by mortals as wives, but nearly always lost by the infringement of taboo. This tale type is the chief survivor in Welsh oral tradition today. The Lake Maidens were beautiful, and like other water spirits, sang and played. They rowed about the surface of their lakes in little skiffs, and they possessed great wealth of cattle.

The Bucca, or Bucca-Boo, of Cornwall seems originally to have been a sea-god, like Davy Jones. Margaret Courtney says: 'Bucca is the name of a spirit that in Cornwall it was once thought necessary to propitiate. Fishermen left a fish on the sands for bucca, and in the harvest a piece of bread at lunch-time was thrown over the left shoulder, and a few drops of beer spilled on the ground for him, to ensure good luck.'[2] He seems to have declined from god-like status to a kind of devil or hobgoblin, for she continues: 'Bucca, or bucca-boo, was, until very lately (and I expect in some places still is) the terror of children, who were often, when crying, told "that if they did not stop he would come and carry them off". It was also the name of a ghost; but nowadays to call a person "a great bucca" simply implies that you think him a fool. There were two buccas—"Bucca Gwidden", the white or good spirit, and Bucca Dhu, the black, malevolent one!'[2]

Bucca's descent into a hobgoblin is even more clearly shown in the *Story of Tolcarn*, where the curiously reticulated rock is supposed to be a fisherman's net stolen by the Bucca. The Paul choir gave chase to him, chanting the creed all the time, and he fled over Paul Hill to Tolcarn, where he turned the net into stone.[3]

[1] J. F. Campbell, ed. cit., Vol. II, p. 205.
[2] M. A. Courtney, *Cornish Feasts and Folk-Lore* (Penzance, 1890), p. 129.
[3] Ibid., p. 79.

In the Fenland of Lincolnshire there was a kind of Nature worship as wild as any in the Celtic countries, but different. The life led there was hard, and the people in the old days were full of fears, graphically described to Mrs. Balfour by an old fenman.

A' can't reetly 'splain to 'ee; but th' fo'ak had idees o' ther o'an an' wa'ays o' ther o'an as a'd kep oop years 'n years, 'n *hunnerds* o' years, since th' toime when ther worn't no ch'och, leastways no cho'ch o' that sort; but tha gi'n things to th' bogles 'n sich, to ke'p un friendly. Ma gran'ther said 's how the bogles 'd wanst bin thowt a deal more on, an' at da'arklins ivery noight th' fo'ak 'd bear loights i' ther han's roon ther ha'ouses, sa'ain wo'ds to ke'p 'um off; an' a'd smear blo'd o' th' doorsil, to skeer awa'ay th' horrors; an' a'd put bre'ad an' salt o' th' flat stouns set oop by th' la'ane side to get a good ha'arvest; an' a'd spill watter i' th' fower co'ners o' th' fields, whan a' wanted ra'in; an' they thowt a deal o' th' sun, fur tha' reckoned as a' ma'ade th' yarth, an' brout th' good an' ill chances, an' a' do'ant know what ahl. A' can't tell 'ee reetly what they b'leeved; for 'twor afore ma gran'-ther's toime, ahl that, an' that's more'na hunnerd n' fifty years agone, seest-tha; but a' reckon tha ma'ade nigh iverythin' as they seed 'n heerd into sort o' gre'at bogles, an' tha wor allus gi'un um things, or sa'ayin' so't o' prayers loike, to ke'ep un fro' doin' th' fo'ak anny evil.[1]

Sun worship is expressly mentioned here as part of the Fen-men's religion, and the strange tale of *The Dead Moon*, also recorded by Mrs. Balfour, is a tale of Moon worship. 'The Tiddy Mun' in another of the tales seems to be a fen spirit, who can control waters and mists and call up pestilence out of the bogs. A certain affection was felt for him, but he could be dangerous if angered. He sounds eerie enough in the description:

He dwelt deep down in the green water holes, and came out at evening when the mists rose. Then he came creeping out in the darklings, limpelty lobelty, like a dearie wee old granther, with long white hair and a long white beard, all matted and tangled, and a long grey gown so that they could hardly see him in the dusk, but they could hear him whistling like the wind and laugh-ing like peewit. He was not wicked like the rest, but he was eerie enough, though the times were when he helped them. For on wet

[1] M. C. Balfour, *Legends of the Cars* (Folk-Lore, Vol. II, 1891), pp. 259–60.

seasons when the water rose to their door steps the whole family would go out together and shivering in the darkness they would call:

> 'Tiddy Mun wi'out a name,
> Tha watters thruff!'

They would call it till they heard a cry like a peewit across the marsh, and then they'd go home. And next morning the waters would be down.

The story is that the draining of the Fens so angered the Tiddy Mun that he brought pestilence on the children and cattle, until he was pacified with lustrations and prayers.[1] In another similar story, *The Strangers' Share*, the Tiddy Men are called the Yarthkins. It seems they must have been minor *dei loci*.

It is doubtful if any of the Norse gods imported by the Saxons and Danes have survived as fairies. The giants, Wade and Wendal, are of Norse origin, and if the nickname of Grim be entirely appropriated by Odin, he may have descended to be a Church Grim; memories of him may also survive in the hooded fairies, in 'Old Carl Hood, who's aye for ill and never for good', and possibly in Robin Hood, whom some people recognize rather doubtfully as a woodland spirit. Generally Odin has become rather a devil than a fairy, and in that character leads the Wild Hunt, the Wisht Hounds, the Devil's Dandy Dogs, and so on. But the line between devils and fairies is indeterminate in the later beliefs.

The earlier Celtic gods and goddesses are better represented among the fairies. Morgan le Fay is generally considered to descend from Morrigan, the War Goddess. Aynia, who is the Fairy Queen in Tyrone, is one form of Anu, who became Gentle Annie on the Scottish Borders and Black Annis in Leicestershire. Queen Maeve, the heroine of the Cattle Raid of Cuilgne, was probably a heroic form of Shakespeare's Queen Mab.

Lesser spirits with whom the young were threatened a short time ago, were perhaps nursery creations, invented by careful mothers to frighten their children away from danger. One of these was Jenny Greenteeth, who lurked in stagnant ponds,

[1] M. C. Balfour, ed. cit., pp. 150–1 (simplified).

grown over with weeds. The Colt Pixy was an orchard spirit who guarded apple trees, and it seems probable that Lazy Lawrence, who laid cramps on apple thieves, served the same purpose.

In Germany there are spirits which guard the cornfields; the only trace of such a belief which I have found in Britain is in a tale told to me in 1959 by Jeannie Robertson, the folksinger, who is one of the travelling people of Aberdeenshire. It was told her by her grandmother as a personal experience. Mrs. Robertson's grandmother, when she was a girl of fifteen, had, like the other girls of her family, a pony of her own. Hers was a little beauty, of whom she was very fond, and she looked after it very carefully. This particular year there was a poor harvest, and the farmers were unwilling to part with their grain, even for money. The girl was determined that her pony should not want, even if she had to steal for it. One night they camped near a fine field, where the corn was standing in shocks, ready to be led. That night, after the rest of the camp was asleep, she stole out and went to the field. It was a bright moonlight night, as clear as day. She stooped to pick up a sheaf, and something moved beside her. She glanced aside, and saw a wee, wee woman, as big as a year-old child, dressed in white silky stuff, with glittering jewels on her. The little creature did not seem to notice her, but jumped on to one of the sheaves, and leapt from shock to shock. The girl drew back. Though her horse starved, she felt she could not steal from that field. Step by step she crept away, and still the little woman leapt from sheaf to sheaf. So the girl went back empty-handed.

Jeannie Robertson was sure her grandmother believed this tale; and she was a very sober woman, and truthful.

These various accounts do not build up to such a number as do those of fairies as ghosts, and yet they cannot be left out of our reckoning.

Five

THE HOST OF THE DEAD

THE great cavalcade of the dead rides in various forms all over Europe, and even in these Islands it takes different shapes. The Wild Hunt is one of the commonest. In early days Woden was the huntsman, later he often became the Devil. An early account of it is quoted from the Anglo-Saxon Chronicle of 1127 by Branston in *The Lost Gods of England.*

> Let no one be surprised at what we are about to relate, for it was common gossip up and down the countryside that after February 6th many people both saw and heard a whole pack of huntsmen in full cry. They straddled black horses and black bucks while their hounds were pitch black with staring hideous eyes. This was seen in the very deer park of Peterburgh town, and in all the woods stretching from the same spot as far as Stamford. All through the night monks heard them sounding and winding their horns. Reliable witnesses who kept watch in the night declared that there might have been twenty or even thirty of them in this wild tentivvy as far as they could tell.[1]

The author is not explicit as to the personality of the huntsman. But presumably he would be supposed to be the Devil, followed by the souls of the dead, though they were rather a small number. In modern times there is no doubt as to the character of the Huntsman. In the West Country the tradition of the Wild Hunt is still alive. It is said to be heard going through West Coker, near Taunton, on Hallows Eve at night. A version of Mrs. Bray's story of *The Old Woman who Went to Market at*

[1] Brian Branston, *The Lost Gods of England* (London, 1957), p. 89.

Midnight was collected by R. L. Tongue at Crowcombe in 1935 and at Vellow in 1940.

In Mrs. Bray's tale there is a solitary huntsman, as there is in some of the Scandinavian legends. He is described as having small horns showing under his hunting cap and one cloven hoof. He rode a headless horse, and his hounds had horned heads and fiery eyes, and their tails whisked about and shone like fire. A strong smell of sulphur hung around them. They were hunting the soul of a lost sinner in the shape of a white hare.[1] In Lancashire the wild geese flying overhead are supposed to be the Wild Hunt, and are called the Seven Whistlers, or the Gabriel Ratchets. Often other lost souls join the hunt. The Dandy Dogs, or Dando and his Dogs, is a name given to the Wild Hunt in the neighbourhood of St. Germans. As Hunt tells the story, Dando was the name of a parson of St. Germans who was given to all forms of riot and was passionately fond of hunting. One Sunday he and his company were out hunting, and as they drove over the estate called Earth they were joined by a strange huntsman on a splendid and fiery horse. It was a hot finish, and Dando called for drink, but he had already exhausted all the flasks of his servants.

'Well, if you can't find any on Earth, go to Hell for it!' he said. The strange horseman bowed, and offered him a golden horn.

'Here is some drink from the place you mention,' he said. Dando drained the whole flask, and declared he had never tasted anything so good. In the meantime the stranger was collecting a large share of the game, quite as a matter of course. Dando was drunk and bellicose, and denied his right to it. The stranger quietly continued to strike it to his saddle. Dando flung himself off his horse and staggered over to the stranger. He grabbed at the game, and fell as the horse swerved. This put him in a passion. 'You shan't have it!' he shouted. 'I'll go to Hell for it rather than you shall get it.'

'So you shall,' said the stranger. He lifted Dando by the scruff of his neck, and carried him off, followed by the hounds in full cry. When they got to the Lynher he leapt into the

[1] K. M. Briggs and R. L. Tongue, *The Folktales of England* (London and Chicago, 1965), pp. 52–4, and A. E. Bray, *The Borders of the Tamar and Tavy* (London, 1859), 2 vols., Vol. II, pp. 114–16.

deepest pool with the hounds close behind him, and went down with a blaze of fire and a great column of steam. That was the last that mortal men saw of Dando and his dogs, but they can still be heard early on Sunday mornings, pelting past in full cry.[1]

Other tales have more definite fairy connections. Wild Edric and his fairy wife were still said to ride the Welsh Border in the nineteenth century with a host of followers;[2] King Herla's or Harlekin's Host in early medieval times was the company of the dead according to Ordericus Vitalis, who tells of a priest, Walchin, who in January of 1091 saw at Bonneval at the Church of St. Aubin in Anjou, the company of Harlequin, a black troop with black horses and banners, noble ladies, churchmen, all conditions of men, many of them known to Walchin in former times.[3] Walter Map supplements this with a real fairy story about them, not unlike *The Return of Oisin*. Herla, a king of ancient Britain, was one day visited by a grotesque creature of pigmy size, riding a goat, and himself goat-footed and hairy like Pan, who announced himself as king of many realms and peoples. He proposed that he should visit Herla and bring him wedding gifts on his marriage, and that Herla should do him like honour in a year's time. Accordingly the little people appeared at Herla's wedding, with a great wealth of gifts and provisions, and waited upon the guests so deftly that King Herla's servants were left with nothing to do. At cockcrow they departed, but a year later the pigmy king appeared and reminded Herla of his promise. King Herla went with him, taking gifts, and for three days he and his company were entertained with feasting and hunting and all merriment. Then King Herla took his leave. Many gifts were pressed upon him, and, last of all the Fairy King gave him a little greyhound to sit on his saddle bow, and told him not to dismount until the greyhound leapt down. King Herla rode home, but everything was changed. He asked a peasant what had happened, and the man could hardly understand him, for three hundred years had passed since he had left the world, and the Saxons had conquered the Britons. When they heard this, some of the

---

[1] R. Hunt, ed. cit., pp. 220–3.
[2] C. Burne and G. Jackson, *Shropshire Folk-Lore* (London, 1883), pp. 28–9.
[3] Ordericus Vitalis, *Historiae Normanorum Scriptores* (Paris, 1619), pp. 693–6.

King's companions leapt to the ground, and as their feet touched the earth they crumbled into dust. King Herla and the rest of his company, warned by their fate, rode on; and they are riding still, waiting for the greyhound to leap down.[1]

There are other such riders. As early as Geoffrey of Monmouth's day King Arthur and his host were said to ride in Wales and Somerset, as Earl FitzGerald rides round the Hill of Mullaghmast.

A tale of a somewhat similar ride of the dead is to be found in Heywood's *Hierarchy of the Blessed Angels*. He does not give the source of the story, but merely calls it a strange History. It is the tale of a centurion in Germany, who, when he was riding out, met a great procession of people nobly mounted, and at the tail of the procession rode his late cook, who had been dead a few days. He was riding a fine horse and leading another, on which he invited the centurion to mount. They were going, he said, to the Holy Land and he knew that the centurion had an earnest desire to go there. Here was the opportunity, and he could not go in better company. The intrepid centurion accepted the invitation, and vanished from the sight of his two servants, who had been riding with him. One would expect that he would be missing for years, in that ghostly company, and would only return when all his contemporaries had died, but, contrary to the common usage of such hosts, he returned next day, having seen all the sights of Jerusalem in that short time, and bringing with him two supernatural presents, a kerchief that could only be cleaned by fire and a poisoned dagger. The description of the hero of the tale as a centurion seems rather an anachronism. Heywood of course describes the ghostly cook as a devil.[2]

It might seem that there is little connection between these ghosts, ancient gods or devils and the fairies, and yet, as I have pointed out already, the distinction between the fairies and the dead is vague and shifting. The Scottish Fairy Rade, described by James VI and Alexander Montgomerie, corresponds closely to Frau Hulde's Ride, and belongs to All Hallowtide, when the fairies, the witches and the dead were all stirring.

[1] Walter Map, ed. cit., pp. 15–18.
[2] T. Heywood, *Hierarchie of the Blessed Angels* (1641), pp. 254–5. The passage is given in *Pale Hecate's Team*, Appendix V.

In the hinder end of harvest, on alhallow even,
Quhen our good neighboures doth ryd, if I reid rycht,
Som buckled on a buinvand, and som one a bene,
Ay trottand in trowpes from the twylycht;

Some saidland a sho ape all graithid into greine,
With mony elrich Incubus was rydand that nycht.

Some hoblard one ane hempstalk, havand to be heicht,
The King of pharie, and his Court, with the elph queine.[1]

In this description the fairies, the witches and the dead come close together.

I have already cited the Fairy Dwellings on Selena Moor as an example of the close connection between the fairies and the dead in Cornwall. In the West Country, too, the little white moths that flutter about the grass in the evening are called 'pisgies' and are said to be the souls of unbaptized children. Will o' the Wisps, under their various names—Spunkies, Pinkets, Jacky Lantern, Joan o' the Wad and many more, are generally reckoned as ghosts. Spunkies and Pinkets are the spirits of unbaptized children, but Will o' the Wisp is often a usurer who has hidden gold, or an unjust man who has moved his neighbours' boundary stones, or in some stories, a man who has been too clever for the Devil, and can get entry into neither Heaven nor Hell.[2] As we have seen, Brownies and other domestic spirits are often thought of as ghosts.

The connection between the Trooping Fairies and the dead is as strong in Ireland as anywhere, as many of Lady Wilde's stories show. A particularly striking tale is *Kathleen*, which I summarize here, but which is beautifully told in the original.

Kathleen was a young girl of Innis Sark who was mourning very bitterly for the death of her lover. One evening, as she sat at the roadside, a beautiful lady appeared to her, and gave her a ring of herbs, telling her that she would see her lover if she looked through it. She looked, and saw him, very pale but crowned with gold, and dancing in a noble company. The lady

[1] Alexander Montgomerie, *Poems* (Scottish Text Society, Edinburgh, 1910), p. 151.
[2] G. L. Kittredge, *Friar's Lantern* (Publications of the Modern Language Association of America, Vol. XV), pp. 415–41.

gave her a larger wreath, and told her that she could visit her lover every night if she burnt a leaf of it, but she must neither pray nor cross herself while the smoke was rising, or he would vanish for ever. After that Kathleen cared for nothing except her visits to Fairyland. Every night she shut herself in her room and burnt a leaf, and while it smouldered she lay in a trance and danced in the bright hills with her lover. But her mother was deeply troubled, because Kathleen would go neither to church nor confession, and was quite changed from the girl she had been. One night she crept up and looked through a chink in the door, and saw Kathleen set fire to the leaf and sink in a trance on her bed. Then the mother knelt down, and prayed aloud to the Holy Mother to save her child's soul. Then she burst open the door, and made the sign of the cross over her. At that Kathleen started up, and cried, 'Mother! Mother! The dead are coming after me! They are here!' And she tossed about like one in a fit.

The priest came and prayed over her, and cursed the wreath, which crumbled into ashes as he spoke. Then Kathleen lay quiet; but there was no strength left in her, and before midnight she died.[1]

This is one of many folk tales which show the danger of longing too much after the dead.

It will be seen that these rides are of different kinds. There is the true Host of the Dead, the Gabriel Ratchets, the Wisht Hounds, the unbaptized children, following as a rule some godlike leader, who later becomes the Devil. There are the euhemerized gods, who are supposed to be wicked huntsmen, compelled to lead their hounds for ever, like Dando, or the wicked squire of R. L. Tongue's story, and finally there is the Fairy Rade, sometimes explicitly connected with the dead, sometimes more innocent and beautiful, like the Nithsdale fairies in Cromek's account, or the beneficent Fairy Queen of the ballad *Alison Gross*:

> But as it fell out on last Hallow-even,
>   When the seely court was ridin by,
> The queen lighted down on a gowany bank,
>   Nae far frae the tree where I wont to lye.

[1] F. S. Wilde, ed. cit., Vol. I, pp. 143–5.

> She took me up in her milk-white han,
>   An she's stroakd me three times oer her knee;
> She chang'd me again to my ain proper shape,
>   An nae mair I toddle about the tree.[1]

It is hard to say when the fairies became mixed in this; whether as descendants of the gods or whether in this context they purely represent the dead; whether their more sympathetic aspect is a modern embellishment or is founded on an old and almost forgotten memory. In this case, as in most others, consistency or logic is not to be looked for in folk tradition; for it is not one voice that transmits it, but many.

[1] F. J. Child, ed. cit., Vol. I, p. 315.

Six

HOBGOBLINS AND IMPS

T HE Puritans of the seventeenth century had no doubt at
all, as I have already said, that Hobgoblins and Brownies, like
Ghosts and Black Dogs, were imps from Hell. A few of them,
such as Baxter, entertained the hypothesis that there might be
such things as 'spiritual animals', creatures of another order
than man, but not necessarily diabolic; but the general puritan
belief was that all fairies were devils. The old folk belief in
ghosts soon flooded back and swamped the theological, in-
tellectualized theories of the Puritans, but the devilish hobgoblins remained, because they belonged to a tradition of evil
and frightening creatures older even than Christianity, primitive man's reaction to the unknown terrors that surrounded him.
The Surrealistic demons painted by Bosch and Breughel, and
less imaginatively portrayed in the crude illustrations to the
writings on witchcraft, find their counterpart in folk tradition.
In a sixteenth century Flemish painting in Bilboa Museum,
reproduced in Baroja's The *World of Witches*[1] there is a most
hobgoblinish little devil in a round cap and long pointed
shoes, with a bushy tail and a broom in his hand, but with the
surrealistic detail that his hands are naked feet. In De Lancre's
Tableau de l'Inconstance (1612) there are devils with butterfly
wings, forerunners of the eighteenth-century fairies. The fuath
Nuckelavee of the Scottish Lowlands would not be at all out of

---

[1] J. C. Baroja, *The World of Witches*, trans. by Nigel Glendinning (London,
1964).

E   55

place in one of Bosch's paintings. He is not a creature to describe to a sensitive child before bedtime.

Nuckelavee was a monster of unmixed malignity, never willingly resting from doing evil to mankind. He was a spirit in flesh. His home was the sea; and whatever his means of transit were in that element, when he moved on land he rode a horse as terrible in aspect as himself. Some thought that rider and horse were really one, and that this was the shape of the monster. Nuckelavee's head was like that of a man's, only ten times larger, and his mouth projected like that of a pig, and was enormously wide. There was not a hair on the monster's body, for the very good reason that he had no skin.

If crops were blighted by sea-gust or mildew, if live stock fell over the high rocks that skirt the shores, or if an epidemic raged among men, or among the lower animals, Nuckelavee was the cause of all. His breath was venom, falling like blight on vegetable, and with deadly disease on animal life. He was also blamed for long-continued droughts; for some unknown reason he had serious objections to fresh water, and was never known to visit the land during rain.[1]

A description founded on that given by an old man who had had an encounter with the monster, is even more terrifying.

The lower part of this terrible monster, as seen by Tammie, was like a great horse with flappers like fins about his legs, with a mouth as wide as a whale's, from whence came breath like steam from a brewing-kettle. On him sat, or rather seemed to grow from his back, a huge man with no legs, and arms that reached nearly to the ground. His head was as big as a clue of simmons (a clue of straw ropes, generally about three feet in diameter), and this huge head kept rolling from one shoulder to the other as if it meant to tumble off. But what to Tammie appeared the most horrible of all, was that the monster was skinless; this utter want of skin adding much to the terrific appearance of the creature's naked body,—the whole surface of it showing only red raw flesh, in which Tammie saw blood, black as tar, running through yellow veins, and great sinews, thick as horse-tethers, twisting, stretching and contracting as the monster moved.

This is perhaps the nastiest of all the demon people of these islands, though there are others that run it close. There is, for

[1] G. Douglas, ed. cit., pp. 160–3; from W. Traill Dennison in *The Scottish Antiquary*.

instance, the barrow-wight described by R. L. Tongue in
Somerset Folklore (Part I, Section 1, p. 13). 'A crouching form
like a rock, with matted hair all over it, and pale, flat eyes,'
or the unpleasant nursery spirit, Bloody Bones (p. 123). 'This
most unpleasant hobgoblin, as we were assured in my childhood, lived in a dark cupboard, usually under the stairs. If
you were heroic enough to peep through a crack you would get
a glimpse of the dreadful, crouching creature, with blood
running down his face, seated waiting on a pile of raw bones
that had belonged to children who told lies or said bad words.
If you peeped through the keyhole he got you anyway.'

There were other vampire spirits of something the same kind
in the country—the Redcaps, who lived in Lowland peel
towers where dark deeds had been done, and re-dyed their red
caps in the blood of travellers who sheltered there,[1] the
Baobhan Sith, who appeared like beautiful women, but sucked
the blood of the men who had intercourse with them,[2] and
many of the water people. The Laird of Lorntie's mermaid was
of the same bloodthirsty character. As he was passing a lake,
some three miles from his house of Lorntie in Angus, he heard a
struggling and splashing in the water, and a woman's voice
calling for help. He jumped into the water to rescue her, but
his manservant pulled him back.

'Bide, Lorntie!' he cried. 'Bide a blink! That wauling madam
was nae other, God sauf us! than the mermaid!'

The laird believed him and turned aside, on which the
mermaid rose in the water and called after him:

> 'Lorntie, Lorntie,
> Were it na your man,
> I had gart your heart's bluid
> Skirl in my pan!'[3]

The Highland Kelpie was as bloodthirsty and as hungry for
human life. Its proper form was that of a horse, but it could
disguise itself as a man. One story commonly told was of seven
little girls who were out walking on a Sunday, and saw a pretty
little horse grazing near the lochside. One after another they

[1] W. Henderson, ed. cit., p. 253.
[2] D. A. Mackenzie, ed. cit., pp. 236-7.
[3] R. Chambers, ed. cit., p. 332.

got on its back, which gradually lengthened itself so that there was room for them all. A little boy who was with them noticed this, and refused to join them. The horse turned its head, and suddenly yelled out, 'Come on, little scabby-head, get up too!' The boy ran for his life, and hid among the boulders where the thing could not get at him. When it saw this it turned aside and dashed into the loch, with the seven little girls on its back. And nothing of them but their entrails ever came to land. This tale is told of Glen Keltney, near Schiehallion, but variants of it are attached to many Highland lochs.

In another tale the Kelpie took the appearance of a handsome young man, but, when the girl whom he was courting discovered him by the shells and weed in his hair, he turned into a horse to pursue her, and would have killed and eaten her if it had not been for a fairy bull which she had reared.[1] A somewhat similar story is told of the Glashtin in the Isle of Man.

Shellycoat is as a rule a less dangerous water spirit than the Kelpie. The Shellycoat of Leith was said to have once played ball with an unfortunate traveller until he was dead, but as a rule they are more mischievous than really dangerous, nearer to the Barguest and Brag of the Northern Counties of England. Scott says of him, 'Shellycoat, a spirit who resides in the waters, and has given his name to many a rock and stone upon the Scottish coast, belongs also to the class of bogles.'[2]

In the footnote he tells a regular bogey-beast tale about Shellycoat.

> Two men, in a very dark night, approaching the banks of the Ettrick, heard a doleful voice from its waves repeatedly exclaim— 'Lost! Lost!' They followed the sound, which seemed to be the voice of a drowning person, and, to their infinite astonishment, they found that it ascended the river. Still they continued, during a long and tempestuous night, to follow the cry of the malicious sprite; and arriving, before morning's dawn, at the very sources of the river, the voice was now heard descending the opposite side of the mountain in which they arise. The weary and deluded travellers now relinquished the pursuit; and had no sooner done so, than they heard Shellycoat applauding, in loud bursts of laughter, his successful roguery.

[1] J. F. Campbell, Vol. IV, pp. 304–6.
[2] Walter Scott, ed. cit., Vol. I, p. 150.

Shellycoat gets his name from the clattering sea-shells in which he is clad. A rather similar spirit called Tangie is dressed in seaweed.

There are some grim figures among the Lincolnshire spirits. One of the most evil of them in character—a true devil with whom everything turned out ill—was Yallery Brown in *Legends of the Cars*. He sounds harmless enough, if not very attractive, in the description of him.

> 'Twas no'an bigger 'n a ye'ar-au'd brat, but a'd long cotted hair an' beard, twisted roun' an' roun' 's body so 'a cudna see 's clouts; an' th' hair wer a'l yaller an' shinin' an' silky, loike a ba'arn's; but th' face o't wor au'd, an' 's if 'twer hunnerds o' years sin' 'twer young an' smooth. Just a he'ap o' wrinkles, an' two bright bla'ack eyne i' tha mid, set in a lot o' shinin' yaller hair; an' tha skin wor tha colour o' tha fresh turned yarth i' tha Spring— brown 's brown cud be, an' 's bare han's an' feet wor brown loike the fa'ace o' un.[1]

It seems likely from the description that the little thing was a Yarthkin; but whatever it was, it was so evil that its gifts brought a curse with them. It had been rescued by the hero of the tale from under a great stone where it was lamenting pite- ously; it spoke him fair and offered him gifts, money or a beauti- ful wife or help with his work; but when he chose help it was given in such a back-handed way that he tried to refuse it, and after that misfortune followed him all his days.

The theme of this tale is the same as *The Fairy Follower*, a tale from the Welsh Marches, heard by R. L. Tongue in the 1920s. It is of a young man who was deeply in love, and was too im- patient to wait and work for his sweetheart; so he tried to obtain a fairy helper. The method he used was very like that described in a seventeenth-century magical manuscript, setting out clear water for the fairies, and afterwards preparing a meal of bread and cheese for them; but he made various blunders in the prepa- rations and procedure, and, though he procured the fairy and she promised to grant his wishes, she did so in a back-handed way that broke his heart. He got his wife and riches, but it was a cross old rich woman he found himself married to instead of his sweetheart, who died in an epidemic through which his

[1] N. C. Balfour, ed. cit., p. 266. Also J. Jacobs, *English Fairy Tales* (Nutt, 1890), p. 27.

great strength carried him unhurt. And the fairy was always by his side, prompting him and giving him no peace; till at length he died of a broken heart, and as he lay on his hearse a cold, clear voice claimed his soul for its own.[1] There is clearly little distinction between this fairy and a devil.

In Highland folk tradition there are held to be two kinds of fairies, good and bad, and this belief is, of course, part of the stock in trade of the sophisticated French fairy stories and their successors; the good and bad fairies are the regular machinery of the plot. Here, as in other features of this type of tale, there is a link with genuine tradition, however much quirks of fancy may have distorted it.

The spectral black dog which is to be found in so many parts of England is supposed to be dangerous as well as ominous, though some black dogs are friendly and helpful. Even the famous Black Dog of Peel Castle, whom it was death to touch, was known to give friendly warning of disasters at sea. On one occasion it held back the skipper of a fishing boat so that he did not put to sea, and so escaped wreck in a sudden storm that sprang up.[2] There are many Black Dog Lanes up and down England. As a rule the Black Dog is described as about the size of a calf, shaggy and with burning, fiery eyes. It is called the Capelthwaite, Padfoot or Shag in the North. It is generally death to touch or strike it. The Creech Hill Bullbeggar is perhaps a black dog, but, if so, it goes on its hind legs. It is described as something tall and black, and it gives eerie shrieks and bursts of laughter. A Bruton man fought it all night with a hazel gad; and when the cock crowed it vanished away. The hazel gad was thought to have saved him from death.[3] A careful survey of the extent and distribution of the black dog beliefs was made by Theo Brown, and appeared in Volume 59 of *Folklore*.

Other hobgoblins are more frightening and mischievous than actually dangerous. The pixy-leading of the West Country is a hobgoblinish trick that is known elsewhere. Blakeborough gives an example from the North Riding of Yorkshire. The Will o' the Wisp here took the form of a pretty girl with a lantern, and the tailor whom she misled well deserved to be teased, for he

---

[1] *The Folktales of England*, pp. 35–6.
[2] W. W. Gill, *A Manx Scrapbook* (London, 1929), p. 242.
[3] R. L. Tongue, ed. cit., p. 122.

had boasted that if he caught a fairy he would put it in a bottle.[1] The Hedley Kow once took the form of two girls, and led a couple of young men into a bog. Merriment rather than malice seems to actuate most of them. There is supposed to be a Galley-Beggar at Over Stowey with a riotous sense of humour. On dark nights its pastime is to toboggan down from Over Stowey to Nether Stowey sitting on a hurdle, with its head under its arm. It shrieks with laughter as it goes.[2] Other creatures, the Hedley Kow, the Picktree Brag and the Buggane of the Isle of Man, tease people by changing their shape like Puck, seeming to be a pot of gold, a bar of silver, a lump of lead and so on, for no reason except for their own amusement. Sometimes they will appear like a headless bear or a ball of fire. In fact, all the metamorphoses ascribed by early pamphleteers to devils and imps are also said to be practised by these impish hobgoblins.

[1] R. Blakeborough, *Wit, Character, Folklore and Customs of the North Riding of Yorkshire* (Saltburn, 1898), p. 138.

[2] R. L. Tongue, ed. cit., pp. 122–3.

Seven

GIANTS, HAGS AND MONSTERS

THE Giants of these Islands, however grotesque they may have been, were generally less formidable than the devilish creatures like the Gruaghs and Ourisks. To begin with they were often extremely stupid. Jack the Giant-Killer's exploits were invariably a triumph of brain over brawn. Often, like the Welsh Giant in that tale, they were cowardly as well as stupid. The Giant Gorm, who was responsible for Maes Knoll, was an outstanding example. One day he was wandering across England with a largish shovelful of earth on his spade. It was the size of a small hill, and he had dug it up goodness knows where and was wondering where to dispose of it. As he strolled along with his head in the air he came to the edge of the Cotswolds, stumbled and dropped his spadeful right into the Avon Valley, where it became Maes Knoll. At the same time, he dug his spade so deep into the earth that he made Wansdyke. Vincent, Lord of Avon, heard all this rumbling and banging going on, leapt on his war-horse and charged straight for the giant. At the sight of him the giant got into a panic and started to run. He had not run more than three steps before he tumbled over his own toes and fell straight into the Bristol Channel. He had not the sense to get himself out, so he drowned, and his great bones made Steep Holme and Flat Holme.[1]

An equally gullible character was the giant who had quarrelled with the Mayor of Shrewsbury, and was carrying a

[1] R. L. Tongue, ed. cit., pp. 126–7.

62

spadeful of earth to dump in the Severn so as to drown the town. The way was longer than he expected, and presently he met a journeyman cobbler with a great bundle of shoes on his back which he had collected to mend.

'How far is it to Shrewsbury?' the giant said.

The cobbler saw that he was up to mischief, and as quick as a flash he answered: 'Shrewsbury, sir! Why, I come from there myself. It's a long road; look at all the shoes I've worn out on the way.'

'Dang it!' said the giant. 'I'm not going to walk no further on such a sweaty day.'

With that he dumped down his spadeful and made the Wrekin; then he wiped his muddy boots on his spade, and that was Wenlock Edge, and then he went back home to where he belonged.[1]

It is obvious that these giants were never believed in at all, but were humorous and fictitious characters. The friendly giants are usually of this kind. Giants friendly to man are to be found occasionally in Irish and Norse tales and in the Tyrol (Motif 531.5.1.), but perhaps they are commonest in England. *The Giant of Grabbist* is a pleasant example from Somerset.

There was once a good giant on Exmoor. He was as big as a hill, but he did no harm, and the people were quite proud of him. He was a great fisherman, and used to wade down Severn Channel and past Lundy Island and scoop up great shoals of fish in his hands, and the fishing boats from Porlock Weir and Minehead and Portishead all followed him, and took what he did not want. He was a kindly fellow, too, for once, when Elijah Crowcombe's old boat, the *Dorcas Jane*, was almost sunk in a storm, he lifted it carefully, and put it safely down in Watchet Harbour, crew, catch and all. When he got back from his fishing he used to sit on Grabbist Hill and wash the Channel mud off his feet, being very careful to keep one foot on one side of Dunster Castle and one on the other and to avoid splashing the Lawn Market. Legends go on to record various contests between the Giant and the Devil, in the course of which Tarr Steps were made and several large standing stones were hurled about, but the Giant won in the end.[2]

---

[1] C. Burne and G. Jackson, ed. cit., pp. 2–3.
[2] *Folktales of England*, pp. 69–73.

This tale is in very much the same mood as the Cornish drolls; long, rambling tales, with which people amused each other on winter nights, round the fireside or at the inn. *Tom the Giant and Jack the Tinkeard* is a typical one. Tom the Giant is something like Tom Hickathrift, but the Giant Blunderbuss, whom he kills, is a more doubtful character, though he has his magnanimous moment.[1] Many of the Giants of Cornwall were ogres and man-eaters, but Holiburn of the Cairn was a gentle creature, who died of grief at the loss of a friend whom he had accidentally killed by patting him approvingly on the head.[2] Holiburn fought for his human neighbours against the Giants of Trecobben. In William of Malmesbury's *Chronicle* there are tales of the Cornish Giants, and of Ordolph of Tavistock.

Tales of these stone-throwing giants are scattered all over the country, wherever there are natural features which call for explanation. In Shetland there were two giants called Herman and Saxe who hurled rocks at each other when they quarrelled. Saxe fetched a midwife as any fairy might have done.[3] The Manx Foawr, a grotesque and humorous character with a wife to match him, was unable to cross running water, like many of the fairies. It is notable that no attempt is made to put these creatures into a period of the past suitable to their employment as landscape builders. They stroll about a country already peopled with mayors, cobblers, tinkers, market-people, church-builders and fishermen. It may once have been seriously supposed that the artificial tumuli and giant standing-stones needed men of greater size and strength than later times produced to build them; that would be the only foundation in real belief that these tales could have. With the ogre giants the situation might be a little different. Cannibalism was almost certainly known in these islands as in most other parts of the world. A group of cannibal bandits was supposed to exist on the Laws near Dundee as late as the fifteenth century. The tale of *The Giants of Stowey* might well be told of a band of outlaws.[4] Tradition has only to work on the strength and size of these man-eaters in order to turn them into giants, and tradition is

[1] R. Hunt, ed. cit. pp. 55–72.　　　[2] Ibid., p. 52.
[3] J. Spence, *Shetland Folk-Lore* (Lerwick, 1899), pp. 152–4.
[4] R. L. Tongue, ed. cit., pp. 128–9.

always ready monstrously to enlarge the size of anyone whom it feels important. Early gods and heroes often became giants. The Welsh Bran was so huge that no ship would carry him, and he had to wade over to Ireland. In rage he became a terrible sight, almost as dreadful as Balor of the Evil Eye, who was one of his race.[1] Akin to him again are the monstrous, one-footed, one-eyed giants, with many heads and strange distortions of shape. Among these are the wizard giants, like that in *Nicht Nocht Nothing*, those who keep their lives in hidden places and own magical treasures. Even the bucolic giant of *Jack and the Beanstalk* had these, whether made by art or stolen from victims is uncertain, though the moral, chap-book version would have it that they were stolen.

Giant-like qualities cling even to the Arthurian heroes. The early Lancelot poem dwells with particularity on the distortion of Lancelot's appearance when he was in a rage.[2] Arthur and Guinevere are supposed to have sat on the two great rocks at Sewing Shields, and Guinevere said something that annoyed her husband so that he threw a stone at her, which she caught on her comb. The stone can still be seen and weighs several tons.[3] This may not be a development, however, but rather an indication of the group of beliefs from which the legends spring. Guinevere is called in Wales 'the Giant's daughter', and even in Malory remnants of the Midir and Etain story hang about her. The Irish hero, Fionn of the Fianna Finn became in later tradition Finn McCool, the giant whose wife helped him to defeat the Scottish Giant who made the Giant's Causeway.[4] Macbeth's grave near Dunsinane is many yards long,[5] and Macbeth was a contemporary of William the Conqueror. In fact, in folk tradition the characters are like those in the Bayeux Tapestry—the important ones are large and the unimportant ones are little. Often monstrous traits

---

[1] *The Mabinogion*, trans. by Gwyn & Thomas Jones (Everyman Library), pp. 33–4; and F. S. Wilde, ed. cit., Vol. I, pp. 40–1.

[2] J. L. Weston, *Sir Lancelot of the Lake*, ed. cit., p. 75.

[3] C. Hole, *English Folk Heroes* (London, 1948), p. 67.

[4] P. Kennedy, *Legendary Fictions of the Irish Celts* (London, 1894), pp. 179–81. See also S. Morrison, *Manx Fairy Tales*, pp. 45–9, in which the Scottish giant has become a Buggane.

[5] J. Sinclair, *The Statistical Account of Scotland* (Edinburgh, 1798), 21 vols., Vol. XX, pp. 224–6.

are attached to heroes, who sometimes seem to have changed from gods to heroes and from heroes to giants. In a learned and penetrating article in volume 69 of *Folklore* Dr. Ellis Davidson has examined the connection between Wade and Weland, and the beliefs we can deduce from various fragments of the story. It well illustrates the connections between the fairies, the giants and the dead. In the course of the paper she says:

> Behind the figure of Weland the Smith it seems possible then to discern a race of supernatural beings thought of in general as giants (but related also to dwarves and elves), who are both male and female, who live in families, who are skilled at the making of weapons and at stone-building, and whose dwellings may be reached by a descent into the earth or under the water. Wade and Weland are associated with certain places in England, and possibly Grendel also. The local traditions of giants who dwell in mounds, caves or stone tombs are of great interest, and Sir Gawain's Green Knight should perhaps now be added to the list.[1]

Occasional hill figures, like that at Cerne Abbas, or the Long Man of Wilmington, have generally gathered some kind of vague giant story to them, whatever their origin may have been. So the Cerne Abbas figure is supposed to be the outline of a giant killed by the local people as he slept a gorged sleep after eating their cattle.[2]

The giant-like hags of Scandinavian legend have become confused in these islands with witch beliefs. Grendel's Mother was undoubtedly one of them, and similar monstrous hags occur in the Fionn legends. The Cally Berry of Ulster is of the same kind— a translation of the Blue Hag of the Highlands. Another is the Witch of Man. She was flying through the air over Glenfernate, carrying a huge rock in her apron to build a castle for the Great Comyn of Badenoch when she passed over a devout gamekeeper, who exclaimed, 'God preserve us!' on which her apron-string broke and the rock hurtled to the ground not far from Kirkmichael. The witch failed to get another string as strong, so she had to abandon her castle-building.[3] This stone-carrying is a really giant-like activity. Madgy Figgy of Cornwall is possibly

---

[1] H. R. Ellis Davidson, *Weland the Smith* (*Folklore*, Vol. 69), pp. 145–59.
[2] J. S. Udal, *Dorsetshire Folk-Lore* (Hertford, 1922), pp. 154–8.
[3] *The Personnel of Fairyland*, p. 175.

another supernatural hag, and one might make out a case for the Witch of Fraddam;[1] but the line between natural and supernatural witches is hard to draw. Perhaps that which turned the ambitious king and his followers into the Rollright Stones and herself became an elder-tree was a supernatural hag rather than a witch.[2]

Many worms and dragons are to be found in the British tradition. As a rule they arrive from nowhere and terrorise the countryside until they are somehow destroyed, like the Gurt Vurm of Shervage Wood in Somerset. He appeared in Shervage Wood one year, as long and fat as three great oaks together. He swallowed sheep and ponies, and when any shepherds or gipsies went up that way he swallowed them too. After a while no one cared to go up there, and the worts were ripening with no one to pick them. There was an old woman who got her living from the worts, and yet she did not dare to go up. So one day when a stranger came along, a wood-cutter from Stogumber, she suggested that there were some nice faggots to cut up Shervage way. She gave him some cider and bread and cheese, but she did not say anything about the great worm. It was a steep pull-up into the wood, and before he set to work the wood-cutter sat down on a great fallen log and took a good draught of cider. The log began to wriggle about. 'You keep still!' said the wood-cutter, and he brought his axe down with such a crack that it went through the trunk like butter, and a great spurt of blood came out of it. It was the Shervage Worm, and one end set out and ran down to Bilbrook and the other to Kingston St. Mary; and since they had set out in opposite directions they never met, so the worm could not join together again, and that was the end of it.[3]

This was a small and insignificant dragon compared to the Worm of Wormington Hill or the Lambton Worm, which coiled three times round the base of a hill. The well-known story of the Lambton Worm gives the origin as well as the death of the dragon. Like the monster to whom Andromeda was to be sacrificed, the Lambton Worm was the punishment of impiety. The young Heir of Lambton was a wild lad, and one Sunday

[1] R. Hunt, ed. cit., pp. 326–7.
[2] *Folk-Lore Record*, Vol. II, p. 177.
[3] R. L. Tongue, ed. cit., pp. 130–1.

morning, when everyone else was going to church, he insisted on sitting fishing in the river, in full sight of the worshippers. When the bell had stopped and the church door was closed the Heir had a catch. A stranger was passing that way, and the Heir called to him to come and look at it. 'It's shaped like an eft,' he said, 'and it has seven holes in its head like a lamprey. What is it?'

'I never saw its like,' said the stranger. 'It seems to me to bode no good.' The Heir took the thing off the hook, and threw it in disgust into the Castle well. He thought no more of it for a long time. But years passed, and the thing grew. The Heir steadied down, and went off to the Holy Land. But while he was away the thing grew too big for the well, and came out and began to ravage the countryside. At length it got so big that it coiled itself three times round Lambton Hill, and every night it had to be given the milk of seven cows to keep it quiet. Many people tried to destroy it, but its breath was venomous, its hide was thick, and when it was cut to pieces it joined up again. At last the Heir came back, and by the advice of a wise man he destroyed the creature, wearing spiked armour, so that it wounded itself when it bit him, standing in the rushing waters of the Weare, so that the dragon's limbs were carried down, one by one as he cut them off, and could not re-unite. But he had to pay for his success by killing the first creature that met him on his return. He failed in this condition, and since then no heir of Lambton has died in his bed.[1]

This is a fairly modern story, but there are ancient elements in it. The human sacrifice motif, for which the animal is an unsatisfactory substitute, belongs to archaic notions such as seemed primitive even in the tale of Jephthah's Daughter; the dragon which joins itself when it is cut and which coils round a hill belongs to an old tradition. We are within hearing of primitive things. The winged, fire-breathing dragon of the St. George story is on the whole less common in England than the mighty worm, and so is the treasure-guarding dragon like the German Fafnir. There is a Somerset tradition of a dragon which guarded a treasure of silver, not gold, but on the whole black dogs, ghosts and giants are more connected with treasure.

[1] W. Henderson, pp. 287–91.

The Celtic imagination has produced some dragon-like monsters not unlike the orcs and sea-monsters that gaped at Beowulf on his under-water adventure. The Welsh afanc is a kind of giant crocodile that dwells in the deepest waters. In the Highlands the boobri is a gigantic bird which comes out of the water and devours sheep and cattle. It has a loud, hoarse voice and webbed feet.[1] The Welsh Llamhigyn y Dwr (the water-leaper) is like a monstrous toad, with wings and a tail instead of legs. It takes the fisherman's bait and breaks his line, but it is so big that it also drags sheep down into the water and devours them. If it is hooked it gives such blood-curdling shrieks as it is dragged to land that the fisherman is in danger of falling into the water and being sucked down.[2] Nearly all these creatures are connected with water, and come, as Andromeda's monster did, out of the sea, or from rivers, lakes or marshes. Only the dry-scaled, fire-breathing, treasure-guarding dragons which live in the roots of the mountains have more connection with fire than with water.

There is another kind of dragon, most commonly to be found in our traditional ballads, which is not intrinsically evil, but is the victim of enchantment, like the werwolf in the medieval romance and the Irish folktale. The Laidly Worm of Spindlestone Heugh was one of these.

> Her breath grew strang, her hair grew lang,
> And twisted thrice about the tree.[3]

Her horrible shape was given her by a malicious stepmother, and her true form was restored by three kisses from her brother. The motif is the same as that in the *Ballad of King Henry* and of the fragmentary *Marriage of Sir Gawayne*. In *Alison Gross* the hero is turned into a laidly worm that toddles about a tree because he refused the blandishments of a witch.[4] The tradition here seems to be a medieval one, late and romantic compared with the ruder monsters.

In a little booklet, *Fee, Fi, Fo, Fum*, H. J. Massingham suggested that both giants and dragons were once beneficent

---

[1] J. F. Campbell, Vol. IV, p. 308.
[2] J. Rhys, ed. cit., Vol. I, p. 79.
[3] F. J. Child, Vol. I, p. 309.
[4] Ibid., pp. 314–15.

characters, as the Chinese Dragon still is; that they sprang from the gentle mind of the neolithic men, and were twisted into malignity by the warlike Celts.[1] On this, as on all other subjects, he writes with vigour and persuasiveness; but the truth of the matter remains everyone's guess.

[1] H. J. Massingham, *Fee, Fi, Fo, Fum* (1926), pp. 90–123.

Eight

FAIRY BEASTS

IT seems as if there were two kinds of fairy beasts, those that are magical in themselves, with special powers and an independent way of life, fairies in animal form that is, and the fairy domestic animals, different from human cattle and often of a superior breed, but appurtenances of the fairies.

The seal people are a prime example of the first kind, a separate race, with their own rulers, owned by nobody, friendly it may be with other sea people, but not their property. Such creatures as the kelpie, though its proper form may be that of a horse, has powers of its own and appears to be no one's servant, though a magic bridle will enslave the kelpie for a time. Grahame of Morphie succeeded in throwing such a bridle over the kelpie and forcing it to work at the building of his castle. When the castle was built and the kelpie was freed it cried, as it galloped off:

> 'Sair back and sair banes,
> Drivin' the laird o' Morphie's stanes!
> The Laird o' Morphie'll never thrive
> As lang's the kelpy is alive!' [1]

But one never hears of the Kelpie working for a fairy master.

Some of the black dogs are the Devil's hounds, but the solitary ones seem to belong to themselves. Moreover there are many creatures which seem to be animals, but which are really fairies in animal form; weasels, cats and toads are often not what

[1] R. Chambers, p. 335.

they appear, and what appear to be birds may really be disguised fairies. In Bottrell's *Fairy Dwellings on Selena Moor* it will be remembered that it was said that the fairies could take the shape of any bird or creature they wished, but that each shape must be smaller than the last.

Cats, in Ireland at least, are regarded almost as fairies in their own right, and generally as evil fairies. The King of the Cats may be basking on your own hearth, and he is often potent for ill. It is only fair to say that the treatment which the cats receive would excuse a good deal of malice on their part. In England, too, there is a King of the Cats, and one of the best versions of Tale Type 113 A is told about him. They say that two young men were once staying in a remote hunting lodge in the Highlands, and one of them had been overtired the day before and chose to stay at home while the other went out shooting. He returned late at night, and all through supper was very quiet and absent, but afterwards, when they were sitting by the fire with the old, black household cat between them, the young man said: 'A strange thing happened to me this evening, I lost my way home, that's why I'm so late, and it fell dark whilst I was still wandering about. At last I saw a light in the distance, and made towards it, thinking it might be some cottage where I could ask my way; but when I got to it I saw that it came streaming out of a hollow oak. Look at that cat!' he said, breaking off. 'I'll swear he understands every word I'm saying.' And indeed, the old cat was looking steadily at him with a very knowing air.

'Never mind the cat,' said his friend. 'What happened?'

'I climbed up the tree and looked down inside. It was much bigger than it looked, and furnished like a kind of church. I was looking down and heard a kind of wailing sound, like singing and howling, and a procession came up into the place—a funeral, a coffin and mourners all in black with torches, but the queer thing was that the mourners were all cats, and they were all wailing and howling together; and on the coffin there was a crown and sceptre, and——' But he got no further, for the old cat had started up, and suddenly shouted—'By Jove, old Peter's dead and I'm King of the Cats!' At that he was up the chimney in a flash, and was never seen again.[1]

[1] *Folk-Lore Journal II*, p. 22.

There are many versions of this tale; in one, the Scandinavian tale of *Knurremurre*, the cat is supposed to be a fairy who has temporarily taken animal form,[1] and there is a Lancashire version in which the dead cat is called Mally Dixon.[2] There are various Irish anecdotes and tales about the King of the Cats, an early one given by Lady Wilde is about the Bard Seanchan who satirized Irusan, the King of the Cats, and nearly paid for it by a hideous death.[3] As a rule in Ireland cats are cruel creatures and cruelly treated, but Lady Wilde has one pleasant tale of a cat who was evidently a fairy. An old woman was sitting up late spinning in her cottage, when there came several knocks on her door. She asked once or twice who it was, and at length a little voice said, 'Ach, Judy agrah, let us in, for I'm cold and hungry.'

She opened the door, and a black cat walked in, followed by two white kittens. The old woman said not a word, good or bad, but sat down to her spinning while the cats washed themselves by the fire and purred loudly. At length the black cat spoke, and warned old Judy to leave off her spinning and be off to bed, for she had already hindered the fairies of their night's pleasure.

'And if it hadn't been for myself and my daughters,' she said, 'it's dead you'd be now. But you've behaved very civil to us, so give us a drink of milk and we'll be off, and mind you don't sit up late again.'

At that old Judy fetched a good bowl of milk; the cats lapped it up, and shot off up the chimney. But something shone bright in the ashes, and when Judy picked it up it was a silver coin big enough to pay her for many a night's spinning. After that she followed the black cat's advice and never sat up late again.[4]

In the Highlands there was believed to be a giant cat, king or god of the cats who appeared to anyone who was barbarous enough to roast a succession of cats alive, and granted wishes or gave knowledge to stop the torture. The Cait Sith, or fairy cat of the Highlands, was dark green with very long ears. In folk traditions there often seems to be a prototype animal who represents all his kind. The Master Otter of Ireland is an

---

[1] T. Keightley, *Fairy Mythology*, pp. 120–1.
[2] J. Harland and T. T. Wilkinson, *Lancashire Legends* (London, 1873), pp. 16–19.
[3] F. S. Wilde, ed. cit., Vol. II, pp. 24–30.
[4] Ibid., Vol. II, pp. 15–16.

example. An inch of his skin will preserve a man scatheless from gunshot or wounds, will save a horse from injury or a ship from wreck. The Master Otter is said to have appeared once at Dhu-Hill, waited upon by about a hundred common-sized otters. The king animal occurs in a good many folk tales.[1]

When we come to the animals kept by the fairies W. W. Gill says in *A Second Manx Scrapbook*:

> Fairies keep all the domestic animals except cats and fowls, and cats they steal, in Denmark. Hen-eggs and their shells, so useful to witches, have always thoroughly mystified the minds of fairy changelings, no matter how long their memories, and although demon cats and witch-cats are plentiful, a fairy-cat is a creature I have never heard of. It is acknowledged that cats have a better vision than other animals for wraiths, ghosts, and other essences of the dusk—better even than the horse—and this gift of hers may have some connection with the Manx belief that the cat was the only member of the family whose presence was tolerated by the fairies when they came into the kitchen at night.[2]

In fact, cats were practically fairies. The crowing of the cock drives away fairies, so that it would seem impossible for them to keep poultry. Yet in the tale of *Childe Rowland* the King of Elfland had a henwife, and indeed a henwife was traditionally a magical character in Scotland.

Fairy dogs are of various kinds, from the miniature hounds which belonged to Elidor's fairies to the rough, wild dogs which were loosed at the woman on the Isle of Sanntraigh. The spectral black dogs are ghosts or demons, and generally masterless, but the true fairy dogs are usually white with red ears, though Lady Wilde records black dogs that belonged to the Cave Fairies, the diminished and conquered Tuatha de Danann. 'Sometimes,' she says, 'the cave fairies make a straight path in the sea from one island to another, all paved with coral, under the water; but no one can tread it except the fairy race. Fishermen coming home late at night, on looking down, have frequently seen them passing and re-passing, a black band of little men with black dogs, who are very fierce if anyone tries to touch them.[3]

[1] W. G. Wood-Martin, ed. cit., Vol. II, pp. 121–2.
[2] W. W. Gill, *A Second Manx Scrapbook*, p. 216.
[3] F. S. Wilde, ed. cit., Vol. I, p. 183.

In Somerset R. L. Tongue collected a recent description of a couple of fairy hounds.

I didn't know any Black Dogs on the Mendips when we were children there, I'm sure there must be some; it's a queer, lonely, haunted area; but not long ago my husband saw, not far from Priddy, two large, white, rough-haired hounds with reddish ears. They were bigger than Irish wolf-hounds, but so like them that his first thought was—'I always thought they were grey.' They passed by him on the other side of the road (and 'lucky for him 'twas so' says our South Cadbury gardener). They made no sound. (Our Irish nanny says death passed him by close and will twice more, since to hear the fairy hounds give tongue is a sinister omen.) He couldn't say where they came from or which way they went, but he somehow felt he must not go on that way; and he retraced his steps. When he had gone about fifty yards he said everything was quite everyday. Our gardener, who came from Cadbury Castle, seemed to recognise their description, but would not talk. Since then my husband has had a very nearly fatal accident. I want to go to Cadbury Castle, but he doesn't. I tell him Nanny says he's safe, but he won't risk it. He says we're going abroad again, and that's risk enough.

Fairy animals are often described as red and white. In *A Second Manx Scrapbook* W. W. Gill says:

The lucky fairy lamb which occasionally appeared among the flocks to the advantage of flockmasters had a fleece which was wholly or partly red. One day, about twenty five or thirty years ago, Mrs. S., who lived at the top of Close Clarke, Malew, went as usual to look after her sheep, which happened to be in the steep, brook-side field containing Chibbert y Wirra, the Holy Well of Saint Mary. Running amongst them she saw a strange lamb wearing a little red saddle and having a red bridle about its head and face. She incautiously stretched out her hand to lay hold of it, but it sprang from her and vanished. If she had touched it, she said afterwards, she would have had a 'poor arm'—withered or paralysed arm. . . . The luck brought by the Manx fairy lamb is understood to have operated chiefly on the health and fertility of the sheep; but the saddle and bridle in the foregoing instance strongly suggest that the fairies rode it.[1]

[1] W.W. Gill, ed. cit., pp. 212–13.

Later he says,

> Red-eared fairy cows came up out of the sea. The little white fairy dog with something red about his head heralded the approach of his owners, especially when they wanted to come indoors for shelter on a cold winter night. He may have been one of them in that serviceable shape.

The fairy horses are of many different kinds. Sometimes they are made of rushes or stems of ragwort transformed at a word, sometimes they are beautiful miniature creatures, which can rise through the air as lightly as a flight of starlings, sometimes they have special powers and wisdom and are enchanted men and women like the dun filly in Curtin's tale of Baranoir.[1] The fairy horses are sometimes dun and shaggy, but more often white, grey or black. In the Fairy Rade described in *Young Tamlane* the horses are black, grey and white, and it is the white horse that carried the human rider. Lady Wilde gives a vivid description of the horses of the Tuatha de Danann, captured in the wars between the King of Munster and Midir of the Danann. They were stabled in the caves of the hills, they were bridled with gold and shod with silver, and a jewel shone in their foreheads like a star. The last of the breed belonged to a great lord in Connaught, and when he died the horse was bought by the English Government; but he scorned to be ridden by a common groom, dashed him to the earth, and fled away like the wind to a lake nearby, into which he plunged, and was lost to the sight of mankind for ever.[2]

King Arthur's steeds, that ride round Cadbury, are shod with silver, and so are those of Earl Fitzgerald.

There seems a close connection between the fairy horses and the water spirits, for Lady Wilde has a story of a herd of fairy horses which were halfway to being kelpies. There was a widow woman with a son, who had a fine farm at a lakeside, and had ripened some of the best corn in the country. But every night it was trampled down by hundreds of horses' hoofs. When the son watched he saw the fairy horses rising out of the lake to graze on the corn; so next night the widow gathered all the neigh-

---

[1] Jeremiah Curtin, *Irish Folk-Tales* (Dublin, 1960. First published in *Bealoideas*, 1941–2), pp. 55–64.
[2] F. S. Wilde, ed. cit., Vol. I, pp. 178–83.

bours with bridles, and they tried to throw them over the horses. They only caught one horse, the finest of the lot, and they took it to the stable, and after that they were troubled no more. But after a year she began to think that the fairy horse should be put to some use; so her son saddled and bridled it and rode it to the hunt. It carried him bravely, and he was the admiration of all there; but on the way home, as they came near the lake, the horse threw his rider, whose foot caught in the stirrup, and the horse dragged him along so that he was torn into fragments, and as the last parted, the horse plunged into the lake. The fairy horses never came back, but the lakeside is haunted by the thundering of hoofs and the screams of the mangled rider.[1]

The wild bogey-horses generally come out of the water, the Each Uisge of Sutherland, or the kelpie of the Highlands, of which J. F. Campbell gives an excellent account.

> The legends of the doings of the water kelpie all point to some river god reduced to a fuath or bogle. The bay or grey horse grazes at the lakeside, and when he is mounted, rushes into the loch and devours his rider. His back lengthens to suit any number; men's hands stick to his skin; he is harnessed to a plough, and drags the team and plough into the loch, and tears the horses to bits; he is killed, and nothing remains but a pool of water; he falls in love with a lady, and when he appears as a man, and lays his head on her knee to be dressed, the frightened lady finds him out by the sand amongst his hair. 'Tha gainmheach ann', 'There is sand in it,' she says, and when he sleeps she makes her escape. He appears as an old woman, and is put to bed with a bevy of damsels in a mountain shieling, and he sucks the blood of all, save one, who escapes over a burn, which, water horse as he is, he dare not cross. In short, these tales and beliefs have led me to think that the old Celts must have had a destroying water god, to whom the horse was sacred, or who took the form of a horse.[2]

The Shetland Shoopiltee and the Orcadian Tangie are of the same nature as the kelpie, and like it they can take a human form. But no fairies ever rode these savage creatures.

The fairy cattle are as a rule of a milder and more domestic nature. *Crudh mara* they are called in the Highlands, and are

[1] F. S. Wilde, ed. cit., Vol. I, pp. 205–6.
[2] J. F. Campbell, ed. cit., Vol. I, pp. lxxx–lxxxi.

sometimes given by the water fairies to their friends to replenish human stock. Sometimes too, fairy bulls go wandering of their own accord and mate with earth-born cows. If so, the offspring should be carefully reared, for they are valuable. They can be distinguished from ordinary cattle by their rounded ears. Cattle of something the same kind were brought as a dowry by the Gwraged Anwn from the bottom of their lakes in the Welsh Fairy Wife stories. Sometimes on a May Day in Ireland a sacred white heifer would appear among the cattle, and this brought the greatest good luck to the farm. Lady Wilde gives a translation of an old Irish song about one of these sacred cows.

> There is a cow on the mountain,
> A fair white cow;
> She goes East and she goes West,
> And my senses have gone for love of her;
> She goes with the sun and he forgets to burn,
> And the Moon turns her face with love to her,
> My fair white cow of the mountain.[1]

There are many Irish legends of cows which rose out of the water. A mermaid caught at Ballycronen gave a gift of three cows as the price of her liberty. The famous Glasgavlen, however, came down from the sky, and gave milk to whoever needed it, until a wicked woman milked her into a sieve, when she left Ireland for ever.[2] Something the same story was told in the North of England about a miraculous cow who gave milk in a time of famine, until a witch killed her by milking her into a sieve.[3] The Dun Cow of MacBrandy's Thicket was a rare case of a mischievous fairy cow.[4]

Sometimes, as I have said in an earlier chapter, the fairies will take a fancy to a mortal cow, in which case it is very unwise to cross them.

A good deal of significance is attached to swine and pigs. In the Highlands and among sailors they are creatures of ill omen, not to be mentioned. The Cailleach Bheur sometimes turns into a wild boar, and in Fife we hear of the Gyre Carling and her Pig. The Gyre Carling is a hag-like Fairy Queen. In Worcestershire

---

[1] F. S. Wilde, ed. cit., Vol. I, p. 195.
[2] W.G. Wood-Martin, ed. cit., Vol. II, pp. 127–8.
[3] J. Harland and T.T. Wilkinson, ed. cit., pp. 16–17.
[4] J. Macdougall, *Folk Tales and Fairy Lore* (Edinburgh, 1910), pp. 281–3.

we have the ballad of *Sir Ryalas* who killed the monstrous wild boar of Bromsgrove, and was attacked by the Wild Woman of the Woods, to whom it was 'her pretty spotted pig'.[1] In all the Celtic legends there is the hunt of an enormous wild boar.

In Wales the goats are almost fairy animals in their own right. The Gwyllion, the mountain fairies of Wales, are special friends of the goats, and comb their beards on Thursdays ready for Friday, which is the fairy Sunday. On the Continent, perhaps more than in England, the goat is the favourite form taken by the Devil. In England and Scotland he chooses a black dog.

Among wild creatures deer are some of the most magical. Often in folk tales they are enchanted humans, but there seem to be magic deer in their own right. In the Highlands they are under the care of the Cailleach Bheur, who herds them and milks them. There is one Highland tale in which the Fairy Wife is a white hind.[2] There are tales and rumours of a sacred white deer, like that seen in the reign of King Henry III. R. L. Tongue collected an account of one from a Women's Institute member at Kilmersdon in 1962.

> In ancient times there were many kinds of deer that wandered in the forest near Kilmersdon, and among them sometimes ran a magical white hind. She was rarely seen, but any woodsman who saw even a flash of her whiteness was fortunate and happy for days. Many seekers tried to get a full view of her, but without success. But one May evening the Lord of Kilmersdon was riding back over Mendip, full of care, for there was a pestilence among his people, when, before him through the forest, sped the fairy hind. It led him on for more than a mile, and then it vanished, and with it went all his fears and heaviness. His heart was filled with great happiness all his life, and in gratitude he built the Lady Chapel at Kilmersdon Church to dedicate his joy to Heaven.

It is probable that this hind was a celestial rather than a fairy vision, like the bird from Paradise in the Saint's Legend, whose song holds the saint for a hundred years. A modern version of this is the Somerset *Stone Mason of the Charltons*. In this tale Old Harry was foiled in an attempt to carry off an old stonemason

[1] R. Bell, *Ancient Poems, Ballads and Songs of the Peasantry of England* (London, 1857), pp. 124–6.
[2] G. Henderson, *Survivals in Belief among the Celts* (Glasgow, 1911), p. 125.

at work on Charlton Makrell Church. The Devil sent two imps disguised as crying children to decoy the old man off holy ground. But while he still had a foot in it he paused to hear a blackbird singing. He stood and listened in great joy for three hundred years, and while he listened the church was built and put to use. At the end of the time the old mason went up a ladder into Heaven in sight of all the congregation.[1] This was an angelic rather than a fairy bird, but the birds of Fairyland have the same powers. It was such a bird that Welsh John heard singing so sweetly in a sycamore tree that he stood entranced to listen to it until the last sap died in the tree, then he returned to his home and crumbled to dust at the touch of human hands.[2]

Of the wild birds, swans, ravens, swallows, robins and wrens have the greatest magical association. Ravens and choughs are reincarnations of King Arthur; swans are often metamorphosed princes and princesses; swallows are sacred and fortunate birds; a robin is also sacred, but ominous of death if he taps at a window or comes into the house. The yellow-hammer was probably once sacred to the sun-god; but, like the wren, he pays for his sacredness by persecution. The yellow-hammer was regarded as the Devil's bird in Scotland, and was said to suck a drop of the Devil's blood every May Day. The scratchy markings on the eggs were said to be a letter written to the Devil. The ritual killing of the wren was accounted for in the Isle of Man by the tale that she was once a wicked fairy who was forced into a wren's shape and was bound to assume it every Boxing Day.[3]

Salmon and trout were the most sacred fish in Celtic tradition. Many of the Celtic wells were haunted by invisible trout which only the second-sighted could see. Sometimes they were to be seen, however, and bold men have even caught and tried to cook them; but when the trout had been grilled on one side and the cook had tried to turn him he always leapt off the gridiron and struggled back to his well.[4] Certain salmon, too,

[1] Collected in the Midlands in 1917 from an East Somerset family.
[2] S. Hartland, *The Science of Fairy Tales* (London, 1891), p. 188.
[3] W. G. Wood-Martin, ed. cit., Vol. II, p. 149; and S. Morrison, *Manx Fairy Tales* (Peel, 1939, 2nd. edition), pp. 134–7.
[4] W. G. Wood-Martin, ed. cit., Vol. II. pp. 108–111.

have magic properties, chiefly those who have lurked in a pool into which the mystic hazel tree drops its nuts. The salmon eats the nuts, and for every nut a white spot appears on his skin. The first taste of such a salmon gives a man taste of hidden things. It was from such a taste that Fionn's tooth acquired its magic power. A white snake has the same magical property in the Scottish tale of Sir James Ramsay of Banff.[1] In many folk tales a crowned serpent has supernatural knowledge.

Tales are also told of huge fish, perhaps more monsters than fairies. One Somerset tale of a monstrous fish seems to suggest something of the witch or fairy about the creature, as it was conquered by cold iron.

My father used to tell us that there was a big fish off Barrow Sands, and it had a huge mouth. It used to swallow all the fish and the sailors too; and what it didn't finish off the conger eels did. They used to bark at those times, and people knew that the big fish was hungry and the fishermen in danger. Well, there was a bold fisherman who went out in his little boat, and the big fish opened its mouth to take him, and he cast his anchor down its throat, and the cold iron finished it.[2]

Conger eels, perhaps because of their barking, are regarded as sinister creatures round the Somerset coast; for there is another tale of a kind of syren who lured the fishermen into the water to feed the congers.

It will be seen that fairy zoology is not easy to bring into a compact system. What with fairies in the shape of animals, monstrous animals with supernatural powers, ordinary wild or domestic animals which are thought to have something unnatural about them, miniature fairy cattle and mortal cattle borrowed by the fairies, the whole subject presents as rich a tangle as any aspect of fairy belief.

[1] R. Chambers, ed. cit., pp. 77–9.
[2] Collected by R. L. Tongue, Brean Women's Institute, 1961.

Nine

FAIRY PLANTS

FROM the earliest times trees have been venerated and have been believed to be the homes of spirits, but some trees are more sacred than others. In these islands it seems as if some trees are personified and some are believed to be the resort of fairies, just as some streams have a personality of their own and others are haunted by water spirits. So it is with trees. Hawthorn trees, for instance, are everywhere thought of as haunted by the fairies, but elders and oaks have a character of their own. May trees are the fairies' favourite dancing place, and not to be cut or uprooted without grave danger. In Ireland solitary trees and bushes are often held sacred to the fairies, whether they are hawthorns or not. In the Parish of Clenor in County Cork there is a sacred ash tree whose branches are never cut though firewood is scarce and the nearest peat hag some three miles off.[1] There is another ash in Borrisokane, the old Bell Tree, or Bael Tree, which, when it was drawn in 1833 was so riven that it looked like two trees, not one. Perhaps the Beltane fires had once been lighted in the middle of it, as they were in the ancient yew at Fortingal in Perthshire. But the local belief was that if even a chip of wood from it was burned in any house, that house would be destroyed by fire.[2] The ash is a sacred tree everywhere, and in Somerset ashen gads were used to protect the cattle against fairies and witches, as rowan, or mountain ash, was in Scotland. Another sacred tree was, in one case at least, an alder,

[1] W. G. Wood-Martin, ed. cit., Vol. II, p. 158.　　[2] Ibid., Vol. II, p. 159.

hanging over a saint's well. A cottager who tried to cut a branch off it twice stopped and went home because he saw his cottage on fire, and twice found that it was a delusion. The third time he determined not to be distracted; he cut the branch and took it home, to find his cottage burnt to the ground. He had been warned.[1]

There is a well-known rhyme:

> Fairy folks
> Are in old oaks

and the oak-men are said to haunt oak coppices, but as a rule oaks are felt to have a personality of their own. A Somerset folk-song runs:

> Ellum do grieve,
> Oak he do hate,
> Willow do walk
> If yew travels late.

The belief behind this is that if one elm tree is cut down the one next him will die of grief, but if oaks are cut they will revenge themselves if they can. The lively way in which shoots spring from the roots of felled oaks probably contributes to this belief. A coppice of this kind is a dangerous place for humans to pass through at night. Willow is the worst of all, for he walks behind belated travellers muttering.[2] There are different opinions about elders; in some parts they are said to be witches in tree form, and if you cut them they bleed; in others they are thought to give protection against the fairies, or to be the refuge of good fairies against evil ones. Whatever was thought of them they were always supposed to be magical trees. Nowadays, however, that belief seems to have died, for elders are so ruthlessly cut that one rarely sees a tree; they are no more than hedgerow shrubs.

After the hawthorn the two most magical trees are the hazel and the apple. In Ireland the hazel was the tree of mystical wisdom, whose nuts dropped into the water and fed the sacred salmon; in England it was associated with fertility. 'Plenty nuts, plenty cratches,' goes the Somerset proverb; and a bag of nuts

---

[1] W. G. Wood-Martin, ed. cit., Vol. II, p. 157. [2] R. L. Tongue, ed. cit., p. 26.

to a bride ensures a fruitful marriage. In the past the Hallowmas nutting expeditions were as full of licence as the May Gathering, and girls who went nutting on a Sunday were said to meet Satan in the woods. Some trace of that belief is to be found in the seventeenth-century play *Grim the Collier of Croydon*,[1] but it is a kindly devil that they meet. The apple was the tree of enchantment in medieval England. It was under a grafted apple tree that Lancelot was asleep when the four fairy queens carried him away, and in the *Romance of King Orfeo* Eurydice was asleep under an apple tree when the Fairy King carried her off. Apples and apple peel are used in several forms of divination, and Avalon, the Isle of the Apples, was the name of the Paradise or Fairyland into which Arthur disappeared. If it was Glastonbury it was none the less Fairyland.

Fairy flowers may be divided into those that give protection against the fairies and those that belong to them.

St. John's wort is the chief of the protective herbs. It heals all the illnesses supposed to be brought on by the fairies, such as stitch, itch and cramp, and it protects the wearer as well as rowan against fairy blight, witchcraft and the power of the Devil. Verbena has the same virtue, and so has ground-ivy.[2]

Cowslips on the other hand are fairy flowers, and have the power to unlock hidden treasures; they are called 'culvers' keys' in the West.[3] Primroses are fairy flowers. In Ireland they are scattered before the house door to keep off the fairies, who are not supposed to be able to pass them, but in Somerset they are the special property of the fairies. Like other yellow flowers they used often to be associated with the Devil. If a nosegay holds less than thirteen it must be protected by violets, or it is unlucky to take it into church, or even into a house. In the Somerset story, *Goblin Combe*, a lost child who had been picking primroses accidentally touched a fairy rock with them, and the fairies came out, gave her presents and showed her the way home. An old miser tried to imitate her, but he took the wrong number of primroses, and was never seen again.[4] Forget-me-nots, too, are carried in searching for hidden

---

[1] Robert Dodsley, *Old Plays*, ed. H. G. Hazlitt (London, 1874), 15 vols., Vol. VIII.
[2] F. S. Wilde, ed. cit., Vol. I, p. 56.
[3] R. L. Tongue, ed. cit., p. 33. See Part I, Section 2, for Plant Beliefs.
[4] *Folktales of England*, pp. 34–5.

treasure, often supposed to be guarded by fairies or spirits. Red campion and devil's-bit scabious are fairy flowers. Periwinkles are called 'sorcerers' violets' in Somerset, and by sorcerers it appears that fairies are meant rather than witches. Wild thyme is a fairy plant and dangerous to bring into the house.

Foxgloves, which Henderson suggests should really be called 'folks' gloves',[1] are universally reputed to be fairy plants. R. L. Tongue gives a modern instance of the belief that it is unlucky to pick them. 'Why don't people allow foxgloves in a house? We saw some lovely ones and stopped the car, and I picked a lot and put them in vases. They looked beautiful, and when my friend came to tea I said, "Aren't my foxgloves lovely?" But she was quite frightened and told me to take them out. She wouldn't go near them, but kept behind the table on the other side of the room.'

The juice of ten foxglove leaves will, however, in the Irish belief, cure a fairy-struck child—perhaps a case of the hair of the dog that bit him.

Lady Wilde tells us that in Ireland the herb-women are supposed to have received their knowledge from the fairies, and it is they alone who know of certain herbs, and who can recognize those that are dangerous. Everyone knows, however, that there are seven herbs that nothing natural or supernatural can injure; they are John's-wort, vervain, speedwell, eyebright, mallow, yarrow and self-help. They are best gathered at noon on a bright day, near the time of the full moon. Of these yarrow is one of the most powerful.[2] A four-leafed clover not only breaks fairy spells, but gives power to see through all glamour.

Two plants that belong entirely to the fairies, and that cannot be used against them, so far as I know, are ragwort and rye grass, in which the fairy host take refuge.[3] It was under a plant of ragwort—a boliaun—that the cluricaune in Crofton Croker's story hid his treasure. The finder tied his red garter to the plant to mark it while he ran to fetch his spade. When he came back every ragwort in the field had a red garter tied to it.[4] Ragwort stalks are used by the fairies for horses. Bluebells

---

[1] W. Henderson, ed. cit., pp. 227–8. (Quoting Hartley Coleridge.)
[2] F. S. Wilde, ed. cit., Vol. II, p. 71.
[3] L. Spence, *The Fairy Tradition in Britain* (London, 1948), p. 61.
[4] T. Crofton Croker, *Fairy Legends of the South of Ireland* (2nd edition, London, 1826), 3 vols., Vol. I, pp. 178–83.

are believed to be fairy flowers. In Somerset they say you should never venture into a wood to pick bluebells. If you are a child you may never come out again, and if you are grown-up you will be pixy-led until someone meets you and takes you out. The same belief is probably known in the North, for Beatrix Potter used it in *The Fairy Caravan*.[1] The Scottish singing game, *The Dusky Bluebells*, is probably a magical or fairy song. There is something a little sinister about the words and fairy-like in the tune. It is danced in and out of a standing ring.

> In and out the dusky bluebells,
> In and out the dusky bluebells,
> In and out the dusky bluebells,
> I am your master.

> Tipper-ipper-apper on your shoulder,
> Tipper-ipper-apper on your shoulder,
> Tipper-ipper-apper on your shoulder,
> I am your master.[2]

In the sixteenth and seventeenth century there was much talk of the fairy fernseed, which men caught on Midsummer-Eve to give them the power of invisibility,[3] but one does not hear so much about it now. Broom was a fairy plant, and used in spells; the *Ballad of Broomfield* shows one use of it.[4] Of garden flowers tulips were special to fairies. People felt it unlucky to cut them, and specially to sell them for money. The West Country tale of *The Tulip Fairies*[5] illustrates this, and it is still believed in Somerset, or was till very recently. Mugwort, in which mermaids take a particular interest, is a magic herb. Running footmen used to wear it in their shoes, for by its help a man can run all day without tiring.[6] The modern housewife might find it useful. Snowdrops are the flowers of death, and are unwelcome gifts in hospitals. Indeed, there are few homely plants that were not, for health or danger, connected with the fairies.

[1] Beatrix Heelis, *The Fairy Caravan* (Philadelphia, 1929), pp. 141–4.
[2] Collected in Perthshire c. 1920.
[3] R. Bovet, *Pandaemonium* (1684), pp. 217–18.
[4] F. J. Child, ed. cit., Vol. I, p. 394.
[5] A. E. Bray, ed. cit., Vol. I, pp. 180–1.
[6] R. L. Tongue, ed. cit., p. 33.

Ten

REGIONAL DIFFERENCES

I N some ways the characteristics of the fairies throughout
these islands are very much the same. Everywhere there seems
some connection between the fairies and the dead; everywhere
secrecy and reserve is needed in the mention of them. Their
favours must not be boasted of, they must not be rewarded, it is
generally not etiquette even to thank them. Everywhere they
are greedy for mortal children, ready to decoy away young girls
and nursing mothers—almost everywhere they need the help
of human midwives to enable them to bring forth children. In
most places they have the power of invisibility, and an ointment
or herb is needed to reveal them to mortals. All over the country
some among them help mortals in their work. If their ways and
wishes are regarded they give rewards of prosperity, or smaller,
more tangible gifts; if they are offended or their taboos are
broken the punishment is out of all proportion to the offence.
These traits are almost universal, but one finds a difference in
type and a variety of emphasis in different parts of the country.

The Irish fairy beliefs are the most explicit and generally
held, and here there are many strands and varieties of belief.
The fairies are of all sizes and various characters. Some are
grotesque, and almost all are formidable, but what strikes one
chiefly is the great beauty of most of the Irish fairies. Again and
again we hear of their magnificence, their love of music and
poetry, their feasts and rides, the beauty of the fairy women
and the fairy horses. There is a close connection between them

and the dead, but their splendour seems to derive from their god-like qualities—in Ireland more than anywhere else one feels the fairies to be shadows of the departed gods of the country.

The heroic tales of the Highlands of Scotland are so like to the Irish that some of them are exactly the same, but the modern fairy beliefs are somehow different. We have an emphasis on the double strain—the good and the bad among the fairies. We have glimpses of the fairy beauty, fairy music sounds out of the hills, and is learned by mortal pipers as it is in Ireland, but the fairies are on the whole diminished, in glamour if not in size, homelier, shyer, and often more grotesque. There is a teeming host of monsters in the Highland beliefs, bodachs, glaistigs, brollachon and so on, shapeless, monstrous creatures looming out of the mist. The Cailleach Bheur in the Highlands is a more elemental and formidable character than the Cally Berry who survives in Ulster tradition. Some of the Highland fairies seem nearer to aboriginal men than to gods, especially in tales of fairy borrowing.

In Wales there seem again to be a variety of shapes for the fairies. The Bendith y Mamau belong to the ordinary fairy pattern; dancing, singing, stealing children and visiting human houses. The fairy wives are perhaps particularly characteristic of Wales, rising out of lakes, won by gifts of bread and cheese, and often bringing dowries of fairy cattle. The fairy wife is an universal concept, but the particular form she takes in Wales is characteristic. Welsh tradition is almost as much haunted by monsters as Highland. The Afanc and the Water Leaper are not as dreadful as Nuckelavee or the Glaistig, but they are bad enough. In Wales there are a great number of tales of the magical passage of time in Fairyland, and of men who crumble into dust on their return. This particular motif is more common in Wales than in stories of the same type elsewhere.

The Isle of Man has names of its own for its fairies and spirits, in the Manx-Gaelic tongue, which is now being sedulously revived. Its fairies are on the whole small—the 'little fellas', but they have the usual characteristics. Like all fairies they must be treated with respect—one should always wish them good night or good day when crossing the Fairy Bridge in the centre of the Island. They are great lovers of music; even the Foawrs, or giants, enjoy dance tunes. They change children and milk cows and play all the fairy pranks. The bogies, the mermaids, the water horses, the water bulls, the domestic goblins are all to be found on the Isle of Man. Mannanan, or Manachan Mac Lir, is the most distinctive of their spirits. It is he who takes the form of the three-legged wheel which is the emblem of Man. He is long dead, however; no appearance of Mannanan has been recorded in living memory. With the Celtic strain there are also some traces of Scandinavian tradition on Man.

In Cornwall the Celtic imagination is rather differently manifested. The fairies as a rule are here small and diminishing people, whether they are regarded as fallen angels or as the dead, and in Cornwall the dead predominate. The fairies, though tiny, are very beautiful; it is perhaps a Puritan strain that makes their beauty illusory and unable to bear the full light of day. Both the domestic fairies and the goblins are represented by the pisgies. There are plenty of bogies—the knockers and bogans and spriggans, but Cornwall is perhaps specially the land of Giants, and of animated standing stones, that go down to the streams to drink, and crush humans who try to pick out the treasures from their empty sockets. Some of the same traits are found in the supernatural beings of other Western counties, particularly Devon and Somerset. Here, too, there are lively standing stones and mischievous pixies. Somerset is said to have lost its true fairies; the last were seen at Buckland St. Mary. Since then there have been plenty of pixies in Somerset, but no fairies.

In Orkney and Shetland the Scandinavian influence is stronger than in the Highlands. The limping trows, which have to be underground by sunrise are in the true Scandinavian tradition. But the water horse and the seal people are to be found in both Orkney and Shetland.

The fairies of the Lowlands of Scotland have their ridings like the Celtic fairies; and, if Cromek is to be believed, they are very beautiful, about half the size of mortal men, with beautiful little horses to match them. The Queen of Elfland, as seen by True Thomas, was also beautiful, but of mortal size. In the Romance we have the change into shrivelled and dreadful looks which may indicate that the beauty was mere glamour. Walter Scott's Alice Brand follows a true tradition.

In Hugh Miller's description of the passing of the fairies the rade is of withered, stunted creatures riding little shaggy ponies. And the descriptions of the fairies in the witch trials are prosaic enough, the braw, broad-faced man who was the King of the Fairies according to Isobel Gowdie, and the stout woman in white who was their Queen. There are fewer giants in the Scottish Lowlands than in other parts of the country, but there are several worms and dragons, and there are mermaids, shellycoats, bogles and redcaps. Brownies are perhaps the most characteristic of the Lowland spirits, laborious, grotesque, touchy creatures, capable of affection and even devotion.

In the North of England there are still Brownies and some fairies, and there is an abundance of grotesque bogies, Brash, Padfoot, Shriker, the Capelthwaite, the Brag, the Hedley Kow, all very much alike in habits and behaviour. A good many of these hobgoblins are supposed to be ghosts, and some are devils outright. We hear little of the theory of the Fallen Angels, too bad for Heaven and too good for Hell, which is mooted in the Celtic Countries.

The fairies in the Eastern Fens are perhaps more individual than any others. In the rest of Lincolnshire there is little difference from other Northern counties; Shagfoal and Shag are of the same nature as the Brash and the Hedley Kow, there are boogart and brownie stories; but the Yarthkins and Tiddy Muns and Tod Lowries are queer, primeval, dangerous spirits, breathing pestilence and having to be constantly placated. The Giants of the Fenland, Wendel and Wade, were a heritage from the Saxons, but the other supernaturals seem to have evolved out of the bogs. With the draining of the fens the belief has gone, and the observances have long ceased. It is difficult to regret the loss of these malign influences, even if they have left the world more materialistic. There was a wild poetry in the descriptions of them, but there seems to have been no beauty in the things themselves.

The Midland fairies are gentler and less formidable than those on the Celtic fringe. In Leicestershire we have Black Annis, the blue-faced hag of the Dane Hills, who ate cattle and children, but not many of them are so malevolent. There are child-stealing fairies, who leave changelings, and Pucks or

90

Pouks who mislead night wanderers and change like bogie beasts into all sorts of shapes to beguile men's wits, there are fairy hills into which people are decoyed; offences against order are punished with pinching and pricking, grain is stolen at night and horses ridden till they sweat; but pinching rather than death is the punishment, the fairies are generally small and beautiful, lovers like the rest of music and dancing, nearer to being flower spirits than spirits of the dead. I say 'are', but perhaps it would be truer to say 'were', for, so far as one can judge, there are no active fairy observances nor living beliefs in the Midland Counties. The last recorded Oxfordshire fairies are said to have been seen going down a hole under the Kingstone at the Rollright Stones. Shakespeare and Drayton were Warwickshire men, who knew the small, flower-loving fairies; Milton, whose roots were in Oxfordshire, recorded the goblins' labours, the pinching fairies, the Will o' the Wisp, the circle of tiny elves seen on a moonshiney night and the lucky fairies who visited a house at birth, but their descendants have banished these fancies. Ghosts abound in the Midland Counties, and Black Dogs are still known; but the fairies have gone to Ireland and Somerset and Cornwall, to Man and the Highlands and Islands.

Just as the landscape and the overhanging clouds change from county to county in these small but varied islands, so the fairies of each district vary subtly in mood and emphasis and colour; but it will be seen that everywhere the characteristics are broadly the same, the same stories are told about them; danger and beauty stream out of all of them.

Part Two

TRAFFIC WITH THE FAIRIES

Eleven

THE FAIRY DEPENDENCE

TALES, descriptions and anecdotes of the fairies from all
over the country and, indeed, from all over the world, make it
clear that they are not generally conceived of as existing in an
independent and self-contained state, but have great concern
with mortal things. Many creatures pursue their own lives and
destinies without any wish to hold communion with mankind,
anxious only to shun human interference. This is not so with the
fairies. However happily they may seem to pass their days in
feasting and riding and the delights of music, however much
they resent human spying or human interference, they are
never thought of as indifferent to men; human help is necessary
to many of their activities, and they greatly desire to influence
human destiny.

There are various accounts of the nature and origins of the
fairies, but they are apparently near enough in kind to mate
with humans—closer in fact than a horse is to an ass, for many
human families claim a fairy ancestress. One of the most widespread of the legends is that of the fairy wife and the fairy
lover; perhaps the commonest of all is that of the changeling,
as if the fairies needed human blood to reinforce their stock.
In Ireland particularly we find the notion that the fairies
need a human to give them strength for their battles and games,
just as the ghosts called up by Odysseus needed to drink blood
to give them strength to answer his questions. Perhaps one of
the most terrible pictures in literature is of the twittering,

mindless things that were once men clustering avidly round to drink the blood which will give them a semblance of life again. Yet the Irish notion is not far removed from it.

In the faction fights in which the Irish fairies, like other inhabitants of Ireland, are fond of engaging, the presence of a human being is almost essential to give strength to their arms, and the same is true of hurling matches.[1] Human food seems to be necessary to them too, either poured as a libation or left out for them at night. Indeed they are everywhere believed to be nourished upon human food, either in its grosser form or in its invisible essence, which they convey away, leaving the unnutritious substance to deceive human senses. They drained the milk from mortals' cattle much as witches were supposed to do. Donald A. Mackenzie has a tale of a man who cut a long hazel switch carried by a little old fairy man. A great spurt of milk came from it, and the milk of all the cows in the neighbourhood, which had been dry for some time, was suddenly restored.[2] Similar stories are told of cattle, which are carried invisibly into the fairy hills while a transformed block is left in their place.

Sometimes the fairies have a vampire-like habit of sucking human blood. It used to be believed in Man that if water was not left out for them to drink they would suck the blood of the sleepers in the house, or bleed them and make a cake with the blood. What was left of the cake they would hide about the house, and if it was not found and given to the sleepers to eat they would die of a wasting sickness.[3]

Sometimes a favourite cow is milked by the fairies. In Hunt's tale the fairies left some milk for the humans,[4] but in the Irish version told by Lady Wilde they took it all. Here the cow was milked by an old woman all in red who came out of a hawthorn tree, and it was disenchanted by being singed with a hot iron.[5] Sometimes the fairies were more kindly, and openly borrowed what they required. Lady Wilde again has such a tale.

> One evening a boy was driving home his father's cows when a fairy blast arose in the form of a whirlwind of dust, on which the

[1] Evans Wentz, ed. cit., p. 44.
[2] D. A. Mackenzie, ed. cit., pp. 219–21.
[3] F. S. Wilde, ed. cit., Vol. I, p. 20.
[4] R. Hunt, ed. cit., pp. 107–9.   [5] F. S. Wilde, ed. cit., Vol. II, p. 47.

cows took fright, and one of them ran upon a fairy rath. The boy followed to turn her back, when he was met and stopped by an old witch-woman.

'Let her alone, Alanna,' she cried, 'she is on our ground now, and you can't take her away. So just run home and tell your father that on this day twelvemonth the cow will be restored to him, and bring a fine young calf along with her. But the fairies want her badly now, for our beautiful young queen down there is fretting her life out for want of some milk that has the scent of the green grass in it, and of the fresh upper air. Now don't fret, Alanna, but trust my words. There, take yon hazel stick and strike the cow boldly three times on the head, that so the way may be clear we have to travel.'

With that the boy struck the animal as he was desired, for the old witch-woman was so nice and civil that he liked to oblige her, and immediately after she and the cow vanished away, as if they had sunk into the earth.

However, the father minded the time, and when that day year came round he sent his son to the fairy rath to see if the witch had kept her promise, and there truly was the cow standing quite patiently, and a fine white calf by her side.[1]

The fairies are great in music and in medicine; yet human musicians are often inveigled into the fairy hills, and it seems necessary for a human midwife to deliver fairy babies. There might be a possible explanation for this, and for the fairy liking for human food. It is hinted at in two stories, one from Wales and one from Ireland. In the Welsh one given by John Rhys the fairy wife is recognized by the midwife attending her as a local girl stolen by the fairies,[2] and in the Irish one the fairy wife who takes food from a farmhouse is a stolen mortal, who still has a chance of being rescued if she refrains from fairy food. It will be remembered that Malekin in Ralph of Coggeshall's story described herself as a human being stolen by the fairies, and she was glad to eat food left out for her. She also had a hope of being freed from Fairyland.[3] The belief, however, in the fairies eating human food is so widespread that it seems impossible to limit the habit to stolen humans; the borrowing is too systematic. In Walter Scott's tale of *The Tacksman's Ox*

[1] F. S. Wilde, ed. cit., Vol. II, pp. 45–6.
[2] J. Rhys, ed. cit., Vol. I, pp. 212–14.
[3] *Ralph of Coggeshall*, p. 121.

all the fairies are concerned in the theft of the human food. Typical references to the habit are to be found in Mary Leather's *Hereford Folklore*. We find, for instance: 'William P—— of Longtown, defined "farises" as "little people that come into folk's houses and steal things".' And later in the same chapter: —'Mrs. D—— of Foxley, said that her mother, now dead, so firmly believed in the existence of the little people that as long as she lived she left the door ajar, and food on the table at night. In return for which they left her money sometimes, and always silver money too.'[1]

Tales of fairy borrowing and lending are widespread. In Hereford, Worcester, Somerset and Northumberland there are tales of the broken bilk or lost peel. Almost always the kindly labourer who mends or makes one is rewarded with a gift of food. In this group of tales it is lucky, not dangerous, to partake of the food. An example of the tale is again to be found in Leather's *Hereford Folklore*.

> One day a man was working in the fields when he heard the fairies talking over their baking; they said they had no peel. He said, 'I'll find a peel.' He made one and left it out in the field where they could easily get it. Next day it was gone, and in its place the fairies had given him a batch of delicious cakes. But they were invisible all the time; he never saw them, only heard them talking. A peel is a flat iron shovel, with a long wooden handle, used for putting bread or loaves into the oven and taking them out.[2]

In this case it seems that the fairies were not frightened away by cold iron, though possibly they might have been unable to work it themselves.

Pans, meal, and occasionally even salt, are borrowed by the fairies, usually those that live underground near a human house. It used to be considered unlucky to lend salt out of the house, but in a tale from Lewis a housewife lent salt to a fairy and no harm came of it. In Campbell's story from the Isle of Sanntraigh a Woman of Peace was in the habit of borrowing a pot, and returning it with the bones left in for payment. Once when the husband was alone in the house he let the pot go

---

[1] E. M. Leather, ed. cit. p. 43.   [2] Ibid., p. 44.

without the necessary spoken conditions, and the pot would have been lost for ever if the Goodwife had not gone to the fairy Bruth and snatched it off the fire. As she went out a fairy man said:

> 'Silent wife, silent wife,
> That came on us from the land of chase,
> Thou man on the surface of the "Bruth",
> Loose the black, and slip the fierce.'

The fairy dogs were loosed and came after her, and she barely escaped. This suggests that the human people were as uncanny to the fairies as the fairies were to them.[1] This is even clearer in a Gaelic rhyme quoted by W. W. Gill in *A Second Manx Scrapbook*. In it an old fairy man complains of a mortal housewife who lived above his fairy house; 'The Dumb Woman from the Land of the Dead took my kettle.'[2] She was dumb, presumably, because she kept the ritual silence which is considered advisable in dealing with the fairies, and from the Land of the Dead because all mortals are doomed to die.

Humankind might well seem uncanny creatures to fairies, with their cold iron and their mastery of Christian words and signs.

Fairy houses are sometimes underneath human hearths, and the hearthstone is often their door. Walter Gill has a story quoted from *The Celtic Review* about a house at Airlie in Angus which was supposed to be haunted by the fairies because cakes baking at the fire sometimes disappeared. At length the house was pulled down, and it was found that the hearthstone was actually the roofstone of an underground house. A number of mouldering cakes were found which had slipped through a crack.[3] There is a naturalistic explanation here, though one cannot help feeling that it is more likely that the cakes had been posted through the crack rather than lost in it accidentally, but in a Shetland folk-tale the hearthstone is raised, and a hand comes up and snatches a cake.

The *Good Neighbours* story, in which a fairy complains to a householder that his slops put out the fairy's fire or make a

---

[1] J. F. Campbell, ed. cit., Vol. II, pp. 52–4.
[2] W. Gill, ed. cit., p. 210.   [3] Ibid., p. 209.

EVANSTON PUBLIC LIBRARY
1703 ORRINGTON AVENUE
EVANSTON, ILLINOIS 60201

puddle in front of his door, is widespread in Scotland, but is not to be found in England, so far as I know. Good luck always follows attention to these complaints, and if they are neglected the stock suffers.[1]

When fairies were no longer believed to visit every house at night they were often supposed to frequent mills. There are two stories of Brownie hauntings at Fincastle Mill in Perthshire recorded in the archives of the School of Scottish Studies. The first sounds rather as if it was a cover for a nest of distillers, and the second which I have already cited is a variant of the Polyphemus story. A very brief Moray tale is also set in a mill. In the *Denham Tracts* there is a Northumbrian story of a fairy-haunted mill.[2]

At Rothley Mill there was a kiln for drying oatmeal, which the fairies used to visit every night to make porridge. The miller's lad one evening thought he would 'gar them loup', and, looking in at the top of the kiln and seeing them sitting round their cauldron stirring the porridge, he took a stone and threw it into the pot, so that the porridge flew about. The fairies all jumped up, and every one of them exclaiming, 'Brunt and scadded! Brunt and scadded!' ran after the lad and overtook him just as he reached a stile between the mill and Rothley. One of them gave him a blow on the back, and from that time he always went lame.

In the Isle of Man, too, the mills were often frequented by the fairies. Gill says, 'Old water mills were dear to the fairies, and Scroundal Mill in Ballaugh, now abandoned to silence and decay, was "full of them" during its busy lifetime, a former miller's last surviving daughter has told me.'[3] Later in the same passage he tells of a mill at Kiondroghad frequented by the fairies at night. Once, in a busy season, the miller's sons decided to work at night, and the broom was thrown across the room. Their mother advised them to leave the mill to the fairies; and they did so, and were no longer annoyed.

Many human occupations were imitated by the fairies. There was a small boat-building yard at Lerwick, and often at dusk

---

[1] R. H. Cromek, *Remains of Galloway and Nithsdale Song* (London, 1810), p. 300.
[2] *Denham Tracts* (F.L.S., 1891), 2 vols., Vol. I, p. 270.
[3] W. Gill, ed. cit., p. 231.

the boss would say, 'Now boys, it's time to be putting away your tools, They'll be wanting to get to work!'[1]

Some of the occupations of humans seems to be independently pursued by the fairies. The Leprechaun, the fairy shoemaker, is a highly skilled craftsman, and in Gloucester Beatrix Potter came across a story of tailoring fairies which she used and transformed in *The Tailor of Gloucester*. The fairies' greatest skill is in weaving and spinning, as such tales as *Tom Tit Tot* and *Habetrot* show. In Man, however, they complain that the fairies are unskilful spinners, and the thread which they spin up and bring back is full of short knotted lengths, and disliked by the weavers. As for their weaving, they say they make a lamentable mess of the looms if they are not dismantled at night.

Skill in various crafts is often a gift of the fairies. The chief of them is the gift of music. *Finger Lock*, a tale about the McCrimmon family collected by Hamish Henderson, is such a one, of the gift of miraculous skill in piping bestowed on an untalented and despised member of that famous family. In Campbell's story of the *Smith's Son Rescued from the Fairies* the boy is given skill with iron work, even though the fairies are frightened of cold iron. Evans Wentz collected a tale from a Barra piper of a fairy gift of skill in carpentry, which again shows the fairy habit of haunting dwellings and workshops.

I heard of an apprentice to carpentry who was working with his master at the building of a boat, at a little distance from his house, and near the sea. He went to work one morning and forgot a certain tool which he needed in the boat-building. He returned to his carpenter-shed to get it, and found the shed filled with fairy men and women. On seeing him they ran away so greatly confused that one of the women forgot her gird (belt), and he picked it up. In a little while she came back for the gird, and asked him to give it her, but he refused to do so. Thereupon she promised him that he should be made master of his trade wherever his lot should fall without future apprenticeship. On that condition he gave her the gird; and rising early next morning he went to the yard where the boat was a-building and put in two planks so perfectly that when the master arrived and saw them, he said to him, 'Are you aware of anybody being in the building-yard last night, for I see by the work done that I am more likely to be an apprentice than the person who put in those two planks, whoever he is. Was it you that did it?'

The reply was in the affirmative, and the apprentice told his master the circumstances under which he gained the rapid mastership of his trade.[1]

It is interesting to note that this gift, unlike the gift of fairy money, was not forfeited when its source was told. ·

As for markets, the fairies not only attend human ones invisibly, to steal butter, and anything that takes their fancy, but they hold markets of their own, the best known being that at Pitminster in Somerset. The first recording of this was by Bovet,[2] but the tradition is still extant. In Ireland the Fairy Fair is called 'The Fair of the Dead', and is held on November Eve, but these dead are sometimes called the Fairies, and their King, Finvarra, is called the Fairy King. The description is just like that of the Fairy Fair. 'They came to the fair, which was filled with a crowd of people he had never seen on the island in all his days. And they danced and laughed and drank red wine from little cups. And there were pipers, and harpers, and little cobblers mending shoes, and all the most beautiful things in the world to eat and drink, just as if they were in a King's palace.'[3]

In Wales a princely tribe of fairies used to come to the markets along the Bristol Channel, and send up prices by their lordly buying; but as a rule the marketing fairies are of a homelier kind, and prefer to take what they want without paying for it.[4]

It will be seen, then, that fairies not only confer benefits upon mankind but also receive them, and might almost be said to live as parasites on men. They bring luck and increase on the farm, they can give presents of silver money, and they keep a jealous eye on the order of the house and farmstead. Certain independent foods they have—berries and leaves and dewdrops dressed up with fairy glamour. They can concoct herbs and ointments, make bread and cakes, spin, weave, make shoes, and sometimes fairy implements, make musical instruments from straws and pipes, and occasionally do metal work, and labour, or seem to labour, in the mines. They have their own

[1] Evans Wentz, ed. cit., pp. 106–7.
[2] R. Bovet, ed. cit. 1684, p. 208.
[3] F. S. Wilde, ed. cit., Vol. I, pp. 145–7.
[4] J. Rhys, ed. cit., Vol. I, p. 161.

cattle, and yet for meat, meal, butter and cheese, they seem to depend chiefly on human resources. They need human nurses and midwives, and must reinforce their blood from human strains. They work and play and fight and dance and hunt, but it sometimes seems doubtful if they are doing more than acting over what they have seen humans do, or anticipating human happenings and disasters.

Twelve

TIME AND SEASONS

THERE are two conflicting beliefs about the fairies and time. In the first place there is an almost world-wide belief that time in Fairyland passes much more quickly than among mortals. In fact, in Fairyland it can hardly be said to pass at all, and the inhabitants partake of the nature of immortality. The Rip Van Winkle or Ossian story is to be found in Japan as well as in Europe and America. The belief is old as well as widespread. The medieval tale of Herlequin which I quote in Part One can be compared with quite modern versions. One such was sent to R. L. Tongue in 1929 by a correspondent who had taken it down from a very old farmer.

'Tis an old ancient tale they do tell about farm (i.e. our farm). There were a queer old chap kept a-hanging round village. Folk did see en to owl-light and night-time; some did zay he shined like a spunky—as you d' call a Jacky-my-lanthorn—but some volks 'll tell 'ee anything. He come in noon-tide too, but all was afeard to speak to 'en, for all his clothes was of strange fashion. Then one noon he come to view outside our varm door, and the old granny couldn't a-bear his sorrow; she ups and speaks to 'en, as priest say she should. 'In the name of the Lord, why troublest thou me?' she say, and then a-called out, 'Yew poor unhappy zoul, come tell I!'

And the old grey ghost he zay, 'Where be my mill then? And my son's cottage by the oak spinney? There be a gurt stone mill by river, and no cottage, and only one gurt aged old oak.'

Then the granny she sees the rights of it.

'Be church there?'

'They've got a new stone one since I went to market this morning, and I did promise Bet I 'oodn't stay late. Where be my dear old wife?'

The granny she see how 'twas, but she kept her peace, and only say, 'WHO did 'ee meet on the road?'

'A queer sort of a chap, and we got to wagering games and old merriment, and he d' want me to stay longer, but I gainsayed 'en. Bet 'ood be a-waiting. Where be my dear wife?'

And then they d'zay there was a light, and a wind that smelled sweet as a primrose bank, and a voice like a throstle in song said, 'Come whoame now, my dear. Yew don't belong down there no more. Come on whoame!' And the sad old ghost he give a bewtiful smile, and he went clean away.

The collector suggested that the Exmoor Forest Demon would be the creature delaying the old man. It is interesting to see the Highland legend used by Barrie in *Mary Rose* turning up here in Somerset.

In this story it does not seem as if the old man actually went into Fairyland; Fairyland closed round him on the Middle Earth. The same is true of those Welsh and Irish tales in which a man stepped into a fairy ring, became invisible to his companion, and, after dancing for a year, thought he had not finished a single reel.[1]

In these fairy ring tales we come to the contradictory part of the fairy time scale. In Fairyland time passes at a very arbitrary rate. Sometimes a year is really nine hundred years, sometimes a night is twenty years, sometimes a few minutes' play, as in this last story, takes a hundred years or more; but this timeless Fairyland is somehow interlocked with mortal time. The ring-bound boy was to be rescued after a year and a day,[2] the fairies pay a seven-yearly teind to Hell,[3] a stolen changeling can win free in twice seven years.[4] It is possible that the fairies can ignore time, but they are bound to seasons. The times for seeing fairies or getting into Fairyland are May Day or Hallowmas; according to Kirk they change their lodgings on quarter days, and these days are to be avoided, as the fairies are

---

[1] S. Hartland, ed. cit., pp. 162–7. Three very valuable chapters are devoted to the miraculous passage of time in Fairyland.

[2] Ibid., p. 163.

[3] F. J. Child, ed. cit., Vol. I, pp. 328–9.   [4] *Ralph of Coggeshall*, p. 120.

travelling then.[1] The time of the full moon and the days before and after it are important to the fairies. Certain times of day belong to them—twilight, midnight and full moon are times when fairies are to be seen. The days of the week are significant to them too. The very mention of Sunday is taboo, as can be seen in the widespread story of the mortal offence taken by them at the suggested addition of Sunday to the fairy song. Friday is the fairies' Sunday, and on Friday they have most power.[2] Yet in the Highlands Thursday, Friday and Saturday are all safe days as well as Sunday, and the fairies can hear nothing that is said of them on Thursdays.[3] This belief is local, for it depends on the sanctity of St. Columba's Day. Wednesday is a day of danger as well as Friday.[4] It seems that, however unconscious of time the bemused mortals in their midst may be, the fairies themselves are pretty tightly kept to a time schedule. Not only are they active at May Day and All Hallows, Lady Day and Lammas, but Midsummer and Christmas also sees them busy. These rival dates are so important and so near to each other as to incline one to guess that the fairies were formerly worshipped by two different sets of people, one which divided the year by June and December, and the other by May and November. Possibly they were respectively agriculturalists and shepherds, for the fairies show interest both in cattle and crops.

When we come, however, to the timeless fairyland another group of opinions seems to come in sight. We are very near to the timelessness of Paradise. These fairies are certainly anxious to allure mortals into fairyland, and to hold them there, if possible, for ever, but their world seems more independent of mortal affairs than that of the seasonal fairies. The agricultural fairies may very plausibly be explained as the dead; those buried under the earth would be in the best position to supervise the growth of seed; but it is equally tempting to think of the timeless fairies as the dead. As we have seen, many of their qualities are shared with the dead. It is a possible supposition that the timeless fairies sprang from the dead who were cre-

---

[1] R. Kirk, *The Secret Commonwealth* (Stirling, 1933), p. 68.
[2] F. S. Wilde, ed. cit.,Vol. II, p. 112.
[3] Evans Wentz, ed. cit., p. 85.
[4] F. S. Wilde, ed. cit., Vol. I, p. 136.

mated, and that those buried under the earth had a more active concern in agriculture. It is another possibility that the timeless fairies were originally gods, and that their entanglement with death was a later notion due to their mingling with the agricultural fairies, and to the kind of confusion which has led to angels being regarded as the souls of the dead. The whole subject calls for investigation on an international level.

Thirteen

FAIRY MORALITY: THE DOUBLE STRAIN

THE good and bad fairy played a great part in the machinery of the sophisticated French fairy tales. They seem so obviously artificial that we are inclined to discount them altogether, and to say that in folklore a good fairy is a fairy in a good temper, and a bad fairy is one that has been offended. This is to a certain extent true, but there is a definite folk tradition of benevolent and malevolent fairies, different in kind, which cannot be neglected. In Leather's *Hereford Folklore*, for instance, we have the beliefs of old Mary Phillips, reported by Mrs. Cummings, housekeeper at Pontrilas Court.

'She told us how to be very careful not to offend the wicked old fairies, or they would do us dreadful injury. These always accompanied the pretty bright fairies, who were always draped in white, with wands in their hands and flowers in their hair.'[1]

This reminds one of the Spriggans, who accompanied the small beautiful fairies in Hunt's story of the Fairy Gump. It is perhaps a belief more prevalent in the Celtic parts of these islands than in the Saxon. It is exemplified in the childhood experience of a man still living, now an eminent lawyer. The tale was told me by his sister. This child, when he was a little boy of about four, lived in a big Manse, near the church, in one of the Islands. He was a solitary little boy, the youngest of

[1] E. M. Leather, ed. cit., p. 45.

all his family, and he wandered about alone, or with the fishermen. One night as he was returning home he saw a great light in the church, and heard the sound of thousands of little musical bells. In a moment the church disappeared, and he saw nothing but a brilliant and many-coloured light. Then it turned to darkness, and the music to horrible and evil wailings. He was terrified and ran into the kitchen, where he told the cook what he had seen and heard. She comforted him, and told him that he was lucky to have seen the fairies. After that he saw the same thing three or four times, but with diminishing vividness. The fear of the dreadful cries haunted him and he began to pine. But he was comforted by an old woman whom he trusted, and who told him that the wailing he heard was that of the bogles, who were being punished by the good fairies for their jealousy of him. The last time he had the vision was from the drawing room window of the Manse. He saw the light and heard the music faintly, and then some deep sighs, and no more. So he knew that the fairies would not appear to him again.

There is something in this which reminds one of Kirk's account of the second-sighted men who involuntarily saw more than they wished to see. 'And glaid would they be to be quite of such, for the hideous Spectacles seen among them; as the torturing of some Wight, earnest, ghostly, stairing Looks, Skirmishes, and the like.'[1] The vision is rather like some of those described by Irish seers to Evans Wentz. It is worth comparing, too, with some psychic experiences about which Kate Christie has written in *Apparitions*. Barrie, though he distorted his matter with whimsy, was working on a true tradition when he made the evil and good fairies hunt in rivalry for the soul of Mary Rose.

The old Barra piper, whose tale to Evans Wentz is quoted in the last chapter but one, made a firm distinction between the good and bad among the fairies.

In my experience there was always a good deal of difference between the fairies and the hosts. The fairies were supposed to be living without material food, whereas the hosts were supposed to be living upon their own booty. Generally, the hosts were evil and the fairies good, though I have heard that the fairies used to *take*

[1] R. Kirk, ed. cit., p. 74.

cattle and leave their old men rolled up in the hides. One night an old witch was heard to say to the fairies outside the fold, 'We cannot get anything to-night.' The old men who were left behind in the hides of the animals *taken*, usually disappeared very suddenly. I saw two men who used to be lifted by the hosts. They would be carried from South Uist as far south as Barra Head and as far north as Harris. Sometimes when these men were ordered by the hosts to kill men on the road they would kill instead either a horse or a cow; for in that way, so long as an animal was killed, the injunction of the hosts was fulfilled.[1]

The *hosts* were generally supposed to be the host of the dead, often at enmity with the living. Presumably the killing would be done by elf-shot, according to the method described by Isobel Gowdie in 1662. In both cases it seems that human beings could do more effective destruction than the hosts themselves. It is strange to see the beliefs which were alive in the seventeenth century persisting into the twentieth.[2]

In Man we find the same idea of the two types of fairies. Gill, in *A Second Manx Scrapbook*, cites Robertson's tour of Man in 1791 for this.

> Robertson was told that the Manx fairies were of two kinds: the playful and benignant, and the sullen and vindictive. The former were gay and beautiful, but shy; the second kind dwelt apart from the others and from men, 'in clouds, on mountains, in fogs, on the hideous precipice, or in the caverns on the seashore'; where they were frequently heard to yell.[3]

Sophia Morrison put it simply in the Preface to her *Manx Fairy Tales*:

> These Little People are not the tiny creatures with wings who flutter about in many English fairy tales, but they are small persons, from two to three feet in height, otherwise very like mortals. They wear red caps and green jackets and are very fond of hunting—indeed they are most often seen on horseback followed by packs of little hounds of all colours of the rainbow. They are rather inclined to be mischievous and spiteful, and that is why

[1] Evans Wentz, ed. cit., p. 106.
[2] R. Pitcairn, *Ancient Criminal Trials in Scotland* (Edinburgh, 1833), Vol. III, Part II, p. 607.
[3] W. Gill, ed. cit., p. 233, note.

they are called by such good names, in case they should be listening!

She then speaks of the Fynoderee, and goes on to the Bugganes.

> Then, far uglier than the Fynoderee, are the Bugganes, who are horrible and cruel creatures. They can appear in any shape they please—as ogres with huge heads and great fiery eyes, or without any heads at all; as small dogs who grow larger and larger as you watch them until they are larger than elephants, when perhaps they turn into the shape of men or disappear into nothing; as horned monsters, or anything they choose.[1]

In fact, according to her, though the best are bad, the worst are worse.

There is a vivid Irish description of the evil fairies of battle in the manuscript narrative of the *Battle of Clontarf* (A.D. 1014). The fairy sweethearts of Dunlaug O' Hartigan and Murrough both tried to detain them, and warned them of the fatal issue of the battle; but their loyalty to their country made them refuse hundreds of years of happiness in the Land of the Ever Young, and choose death instead. For the battle all the evil hosts of the O'Shee, led by Baod, the Goddess of War, were mustered.

> There arose a wild, impetuous, precipitate, mad, inexorable, furious, dark, lacerating, merciless, combative, contentious *badb*, which was shrieking and fluttering over their heads. And there arose also the satyrs, and sprites, and the maniacs of the valleys, and the witches, and goblins, and owls, and destroying demons of the air and firmament, and the demoniac phantom host; and they were inciting and sustaining valour and battle with them.[2]

Here we have an example of god-fairies; for the raven Badb was the Goddess of War.

In every country and county one hears of the mischievous and malignant fairies, Kelpies, Bogles, Brags, Boggle-boos, Rawhead-and-Bloody-Bones, Redcaps, Spriggans, and so on; but the morality of even the ordinary, decent, well-wishing fairy is of a brand of its own, and not perhaps the same as that

---

[1] S. Morrison, ed. cit., pp. v–vi.
[2] Evans Wentz, ed. cit., p. 306.

incumbent on mortals. According to Elidurus the fairies were great lovers and respecters of truth, and indeed it is not wise to attempt to deceive them, nor will they ever tell a direct lie or break a direct promise, though they may often distort it. The Devil himself is more apt to prevaricate than to lie, and the worst of the fairies are at least equally scrupulous. Order more than morality is part of the fairy code. They are great lovers of cleanliness, tidiness and established ways. The second thing that they require of human beings is liberality; their chief villain is the miser and the covetous man, and such are almost certain to be punished if they come across them. There is an example, for instance, given by Lady Wilde, of the old hag who was chopped into pieces to make a fairy banquet.

> When she was there above in the world she was a wicked miser, hard to the world, and cruel and bitter in her words and works; so now we have her here, and her soul will never rest in peace, because we shall cut up the body in little bits, and the soul will not be able to find it, but wander about in the dark to all eternity without a body.[1]

The fairies set a high value on courtesy and respect, though this is sometimes better observed by ignoring them than by thanking them. The etiquette is uncertain here, but discourtesies and practical jokes are always discouraged.

On sexual matters the fairies are very lax, and we can perhaps trace here some indication of fertility rites attached to them. Campion's poem, *The Fairy Queen Proserpine*, invokes the fairies as patrons of complacent lovers.[2]

As early as the seventeenth century 'fairy' was used as a synonym for a lady of easy virtue. There is an example of this in one of the Bodleian manuscripts in a poem to The Lady Berkeley which begins:

> You British Faeries, Saffron-coloured elfes,
> You stuftout puppetts, least parts of your selfes.[3]

The word is still occasionally used in the same meaning, though it is now more generally applied to homosexuals.

---

[1] F. S. Wilde, ed. cit., Vol. I, p. 138.
[2] *The Works of Thomas Campion*, ed. by A. H. Bullen (London, 1889); *A Book of Airs*, pp. 21–2.
[3] *MS. Bodley Malone*, 14. f. 16 v.

A flavour of bawdiness hung about them, as in a sly tale told in *Round About Our Coal Fire,* a little pamphlet of the early eighteenth century.

A Gentlewoman and her Husband were going into the Country, and thought it best to retire out of Town four or five Miles the Night before, to receive the Stage-Coach, and avoid the Ceremony of taking leave of their Friends, which are generally more troublesome than welcome on that Occasion, and being gone to Bed in a Country-Town where Fairies walk'd; about Twelve-a-Clock, up comes a little Woman, not much bigger than one's Thumb, and immediately follows a little Parson, also a great Number of People, and a Midwife with a Child in her Arms; and I suppose by their Power Chairs were set for them. But it happen'd that they wanted a Godmother for the Child, for it was to be christen'd that Night; so says the good Fairy Father, the Gentlewoman in the Room will do us that Favour; ay, says the rest of the Company, 't is a good Thought; and up brisk'd the Fairy Father to the Bed-side, and called out the Lady, who did the Office; for which the Father gave her a large Diamond Ring. All this while the Lady's Husband was as fast as a Church, and knew nothing of the Matter. But in the Morning, good lack, the Case was alter'd; he espied the fine Ring upon his Wife's Finger; How come you by that, My Dear, says he? Why my Love, replies she, the Fairies have been here to Night, and told him the story of the Christening.[1]

Both male and female fairies are often amorous of mortals; the counter-accusations of Oberon and Titania are in the true folk tradition; but they are also ready to further human love affairs, and such fairy rites as those attached to the May Day celebrations and the Hallowmas nut-picking have an amorous intention behind them.

The fairies, as one would expect, have no special bias towards respectability, and a genial rogue is as likely to receive their favours as anyone else. In a story recorded by R. Macdonald Robertson an old whiskey distiller was a great friend of the fairies who danced on the White Wells near Assyat House; they taught him the use of the grandavy plant which cures eczema. One night Donald Fraser unwittingly made an assignation with the Devil, to conduct him to his distilling bothy, and that night, as he passed the White Wells, he heard

[1] *Round About Our Coal Fire* (1740), pp. 43–4.

the Little People whispering, 'Be careful, Donald Fraser, Be careful, Donald Fraser.' He did not understand the warning, however, and he and his companions would have been done to death by the Fiend if they had not been saved by a white ptarmigan which he had rescued that winter. On his safe return from his adventure he heard the Little People rejoicing at his escape, and they came and helped him down with his kegs of whiskey.[1]

So far as respect for human goods is concerned honesty means nothing to the fairies. They consider that they have a right to whatever they need or fancy, including the human beings themselves. On the whole it may be said that if they are suitably propitiated and treated with respect, allowed to take what they fancy and feed where they like, unmolested in their revellings and unhindered in their journeys, the fairies have a kindly feeling towards mankind, will help them if they can, and enjoy their companionship.

[1] R. Macdonald Robertson, *More Highland Folk Tales* (Edinburgh, 1964), pp. 66–70.

Fourteen

CHANGELINGS AND MIDWIVES

T HE thing that everyone knows about the fairies is that they covet human children and steal them whenever they can. No account of fairies is complete without the mention of this practice. From the early chronicles of Gervase of Tilbury and Ralph of Coggeshall, through the Elizabethans down to modern times, and in both Celtic and Saxon areas, the tale is substantially the same.

There are variations in the reason for the interchange, and the character of the substituted changeling, but the main outline is generally accepted. The most usual reason given is that golden-haired, beautiful children are desired by the fairies to improve the fairy stock, who tend to be dark and hairy; sometimes it is said that the fairies owe a tribute to Hell, and do not wish to pay it out of their own people; sometimes human beings seem to be taken as servants. Mortals of all ages and both sexes are enticed into Fairyland; but unchristened children, 'little pagans', are particularly liable to be carried off unless certain precautions are taken, an open pair of scissors hung over them, a pin stuck into their clothes, the father's trousers laid across the cradle, a circle of fire drawn round them. These precautions may well have been older than Christianity. The explicitly Christian signs, the sprinkling with holy water and the sign of the cross, were certainly believed to be potent, but even in Pagan times the nameless state of the baby may have been thought to expose him to danger; for in some stories, such as *Short-Hoggers of Whittinghame*, the giving of a nickname was considered enough to liberate the little spirit.[1]

The substitutes left in the place of the little humans are variously described. Sometimes they are said to be fairy children who do not thrive and need human milk, sometimes old, old fairies near to dotage, sometimes they are pieces of wood, or roughly moulded figures that show an illusory animation that soon ceases. Such a one, for instance, is probably exemplified in the Shetland tale *Mind the Crooked Finger*. A newly-made father observed a group of fairies busy about something just outside his house, and heard one say to another, 'Mind (that is remember) da crooked finger.' His own wife had a crooked finger, and the fairies were making a model of her. Warned by this the husband managed to save his wife, and the log of wood shaped in her form was used as a chopping block for many years.[2] In another tale the fairies give a rhyming description of the parents whose features are to be imitated.

An unusual tale of a fairy mother who preferred her own child, ugly though it was, to any changeling is told in Lady Wilde's *Ancient Legends of Ireland*. The mother of a newly-born child was lying one night with her husband asleep beside her when the door burst open and a tall, dark man came in, followed by an old hag with a wizened, hairy child in her arms. They sat down by the fire, and then the man got up and looked into the cradle. The mother woke her husband, who jumped out of bed and tried to light a candle. It was twice blown out, but he got hold of the tongs and attacked the old hag, and finally pushed her out of the house. He lit the candle, and then they saw that their baby was gone, and the little misshapen imp was in its place. They burst out into loud lamenting and bitter crying. Presently the door opened again, and a young woman with a red handkerchief round her head came in. She asked them why they were crying, and they showed her the thing in the cradle. She laughed for joy when she saw it, and when they asked her why, she said, 'Because this is my child that was stolen from me to-night; for I am one of the fairy race who live under the hill, and my people coveted your beautiful baby, but I would sooner have my own. I will take him now, and I will

[1] R. Chambers, ed. cit., p. 334.
[2] *Scottish Fairy and Folk Tales*, pp. 123–4. From J. G. Ollason's MS.

tell you how you can win your own child back.' She told them to take three sheaves of corn to the fairy hill, to burn them one by one, and to threaten to burn the hill in the same way if their child was not given back. And she warned them to keep the child carefully, and to hang a horseshoe nail round his neck for a protection. They did as she said, and as the father set fire to the third sheaf an old man from the fairy hill brought his child back to him, and warned him besides to draw a circle with a hot coal round the cradle that night. He did as he was told, and there was peace from that time between him and the fairies, and he would never allow the fairy hill to be molested.[1]

There is another, more elaborate tale collected by Lady Wilde in Innis Sark, in which the fairy mother again prefers her own child. In this tale there is a visit of the human mother to the fairy court, and an element of glamour and enchantment that is reminiscent of some parts of the Arthurian Legends.[2]

As a rule the fairy changeling is old, and the ruse for unmasking him is one by which he is tempted into betraying his age—'I am old, old, ever so old,' or 'I have seen three forests grow and wither, but I never saw ale brewed in an eggshell before.' This tale of the brewery of eggshells is the most usual one, but occasionally the changeling betrays himself out of boredom, confiding in an unwary way in a visiting tailor. Generally in these stories the desire to play on the pipes has grown too strong for him. Occasionally there are two changelings, who are overheard in precocious conversation. When the changeling had been detected the usual means of getting rid of it were harsh and fierce. Many human children suffered from them. Children with marked thyroid deficiency and those infected with infantile paralysis would be most likely to be suspected of being changelings. If parents and neighbours had been content to try the traditional tests and wait for the miraculous speech, things would have been bad enough for the child; but they were not always so patient. Even at the beginning of this century a child was burned to death in Ireland when the neighbours put him on a hot shovel, and there have been several cases of children who were put outside on the dungheap, and died of exposure. Occasionally the mother was told to look

[1] F. S. Wilde, ed. cit., Vol. II, pp. 149–52.
[2] Ibid., Vol. I, pp. 119–24.

after the changeling carefully, so that her own child would be equally well cared for. In one tale, from Scandinavia the fairy mother said with a rare magnanimity, on returning the human child: 'Here is your baby; I looked after it better than you looked after mine.'[1]

An example of the normal story of the changeling, as it is told all over the country, is to be found in E. M. Leather. This is from Jane Probent of Kington, and was told in the Hommel Hopyard at Weobley in September 1908. The teller believed the tale because she had heard it from someone else, who 'believed it to be true'.

A woman had a baby that never grew; it was always hungry, and never satisfied, but it lay in its cradle year after year, never walking, and nothing seemed to do it any good. Its face was hairy and strange-looking. One day the woman's elder son, a soldier, came home from the war, and was surprised to see his brother still in the cradle. But when he looked in he said, 'That's not my brother, mother.' 'It is indeed,' said the mother. 'We'll see about that,' he said. So he obtained first a fresh egg and blew out the contents, filling the shell with malt and hops. Then he began to brew over the fire. At this a laugh came from the cradle. 'I am old, old, ever so old,' said the changeling, 'but I never saw a soldier brewing beer in a egg shell before.' Then he gave a terrible shriek, for the soldier went for him with a whip, chasing him round and round the room, what had never left his cradle! At last he vanished through the door, and when the soldier went out after him he met on the threshold his long lost brother. He was a man twenty-four years of age, fine and healthy. The fairies had kept him in a beautiful palace under the rocks, and fed him on the best of everything. He should never be as well off again, he said, but when his mother called he had to come home.[2]

There are numerous stories of the fairy attempts at kidnapping being thwarted. In one told by Lady Wilde the witches are in collusion with the fairies, for a man passing a house late at night heard two women talking, and one said, 'I have put the dead child in the place and carried away this one. Wait till the moon rises and then take it to the fairy queen, and you shall have the payment I promised.'

[1] T. Keightley, ed. cit., p. 126.
[2] F. M. Leather, ed. cit., pp. 46–7.

Printed for John Bell, British Library Strand, London, Dec. 27. 1781.

2 Title-page to Tickell's 'Kensington Gardens'.
Thomas Stothard. *Bell's English Poets* 1789 (*see* chapter 18)

3 'The Rape of the Lock.' Thomas Stothard.
Du Roveray edition, 1798 (*see* chapter 18)

In the meantime they went to eat, and the man reached in at the window and lifted out the sleeping child, and took it for his mother to keep. In the morning there was great lamentation in the village, for the lord's beautiful baby boy, who had just been born, had died in the night, and lay there a wizened corpse, so changed that no one knew it. The man who had found the baby went with the other mourners to look at the little corpse, and laughed aloud when he saw it. He persuaded the lord to have a fire lit, and then went up to the cradle, and said to the still form there: 'If you don't get up out of this I'll throw you on the fire.' The thing grinned, opened its eyes and shot out of bed; but the man was too quick for it. He caught it and threw it on the fire. As soon as the flame touched it it turned into a black kitten and shot up the chimney. Then the man brought his own beautiful child back to the lord, and it was fortunate all its days, after the escape from the fairies.[1]

Children as well as babies were sometimes carried away by the fairies; but next to unchristened children, nursing mothers who had not yet been churched were in the greatest danger. These were carried away into Fairyland to give suck to fairy babies. Sometimes they were carried great distances, for there is a story of a Highlander who saw a cluster of fairies carrying something, and with great presence of mind threw his cap among them, crying out, 'Change this for that!' It is not etiquette for the fairies to refuse such an offer, so they seized his cap and dropped their burden, who proved to be a beautiful and delicate lady in a deep sleep. The Highlander carried her home, but even when she waked he was none the wiser, for he had no English and she had no Gaelic. He and his wife kept her with them for some years, till a fortunate chance brought her husband and son to the place, officers employed over General Wade's roads. The fairies had travelled with their burden from the Lowlands.[2] It is unusual, however, for them to go so far afield for their prey; it is the fairies in the neighbouring hillock who are usually the danger. There are many stories of such abductions, sometimes ending happily in the rescue of the woman, as in Mary Nelson's rescue by her brother, told by Sir

[1] F. S. Wilde, ed. cit., Vol. I, pp. 170–2.
[2] R. Grant Stewart, *The Popular Superstitions of the Highlands* (1823), pp. 116–20,

Walter Scott,[1] more often perhaps, tragically, when the rescue fails, sometimes through the jealousy of a second wife, too hastily married by the supposed widower.[2]

Human milk is much esteemed by the fairies; there seemed to be a notion that it might give fairy babies the chance of a human soul. Cromek has a story of a nursing mother who was visited by a fairy with a child to which she begged her to give one suck of her milk. The mother did so, and was blessed and rewarded by the fairy.[3]

The human midwife is almost as important to the fairies as the nursing mother; it seems sometimes as if fairy babies could not be delivered without human aid. The very earliest story of this, that given by Gervase of Tilbury about the Dracae, is typical of a hundred others. Here we have the midwife fetched at night, the fairy ointment and the blinding of the seeing eye. The same tale, with variations, is told in Somerset, in the Scottish Lowlands, in the North of England and Ireland. A Welsh story, told by John Rhys in *Celtic Folklore*, gives a possible explanation both for the desire for a human midwife and for the use of the fairy ointment. It was written down in Welsh by William Thomas Solomon, the old man who told it, and John Rhys gives both the original and the translation in his book.

An old man and his wife lived at the Garth Dorwen in some period a long while ago. They went to Carnarvon to hire a maid servant at the Allhallows' Fair; and it was the custom then for young men and women who stood out for places to station themselves at the top of the present *Maes*, by a little green eminence where the present Post Office stands. The old man and his wife went to that spot, and saw there a lass with yellow hair, standing a little apart from all the others; the old woman went to her and asked if she wanted a place. She replied that she did, and so she hired herself at once and came to her place at the time fixed. In those times it was customary during the long winter nights that spinning should be done after supper. Now the maid servant would go to the meadow to spin by the light of the moon, and the *Tylwyth Teg* would come to her to sing and dance. But some time in the spring, when the days had grown longer, Eilian escaped with the

---

[1] Walter Scott, ed. cit., Vol. II, pp. 372–5, note.
[2] S. Morrison, ed. cit., pp. 79–81.
[3] R. H. Cromek, ed. cit., p. 302.

Tylwyth Teg, so that she was seen no more. The field where she was last seen is known to this day as Eilian's Field, and the meadow is called the Maid's Meadow. The old woman of Garth Dorwen was in the habit of putting women to bed, and she was in great request far and wide. Some time after Eilian's escape there came a gentleman to the door one night when the moon was full, while there was a slight rain and just a little mist, to fetch the old woman to his wife. So she rode off behind the stranger on his horse, and came to Rhos y Cwrt. Now there was at that time at the centre of the *rhos*, somewhat of rising ground that looked like an old fortification with many big stones on the top, and a large cairn of stones on the northern side: it is to be seen to this day, and it goes by the name of Bryn i Pibion, but I have never visited the spot. When they reached the spot, they entered a large cave, and they went into a room where the wife lay in her bed; it was the finest place the old woman had seen in her life. When she had successfully brought the wife to bed she went to the fire to dress the baby; and when she had done the husband came to the old woman with a bottle of ointment that she might anoint the baby's eyes; but he entreated her not to touch her own eyes with it. Somehow, after putting the bottle by, one of the old woman's eyes happened to itch, and she rubbed it with the same finger that she used to rub the baby's eyes. Then she saw with that eye how the wife lay on a bundle of rushes and withered ferns in a large cave, with big stones all round her, and with a little fire in one corner; and she saw also that the lady was only Eilian, her former servant girl, whilst, with the other eye, she beheld the finest place she had ever seen. Not long afterwards the old midwife went to Carnarvon to market, when she saw the husband, and said to him, 'How is Eilian?'

'She is pretty well,' said he to the old woman. 'But with what eye do you see me?'

'With this one,' was the reply; and he took a bulrush and put her eye out at once.[1]

Professor Rhys adds that in the spoken tale Solomon had mentioned that an immense amount of spinning was done when Eilian span with the fairies. Old Solomon had the tale from his mother, who had heard it from an old woman at Garth Dorwen some eighty years before. Eilian's yellow hair presumably made her specially attractive to the fairies. This may well be the only complete Fairy Midwife story, beginning with the

[1] J. Rhys, ed. cit., Vol. I, pp. 211–13.

abduction of the human bride, already somewhat set apart from her contemporaries at the time when she was hired, going on to the birth of the half-human child, and the calling in of the human midwife. It might be argued that all the Fairy Midwife tales are the second part of this story; that the human midwife is needed for the human wife, and that the fairy ointment is only needed to give fairy sight to half-human fairies. We may presume that it had never touched Eilian's eyes, and that the glamour thrown over the place was for her benefit.

It will be remembered that in the seventeenth-century pamphlet, *Robin Goodfellow*,[1] which Alfred Nutt considered to be the last of the tales of god-born children, Robin had by inheritance the tricksy nature of the fairies, but had to be given the fairy powers by his superhuman father. It may well be that in Hunt's closely-connected stories, *The Fairy Widower* and *Cherry of Zennor*, the Widower's first wife had been as human as Cherry, and had therefore died; and because he was half-human the little fairy boy needed the ointment to quicken his sight. This would rationalize the whole position; but how far rationality is characteristic of folk tradition is another matter.

[1] *Robin Goodfellow: His Mad Prankes and Merry Jests* (London, 1628).

122

Fifteen

FAIRY WIVES AND FAIRY LOVERS

T HE end of the last chapter brought us directly to the amorous relations between fairies and humans, to the human wives stolen by fairy husbands, and from them to the fairy wives seized or decoyed by human husbands. There are also the less regularized relations of visiting fairy sweethearts of both sexes. Lady Wilde gives us a full account of the stolen humans:

> The evil influence of the fairy glance does not kill, but it throws the object into a death-like trance, in which the real body is carried off to some fairy mansion, while a log of wood, or some ugly, deformed creature is left in its place, clothed with the shadow of the stolen form. Young women remarkable for beauty, young men, and handsome children, are the chief victims of the fairy stroke. The girls are wedded to fairy chiefs, and the young men to fairy queens; and if the mortal children do not turn out well they are sent back, and others carried off in their place.[1]

The episode of the Fairy Wife has received greater publicity because her drama has been enacted directly under human observation. Some people have gone so far as to suggest that there are no male fairies, and that fairy beliefs represent a very primitive state of human culture, when the birth of a child but not its procreation was understood. An examination of the Fairy Wife stories themselves would show this to be a fallacy. For instance, in the tale of the *Fairy of Llyn y Fan Fach* the father

[1] F. S. Wilde, ed. cit., Vol. I, p. 52.

123

of the fairy appears, to strike a bargain with his future son-in-law.[1] In the Welsh stories the supernatural brides are always fairies, very often lake maidens, in the Highlands of Scotland they are generally seals, with a previous seal husband, whom they prefer; and they are secured, not by courtship or gifts, but by the theft of their skins, thus bringing them nearer to the Swan Maidens, a tale widely spread on the Continent, which is also to be found in Scotland in some versions of *Nix Nought Nothing*, a story in which the father is, of course, very important.

Eilian, in the tale told in the last chapter, appears to have been a willing bride, as Cherry of Zennor would have been if she had not broken the ointment taboo and been ejected from Fairyland. As a rule, however, maidens taken into Fairyland are taken there unwillingly, often on the eve of a human wedding. A theft of this kind was frustrated in Crofton Croker's *Master and Man*,[2] in the Ulster tale of *Jamie Freel*,[3] and in *The Stolen Bride*, told by Lady Wilde.[4]

The most poetic story of a bride desired by a fairy husband and carried off into Fairyland at last is the Irish legend of Midhir and Etain.[5] In the old version of the tale Etain was originally the fairy bride of King Midhir, who had been turned into a midge by a jealous rival, swallowed by a mortal woman and reborn as a mortal. Midhir searched for her through the upper world, and at last found her married to King Eochaid, and won her by magical power at chess play. This is the version used by Fiona Macleod in *The Immortal Hour*, and in this the original right is Midhir's, though King Eochaid is innocent of any wrong in the matter. The complicated way in which people were re-born in ancient Irish beliefs made life difficult for everyone.

The written legend has survived into oral tradition, and Lady Wilde collected an example of it with a slightly different focus, which is among the traditions of the Cave-Fairies, believed to be the last survivors of the Tuatha de Danann.

The King of Munster once saw a beautiful girl bathing and

[1] J. Rhys, ed. cit., Vol. I, pp. 2–12.
[2] T. Crofton Croker, ed. cit., Vol. I, pp. 159–69.
[3] W. B. Yeats, *Irish Fairy and Folk Tales*, (n.d.), pp. 52–9. 'Jamie Freel and the Young Lady.' Told by Laetitia Maclintock.
[4] F. S. Wilde, ed. cit., Vol. I, pp. 49–51.
[5] Augusta Gregory, *Gods and Fighting Men* (London, 1910), pp. 88–100.

chose her to be his queen. Her name was Edain, and she was the most beautiful woman in all Ireland. King Midar of the Tuatha de Danann heard of her, and, in disguise, going to the King of Munster's palace, he challenged him to a game of chess. The winner was to name his prize. Midar won, and claimed Edain, but said he would not fetch her for a year and a day. The King of Munster marked the time, and when the day came he had his palace ringed with a triple ring of men and his palace crowded with warriors. But suddenly Midar was there, though only the King could see him. He struck the golden harp in his hand and sang to the Queen, inviting her to go with him to the Land of Fair Lovers. He put his arm round her and she went with him, like one with no will nor strength to resist, while the King of Munster sat powerless to stop them. When they were gone he waked up as if out of a trance, and summoned all the Kings of Ireland to dig the fairy mounds and destroy the fortresses of the Danann, for he knew by the way that Midar had vanished that he was one of the chieftains of the Tuatha de Danann. He tried to wall up the stables of the fairy steeds and starve them to death, but they broke out, and at the sight of them the Kings stopped thinking of Edain, and only tried to catch the marvellous steeds for themselves. Then the King summoned the chief Druids, and made them use all their magic to find out where Edain was hidden. They found out at last that she was in the centre of Ireland, in the fortress of King Midar. Then the King dug and burnt till the fortress was levelled to the ground. And when they reached the very gate of the fairy palace it opened, and fifty beautiful women came out, each one so like Edain that the King was baffled. But when Edain saw her husband the spell was lifted from her, and she went to him, and he swung her up on to his horse, and they rode away together to the Palace of Tara, where they lived happily all their days. But after this time the powers of the Tuatha de Danann declined, till they became no more than the Cave-Fairies who haunt Ireland to this day.[1]

Here we see the shift of sympathy from the fairies to the mortals, so that it is Eochaid and not Midhir who has the right to Edain.

W. W. Gill notes in *A Second Manx Scrapbook* that on the

[1] F. S. Wilde, ed. cit., Vol. I, pp. 179–82.

Isle of Man certain abnormal states are still privately regarded as the effects of intercourse with fairies or spirits. In Lezayre, some time ago, a girl grew thin and listless, and her mother suspected her of intercourse with spirits. The girl denied it, but the mother watched her secretly, and at length saw her dancing among the fairies on the hillside above the church. She dared not go nearer, but in the morning she gave her daughter a severe beating, which the poor girl was little able to stand. Shortly after she died, and the general belief was that she had gone to the fairies for good.[1]

There is less in modern tradition about young men being carried off to Fairyland to live with fairy sweethearts, as Ossian was. Lady Wilde, however, records one case.

A young man died suddenly on May-Eve while he was lying asleep under a hay-rick, and the parents and friends knew immediately that he had been carried off to the fairy palace in the great moat of Granard. So a renowned fairy-man was sent for, who promised to have him back in nine days. Meanwhile he desired that food and drink of the best should be left daily for the young man at a certain place on the moat. This was done, and the food always disappeared, by which they knew the young man was living, and came out of the moat nightly for the provisions left for him by his people.

Now on the ninth day a great crowd assembled to see the young man brought back from Fairyland. And in the midst stood the fairy doctor, performing his incantations by means of fire and a powder which he threw into the flames that caused a dense grey smoke to arise. Then taking off his hat, and holding a key in his hand, he called out three times in a loud voice, 'Come forth, come forth, come forth!' On which a shrouded figure slowly rose up in the midst of the smoke, and a voice was heard answering, 'Leave me in peace; I am happy with my fairy bride, and my parents need not weep for me, for I shall bring them good luck, and guard them from evil evermore.'

Then the figure vanished and the smoke cleared, and the parents were content, for they believed the vision, and having loaded the fairy-man with presents they sent him away home.[2]

There was a contradiction here which might have made the parents a little uneasy. The food was left out so the young man should not be forced to eat fairy food, which would bind him to

[1] W. Gill, ed. cit., pp. 228–9. [2] F. S. Wilde, ed. cit., Vol. I, p. 200.

Fairyland for ever. If he took it nightly it would seem to be a sign that he wished to be freed, and yet when he was summoned he begged to be allowed to remain. If the parents had not suspected the fairy doctor of trickery they might well have feared that their son was being coerced by the fairies. However, it was as well that they were satisfied.

The visiting fairy sweetheart is not so common in tradition as the fairy wife or husband. There was one case reported by Evans Wentz of an importunate fairy mistress who followed her lover to America,[1] and we hear of the Lhiannon-Shee, or fairy follower, in the Isle of Man. She belongs to the same class as the Lamia or Succuba. Like the Lamia she often haunts wells and pools. She is a kind of vampire, and ruins the man to whom she attaches herself, body and soul. The Shropshire Fairy Follower, whose story I have given in Part I is of very much the same kind. The fairy lover who paid secret visits to his sweetheart is to be found in a tale collected by John Gregorson Campbell in *Waifs and Strays of Celtic Tradition*, Vol. V. It is a strange tale, which throws light on various by-gone customs and ways of life in the Highlands. There were once two sisters in Mull, Lovely Margaret and Dark Ailsa. Lovely Margaret had a fairy sweetheart who visited her in secret. She was so full of happiness in her love that she confided it to Ailsa, begging her to tell no one. Ailsa said, 'The secret will as soon go from my mouth as from my knee'; but she broke her word, and soon the whole town knew of Lovely Margaret's fairy lover. People peered and whispered, and the fairy was offended and left Margaret for ever. After the loss of her lover Margaret never more came into a human house; she wandered about among the hills, and shepherds saw her sometimes, and heard her crooning a lament for her loneliness, without father or mother, and with a sister who had betrayed her. She laid a curse on Ailsa, wishing her want and ill-luck, and prophesying that evil would come on her or her descendants for her treachery. For the present no evil came, and Ailsa married and had one son, who was called Torquil. At this time Margaret, or her wraith, was heard again lamenting that Ailsa had a son, who could climb and fish and reap better than any other. Her words proved true, for when he came to manhood Torquil could reap as much as

[1] Evans Wentz, ed. cit., pp. 112–13.

any other seven men, and this gift proved his undoing. For one hot harvest time when the corn grew thick in all the fields, a fairy maiden came out of the cairn, and whatever field was ripe she would reap, and at night, between sunset and sunrise she would do the work of seven men. Torquil took this as a challenge to himself, and he was eager to see the Cairn Maiden, but he could never get a glimpse of her, till, one Sunday evening in the first moonlight, as he was passing one of his fields, he saw her setting to work. He ran to fetch his sickle and began to reap the furrow next to her, saying, 'You will be a good reaper, but I will keep up with you.' He reaped his hardest, but she was ahead of him. He called out, 'Maid of the Cairn! Wait for me! Wait for me!'

But she called back, 'Handsome, brown-haired boy, overtake me, overtake me!' He worked with all his might till a cloud covered the moon, and he called out, 'The moon is smothered with clouds, Wait for me! Wait for me!'

But she answered, 'I have no other light. Overtake me! Overtake me!' Then he called, 'I am wearied with yesterday's reaping. Wait for me! Wait for me!'

And she answered, 'I climbed the hill of seven steep summits; Overtake me! Overtake me!'

The night wore on till it was nearly dawn, and he cried after her, 'My sickle wants sharpening. Wait for me! Wait for me!'

And she replied, 'My sickle would not cut garlic. Overtake me! Overtake me!' And at that she reached the end of her last furrow and waited for him to come up. He came up with her, and grasped the last sheaf of corn, the Corn Maiden, in his hand and cut it. They faced each other, and he said to her, 'You have put the Old Woman of Want far from me this year. I have cause to be pleased with you.'

But she answered, 'It is an evil thing to reap the Corn Maiden early on a Monday morning.' And at her words he dropped dead at her feet, with the sheaf of corn in his hand. And so the treachery of Dun Ailsa was avenged. The maiden went back to her Cairn, and was never seen again.[1]

The tale is full of atmosphere. One can see the upland corn-field and feel the sea-laden air, and hear the two voices calling

---

[1] J. G. Campbell, *Clan Traditions and Popular Tales*, Waifs and Strays of Celtic Tradition, Vol. V (London, 1895), pp. 95–9.

to each other as moonlight pales into dawn, and yet it is mysterious. It is uncertain whether the Cairn Maiden was Margaret, or her wraith, or a daughter born to her after her lover's desertion. It seems that in a manner Margaret withdrew into Fairyland, though she was never reunited with her fairy lover. This tale is a late and fragmentary version of the Cupid and Psyche legend.

In the Highland custom the Old Woman of Want was not merely a symbolic figure. If there was any old woman without kindred or means of subsistence the man who reaped the last strip of cornland was obliged to take her into his house for the winter.

The lover in this tale was implacable but not essentially malevolent. Pretty girls in the Celtic countries were likely to meet more dangerous characters. The Love Talker of Ireland used to wander the glens in the likeness of a handsome young man with a pipe in his mouth. Young girls found him irresistible, but he vanished after intercourse with them, and they never saw him again, but pined away and died. A Somerset song, 'My Love wore a garland of clay', might well relate to a human lover, but it is traditionally supposed to be about a fairy of the same kind as the Love-Talker. The words are given in full in *Somerset Folklore*. The first verse goes:

> O my love wore a garland of may,
> O my love wore a garland of may,
> And she looked so nice and neat
> To her pretty little feet
> When she met her false lover in the dew.[1]

May is, of course, a fairy blossom, and not safe for humans to wear.

In the Highlands of Scotland the Water Horse is even more dangerous. It often takes the form of a young man, who can be detected for what he is by the sand and seashells in his hair. It is his practice to carry his sweethearts into the water and devour them. Mermaids and river spirits are equally dangerous to young men, but I have already written of these among the water spirits, who are ordinarily more dangerous than friendly.

[1] R. L. Tongue, ed. cit., pp. 207–8.

Sixteen

FAIRY ENCOUNTERS AND ODD
EXPERIENCES

Eₙcₒᵤₙₜₑᵣₛ with the fairies are almost necessarily brief, for under ordinary circumstances men are supposed to see them only between one blink of the eye and the next. In old times children were often exhorted not to fix their eyes because this was taken to be an attempt to see the fairies, or at least a condition in which they might be seen; and such sights were thought to be dangerous. This peculiar quality of the fairies makes proof of their existence difficult; but in many quite modern descriptions of them it still holds good. For instance, in Walter Gill's *A Second Manx Scrapbook* there is an account of a fairy experience of a friend of his from Liverpool, who had lived in Man for a considerable time and had been known to Mr. Gill for thirty-five years.

About 34 years ago, when he was 23, at 10 a.m. of a brilliantly sunny summer morning he was walking on the short grass below the débris at the west side of the Glen Aldyn slate-quarries, which lie far above the inhabited part of the Glen. Here he came to a sudden stop to avoid stepping on something alive between two and three yards in front of him. It was five little creatures dancing in a ring, hand in hand. They stood a foot or 18 inches high and were greyish in colour like fungus, their bodies seeming to be swollen in front, their limbs and eyes clearly distinguishable, and their heads moving as they danced. He speaks of them as 'little

130

men' because they gave him a strong impression of being of the
male sex. After he had watched them for a short time they vanished
from his sight, and there was nothing there but the grass. Thinking
his eyes or brain might have played him a trick, he went to the
same spot a couple of mornings later, and there they were again,
just as before. He has hardly ever spoken of it to anyone for fear
of ridicule.[1]

This curiously prosaic and matter-of-fact account reminds
one of some of the early descriptions of the fairies, and has the
same convincing quality. Evans Wentz obtained an unusual
description of the fairies from a member of the House of Keys,
in which the fairies, unlike those often described, appeared
to be very tiny. Another Manx fairy encounter told by W. Gill
is also connected with a quarry. 'A friend used to be telling
him he went early in the morning to a quarry in a field yonder,
and this man came across two of Them. Little fellows they were,
between two and three feet high; they were wearing red caps,
and they ran away when they saw he was looking at them.'[2]
It was believed to be important to see the fairies before they
saw you. In this respect they were like basilisks and wolves.

In a Somerset description of fairies seen in the same way in
the twinkling of an eye, they were smaller, about the size of
partridges and of a reddish brown colour.

A farmer's wife near Timberscombe described a meeting
with a fairy to R. L. Tongue in 1962. 'I've never seen a ghost,
but I *did* see a fairy. It was on the Berkshire Downs, and we'd
lost our way, and didn't know what track to take. When I
looked round, there was a small man in green standing at my
elbow. He had a round smiling face, and he said, "You take
that one; you'll be all right." Then he didn't disappear, but he
just wasn't there any more. Did I see him? Or didn't I?' A
visitor from Hampshire suggested that it was a derrick. Derricks
are ill-natured fairies in Devonshire, but it seems that in
Hampshire they must be considered friendly.

An experience rather like this was told me by a friend, a
clergyman's widow. She suffers from an injured foot, and one
day she was sitting on a seat in Regents Park, wondering how
she would find strength and courage to go home. Suddenly she
saw a tiny man in green, who looked at her very kindly and

---

[1] W. Gill, ed. cit., pp. 230–1.   [2] Ibid., p. 211.

said, 'Go home. We promise that your foot shan't pain you tonight.' Then he disappeared, but the pain, which had been considerable, was quite gone. She walked home easily, and all that night she slept painlessly. On another occasion she had seen a group of fairies dressed in flowers dancing together on one side of the flower-beds, but this had only been a momentary glimpse and she had heard nothing.

A more alarming experience was described, again to R. L. Tongue, by a President of the Women's Institute in Wellington.

> When we were on holiday in Cornwall my daughter and I came down a winding lane, and all of a sudden there was a small green man by a gate watching us. All in green, with a pointed hood and ears. We both saw him, and my little girl screamed—she's psychic —and we were cold with terror. We ran for the ferry below. It was going across, but it came all the way back to pick us up. No one said a word, but they didn't think we were silly. I don't think I have ever been so frightened.

Here—for what the Manx belief is worth—the fairy had seen them before they had seen it, and it was therefore dangerous.

One of Mr. Hawker's parishioners had an encounter with the pixies, reproduced by S. Baring Gould in *The Vicar of Morwenstow*.

'This man had been to Stratton market. On his way home, as he was passing between dense hedges, suddenly he saw a light, and heard music and singing. He stood still, and looked and listened. Passing through the hedge he saw the little people in a ring dancing, and there sat on a toadstool an elf with a lantern in his hand, made of a campanula, out of which streamed a greenish-blue light. As the pixies danced they sang.

' "Sir"—this is the man's own account—"I looked and listened awhile, and then I got quietly hold of a great big stone and heaved it up, and I dreshed in amongst them all, and then I up on my horse and galloped away as hard as I could, and never drew rein till I came home to Morwenstow. But when the stone fell among them all, out went the light. You don't believe me? But it be true, true as Gospel, for next day I went back to the spot, and there lay the stone, just where I had dreshed it." '[1]

[1] S. Baring Gould, *The Vicar of Morwenstow* (1876), p. 164.

The fairy with the campanula lantern is in the Shakespeare tradition, one of the small flower fairies. By all traditions the man who so unkindly threw a stone into the midst of this harmless company should have been punished with lameness at least.

At the end of the last century the small, lively, green fairies were to be found in the North of England as well as in the South West. In the first volume of the Folk-Lore Record an account is printed of the fairies seen by the bathman at Ilkley Wells. It was reported to Charles Smith by John Dobson.

'William Butterfield' he continued, 'always opened the door the first thing in the morning, and he did this without ever noticing anything out of the common until one beautiful quiet mid summer morning. As he ascended the brow of the hill he noticed rather particularly how the birds sang so sweetly, and cheerily, and vociferously, making the valley echo with the music of their voices. And in thinking it over afterwards he remembered noticing them, and considered this sign attributable to the after incident. As he drew near the Wells he took out of his pocket the massive iron key, and placed it in the lock; but there was something "canny" about it, and instead of the key lifting the lever it only turned round and round in the lock. He drew the key back to see that it was all right, and declared "it was the same that he had on the previous night hung up behind his own door down at home." Then he endeavoured to push the door open, and no sooner did he push it slightly ajar than it was as quickly pushed back again. At last, with one supreme effort, he forced it perfectly open, and back it flew with a great bang! Then whirr, whirr, whirr, such a noise and sight! all over the water and dipping into it was a lot of little creatures, all dressed in green from head to foot, none of them more than eighteen inches high, and making a chatter and jabber thoroughly unintelligible. They seemed to be taking a bath, only they bathed with all their clothes on. Soon, however, one or two of them began to make off, bounding over the walls like squirrels. Finding they were all making ready for decamping, and wanting to have a word with them, he shouted at the top of his voice—indeed, he declared afterwards he couldn't find anything else to say or do—"Hallo there!" Then away the whole tribe went, helter skelter, toppling and tumbling, heads over heels, heels over heads, and all the while making a noise not unlike a disturbed nest of young partridges. The sight was so unusual that he declared he either couldn't or daren't attempt to rush after them.

He stood as still and confounded, he said, as old Jeremiah Lister down there at Wheatley did, half a century previous, when a witch from Ilkley put an ash riddle upon the side of the river Wharfe, and sailed across in it to where he was standing. When the well had got quite clear of these strange beings he ran to the door and looked to see where they had fled, but nothing was to be seen. He ran back into the bath to see if they had left anything behind; but there was nothing; the water lay still and clear as he had left it on the previous night. He thought they might perhaps have left some of their clothing behind in their haste, but he could find none, and so he gave up looking, and commenced his usual routine of preparing the baths; not, however, without trotting to the door once or twice to see if they might be coming back; but he saw them no more.'[1]

In this engaging account of the fairies no wings are mentioned; they bound like squirrels, they do not fly like birds; and yet their voices and the whirr that they make seems birdlike. The twittering and indistinct speech of the fairies is to be noted here, as in earlier accounts.

A later, psychic believer in fairies gives some of them wings, though he says they do not use them for flight. His description sounds curiously like a nineteenth-century fairy illustration. It is dated The Lake District, August 1922.

A group of fairies are gambolling and dancing on a little plateau on the other side of the stream. Their bodies are female, their main clothing is pale blue; their wings, which are almost oval in shape, are constantly fluttering as they dance in a ring hand in hand. Some of them wear a loose girdle, from which is suspended an instrument like a horn. All are draped with a material which serves to conceal the form more completely than is usual with this type of nature-spirit. Their height is probably six inches.[2]

This observer, unlike others who have had fairy visions, seems able to watch them at his leisure.

The travelling people still describe occasional fairy encounters. One recorded by Walter Johnson, in the Archives of the School of Scottish Studies, is of a fairy seen in the Sma' Glen in Perthshire. He described it as 'a wee green man with

[1] *Folk-Lore Record I* (1878), pp. 229–31.
[2] G. Hodson, *Fairies at Work and Play* (Theosophical Publishing Press, 1925), p. 80. For the Cottingley Fairies, see Appendix III.

4　'Titania's Awakening.' Johan Fussli. The Boydell
Shakespearian Gallery, 1790 (*see* chapter 18)

5 'Titania and Bottom.' Johan Fussli. The Boydell
Shakespearian Gallery, 1798 (*see* chapter 18)

peakit boots, with a cap like an old gramophone horn on his head'. In fact, dressed in exactly the traditional fairy way. Its face was dark and furrowed. He and his father saw it across the burn. The rocks opened and it disappeared.

About ten years ago he had another fairy experience. He found a ruined house with a wee well at Tom na Toul. He went to dip his can in it, and saw a light coming out of the bushes. Two wee men came out, about six inches tall, carrying a coffin between them. Curiously enough they were wearing bowler hats. This is one of the occasional mentions of fairy funerals. Another one was collected by T. F. G. Paterson from Ulster, where such traditions can still be found among the old people. 'A man once followed a fairy funeral. He was up late at night an' heard the convoy comin'. He slipped out an' followed them an' they disappeared into Lisletrim Fort (a triple-ringed fort near Cullyhanna). He heard the noise of them walking plain, but he saw none of them.'

Sam Hanna Bell, in *Erin's Orange Lily*, records some broadcasts of fairy experiences he took from the Ulster people. In one a woman from the Glens of Antrim tells of a conversation with an old woman from Waterfoot.

'Mary,' says she, 'I saw a fairy with my own two eyes.'
'Augh,' says I, 'You surely didn't see a fairy?'
'I did—as sure as I have to face my God I saw a fairy. . . . My brother John and I went up for the cows one Summer evening, and we both saw the wee woman, and she wasn't more than two feet high, with her wee red cap on her head and the short skirt, and she walked along the stone ditch, and she never moved a pebble of it.'[1]

Odd happenings attributed to the fairies are more common than the actual sight of them. Sophia Morrison, in her *Manx Fairy Tales* published in 1911, gives an account of such an experience, related by one, James Moore.

I'm not much of a believer in most of the stories some ones is telling, but after all a body can't help believing a thing they happen to see for themselves.

I remember one winter's night—we were living in a house at the time that was pulled down for the building of the Big Wheel.

[1] S. Hanna Bell, *Erin's Orange Lily* (London, 1925), p. 89.

It was a thatched house with two rooms, and a wall about six foot high dividing them, and from that it was open to the scrabs, or turfs, that were laid across the rafters. My Mother was sitting at the fire busy spinning, and my Father was sitting in the big chair at the end of the table taking a chapter for us out of the Manx Bible. My brother was busy winding a spool and I was working with a bunch of ling, trying to make two or three pegs.

'There's a terrible glisther on to-night,' my Mother said, looking at the fire. 'An' the rain comin' peltin' down the chimley.'

'Yes,' said my Father, shutting the Bible; 'an' we better get to bed middlin' soon and let the Lil' Ones in to a bit of shelter.'

So we all got ready and went to bed.

Some time in the night my brother wakened me with a: 'Shish! Listen boy, and look at the big light tha's in the kitchen!' Then he rubbed his eyes a bit and whispered: 'What's Mother doin' now at all?'

'Listen!' I said, 'An' you'll hear Mother in bed; it's not her at all; it must be the Little Ones that's agate of the wheel!'

And both of us got frightened, and down with our heads under the clothes and fell asleep. In the morning when we got up we told them what we had seen, first thing.

'Aw, like enough, like enough,' my Father said, looking at the wheel. 'It seems your mother forgot to take the band off last night, a thing people should be careful about, for it's givin' Themselves power over the wheel, an' though their meanin's well enough, the spinnin' they're doin' is nothin' to brag about. The weaver is always shoutin' about their work, an' the bad joinin' they're makin' in the rolls.'

I remember it as well as yesterday—the big light that was at them, and the whirring that was going on. And let anybody say what they like, that's a thing I've seen and heard for myself.[1]

Many more recent odd experiences were collected by R. L. Tongue on her visits to Women's Institutes. Everyone has some unexplained happenings in his own life, often quite trivial; the point of interest in these is that they were all attributed, hesitantly or undoubtingly to fairy agency.

The Vice-President of Eddington Women's Institute in 1962 said:

'My cottage is on the old Pilgrim's Way to Glastonbury, and all sorts of odd things happen,—not frightening, just odd. One

---

[1] S. Morrison, ed. cit., pp. 3–5.

of the bedroom doors shuts itself, and I find I can't open it however much I try, it is just as if it was bolted. *But* if asked politely it will open for me quite easily, often without being touched. An old friend from the moor below said that it was known that "They" came there at times.'

Another member volunteered at this:

'They used to have a dancing circle in Loxley wood, and they'd visit houses they liked near by.'

Another member of Eddington Institute described a fairy experience in Surrey.

'When we were living in Surrey lately we went out for a picnic. My small boy took his precious bag of marbles in his pocket. After tea he wanted to go exploring, so he put them very carefully beside the hamper. I did not go out of sight of the hamper, but when it was time to go, and he came back, the marbles had gone. We all searched for them a long time because he was so upset. On the way back to the bus stop he suddenly stopped and said, "They *are* there, I must go and get them." He ran back the half-mile; I watched him, and no one was anywhere about. He came back shouting, "Here they are, Mummy, and *two* new ones!" Since I came here I have heard it is a tricksy place, where everybody loses something.'

The Vicar's wife at Kilve had an anecdote about a Devonshire cottage at which she stayed a few years before 1962.

'My husband exchanged pulpits for our holiday a few years ago, and we went to a little church in Devon on the edge of Maldon. The house was very old indeed, long and low and thatched. It was always very dark, but I liked it, though queer things occurred. One day I was going to light the fire, and put on a stew for us, for our supper at night when we returned after a day's outing. Something disturbed my attention, and I went off, forgetting to light the fire. We came back that evening, resigned to bread and cheese. The fire was alight and the stew was hot. We had been within sight of the house all day. We had seen nobody go there, nor had we seen any smoke. Another time the same thing happened in reverse. I forgot to take off the evening meal, which was cooking, and put it aside to be heated again. I remembered it in the afternoon, by which time it should have been a crisp. We arrived to find it taken off the stove and waiting to be warmed up. I was advised, if I wanted the fire to burn up brightly, to shout up

the chimney for help. It always came. The only time They dis-
approved was when I found a delightful nook in the heather, and
settled down to sew in the sun. That afternoon I lost two needles in
quick succession, and then the needlebook disappeared too. I
took the hint, and we left the nook to its owners.'

In holiday time, at least, this lady seems to have been a
rather casual housewife. It is as well that she found a domestic
spirit to help her.

Pixy-leading is perhaps the commonest of the fairy experiences in modern times. Not long ago a Methodist preacher
gave an account of it on the wireless. R. L. Tongue records two
experiences, one from a member of Nettlecombe Women's
Institute in 1961, and one from its President.

'I were pixy-led once in a wood near Budleigh Salterton. I
couldn't find my way out, though 'twas there, plain to see. I went
all around about it three times, and then somebody coom along
to find me, and I thought how could I miss the path. They said
others was pixy-led there too.'

The President's account was more sophisticated and cir-
cumstantial, but it amounted to the same thing.

'I went a journey to a house in Cornwall to do some secretarial
work. When the farm came in sight I walked in and asked if I
were on the right track to the Manor. They all looked a little
queer,—I thought it was because they never saw any strangers,—
but the farmer's wife was very kind and gave me careful directions.
I was to cross certain fields, and then go down a certain track to
where there were *two* gates, and I must take the white one. She
was so insistent on this that I had visions of a bull in the other
field, or fierce watch-dogs; and the farm men who sat by (they
were having a meal) all agreed in silence. Well, I came to the
bridle track; it was a misty, snowy, depressing day and I didn't
want to be late,—I had to walk home after. Then I came to a gate
at the end, set in a thick hawthorn hedge, *one* gate, and it wasn't
white, and I had a most creepy feeling. I was determined not to
lose that job. I was just starting work and I needed the pay. Well,
I went all along that hedge, and I pricked my fingers too, but there
was only one gate. Then somebody came up the bridle track
whistling, and the thick mist cleared, and there was no hedge. It
was one of the farm lads sent after me who knew what to do.
"Here's your white gate, Miss," he said, and, sure enough, there it

138

was, beside the other one. He didn't stop for thanks, but turned back to the farm, still whistling loudly. The old Manor House was there, right in front of me, and I went in at a run. My job didn't take me more than an hour, and I simply ran past the farm. The woman looked out, and I waved and hurried on. I wish now I'd had the courage to ask if her boy wore hob-nailed boots, or carried salt in his pocket, or if he had been told to sing or whistle.'

No doubt most of these experiences could be explained, and those that seem inexplicable possibly owe something to the human love of wonders, and to the way in which memory unconsciously embroiders a tale and makes it more interesting. This tendency is noticeable even in essentially truthful and undramatic people, those with a self-dramatizing temperament will often elaborate a tale until it becomes almost unrecognizable after a few years. The significant thing here, as I have already pointed out, is that the explanation offered for these happenings is the fairy agency. I know a small wood in Surrey where it is extremely difficult for a stranger to find his way. One might well feel he was pixy-led as he strayed about it; but the local explanation is that this was a smugglers' wood, and the intersecting paths formed a maze in which the Preventive Men would be misled. Historical and ghostly traditions are generally held to be more alive in England than fairy beliefs, which have been treated as moribund for five hundred years. It is therefore interesting to see the ancient belief raising its head once more.

Seventeen

HUMAN OPINIONS

Those people who believe, or used to believe, in the real existence of fairies have advanced various opinions to account for them. In the time of the witchcraft trials, when all psychic experiences were deeply suspect, ghosts, fairies and second sight were thought to be part of the diabolic machinery for ensnaring the souls of men. Ghosts were devils in masquerade, fairies were familiar spirits, and all those who saw things not seen by other men were liable to suspicion as witches. Even among people of Puritan leanings this belief was sometimes modified, but it was generally held.

In many of the witch trials—in Dorset, in the North of England, in Scotland and the Isle of Man—fairies and witches were believed to work together. In Ireland fairies and witches are still said to dance together on All Hallows Eve, and several fairy practices, such as elf-riding horses and stealing the milk of cows, were ascribed to the witches as well as the fairies. They were even said to steal babies out of their cradles and sell them to the fairies. There was some confusion, too, between the superhuman hags and the witches. The Cailleach Bheur, under the name of Cally Berry, still figures in Ulster, where she seems to be regarded as a human witch. From the earliest times fairies and enchantresses were intermingled. In Malory at least Morgan le Fay was a human half-sister of Arthur's, though in the earlier tradition on which he drew it is probable that Arthur and all his family were supernatural. In the

140

seventeenth century the fairy ladies of Holinshed turned into witches.

When the witch fever abated, however, the fairies went back to their old place in the popular regard. A truly valuable piece of investigation on the fairy beliefs of the Celtic parts of these islands was undertaken by Evans Wentz at the beginning of this century. He published his conclusions in 1911 under the title *Fairy Faith in Celtic Countries*. In the course of his investigations he travelled in the Highlands and Islands, often on foot, in Ireland, Wales and Cornwall, and he concluded by visiting Brittany. In all these places he went first to well-known folklorists, such as Douglas Hyde in Ireland and Alexander Carmichael in the Highlands, but followed this up by visits to priests, schoolmasters, crofters, fishermen, to anyone indeed whom he could hear of as likely to know something of fairy traditions. He gives a careful account of each witness, so that one can understand clearly the different degrees of sophistication. Wherever possible he tried to get not only anecdotes of the fairies but opinions about them. The theories which he collected fall under several heads. The greatest number of believers in all the countries spoke of them, though rather doubtfully, as the spirits of the dead. For instance, in the Isle of Barra Mary Maclean, after speaking of the Hosts, who are identified by Alexander Carmichael with the dead, was asked if the fairies were anything like the dead, and hesitated before answering. 'She thought they were like the dead, but not to be identified with them. The fallen-angel idea concerning fairies was an obstacle she could not pass, for she said, "When the fallen angels were cast out of Heaven God commanded them thus:— 'You will go to take up your abode in crevices, under the earth, in mounds, or soil, or rocks.' And according to this command they have been condemned to inhabit the places named for a certain period of time, and when it is expired before the consummation of the world, they will be seen as numerous as ever." '[1]

Sometimes, in the Highlands, in Wales and in Cornwall, fairies were vaguely called 'spirits', with a kind of implied suggestion that they were the spirits of the dead. Sometimes they were described without qualification as the dead, or said to have

[1] Evans Wentz, ed. cit., p. 109.

the dead among them. More often they are qualified as a special kind of dead. John Graham, an old man living near Tara, said that the fairies were those killed before their time, who had to live in Fairyland till their allotted time of death.[1] Possibly John Graham may have brought the belief, with his name, from Scotland, for it was current in Scotland at the time of the witchcraft trials. In Cornwall the Pisgies were sometimes thought to be the spirits of stillborn children. The commonest explanation was that the fairies of various kinds are spirits of long-dead or extinct races. John Boylin of County Meath suggested that the different tribes of fairies were accounted for by some of them being spirits of the Fir Bolgs, some of the Milesians, some of the Tuatha De Danann. All of them were to be seen round the slopes of Tara dressed in ancient costume.[2] An old Welshman living near Strata Florida evidently thought of the Tylwyth Teg as spirits of prehistoric people. His grandfather had heard singing in a certain field, and later dug into a burial place where he found bones and funerary urns. Because of the singing he decided that they belonged to the Tylwyth Teg.[3]

A folklorist in Cardiganshire said: 'By many of the old people the *Tylwyth Teg* were classed with spirits. They were not looked upon as mortal at all. Many of the Welsh people looked upon the *Tylwyth Teg*, or fairies, as the spirits of Druids dead before the time of Christ; who being too good to be cast into Hell were allowed to wander freely about on earth.'[4]

In Ireland, Scotland and Wales various accounts of the origin of the fairies were given, but in Cornwall they seemed to be almost universally regarded as the spirits of the dead, of one kind or another. The Knockers, who haunted the mines, were supposed to be the souls of Jews deported there by the Romans for their part in the crucifixion; the Tolcarn Troll was supposed to date back to the time of the Phoenicians, and to have plied to and fro in their boats. Pisgies, or Pixies, were believed to be the souls of the prehistoric inhabitants of the land. Mr. Henry Madden, an architect, who had learned his pixy-lore as a child from his old nurse, said in his evidence: 'Pixies were often supposed to be the souls of the prehistoric dwellers of this country. As such, pixies were supposed to be getting smaller and

---

[1] Evans Wentz, ed. cit., p. 32.   [2] Ibid., pp. 32–3.
[3] Ibid., p. 148.   [4] Ibid., p. 147.

smaller, until finally they are to vanish entirely.'[1] This evidence agrees with such tales as *Fairy Dwellings on Selena Moor*. The dwindling of the pixies would represent their loss of power, and account for their eagerness to get hold of human changelings and reinforce their weakening stock. In Lady Wilde's stories it is apparent that the belief in the fairies as the dead is as widespread in Ireland as elsewhere. In the Isle of Man, too, it was suggested that the fairies, or 'Themselves', were the spirits of those drowned in Noah's Flood. Of course, among all these antique fairies would be those of more modern times, who had been stolen or decoyed into fairyland, and held captive there by being persuaded to eat fairy food.

The Christian theory that the fairies are fallen angels seems to be next in popularity and width of distribution. Evans Wentz collected evidence of this in several different parts of Ireland. The most explicit was from Patrick Waters in County Sligo. 'The *gentry* are the most noble tribe of all; and they are a big race who come from the planets—according to my idea; they usually appear white. The *Daoine Maithe* (though there is some doubt, the same or almost the same as the *gentry*) were next to Heaven at the Fall, but did not fall; they are a people expecting salvation.'[2]

In his introduction to the Highland Section of the book Alexander Carmichael gives the full story of the fairies and the Fall, as told to J. F. Campbell of Islay in 1871.

The Proud Angel fomented a rebellion among the angels of heaven, where he had been a leading light. He declared that he would go and found a kingdom for himself. When going out of the door of heaven the Proud Angel brought prickly lightning and biting lightning out of the doorstep with his heels. Many of the angels followed him—so many that at last the Son called out, 'Father! Father! the city is being emptied!' Whereupon the Father ordered that the gates of heaven and the gates of hell should be closed. This was instantly done. And those who were in were in; and those who were out were out; while the hosts who had left heaven and had not yet reached hell flew into the holes of the earth like stormy petrels. These are the Fairy Folk—ever since doomed to live under the ground, and only allowed to emerge where and when the King permits. They are never

[1] Evans Wentz, ed. cit., p. 176.   [2] Ibid., p. 53.

allowed abroad on Thursday, that being Columba's Day; nor on Friday, that being the Son's Day; nor on Saturday, that being Mary's Day; nor on Sunday, that being the Lord's Day.

> God be between me and every fairy,
> Every ill wish and every druidry;
> To-day is Thursday on sea and land,
> I trust in the King that they do not hear me.

On certain nights when their *bruthain* (bowers) are open and their lamps are lit, and the song and dance are moving merrily, the fairies may be heard singing light-heartedly:

> 'Not of the seed of Adam are we,
> Nor is Abraham our father;
> But of the seed of the Proud Angel,
> Driven forth from Heaven.'[1]

More than a quarter of a century later Murdoch Maclean of Barra confirmed this in giving evidence to Evans Wentz. 'My firm belief,' he said, 'is that they are not the spirits of dead men, but are the fallen angels.'[2]

The same tale was told in Man by William Cashen, keeper of Peel Castle. 'My father's and grandfather's idea was that the fairies tumbled out of the battlements of Heaven, falling earthwards for three days and three nights as thick as hail; and that one third of them fell into the sea, one third on the land, and one third remained in the air, in which places they will remain till the Day of Judgement. The old Manx people always believed that this fall of the fairies was due to the first sin, pride; and here is their prayer against the fairies: "Jee saue mee voish cloan ny moyrn" (God preserve me from the children of pride).'[3] This is repetition of a belief expressed by several sixteenth- and seventeenth-century writers, Thomas Heywood, for instance.

In Pembrokeshire a similar belief was expressed.

> 'I think the spirits about us are the fallen angels, for when old Doctor Harris died his books on witchcraft had to be burned in order to free the place where he lived from evil spirits. The fairies, too, are sometimes called the fallen angels. They will do good to those who befriend them, and harm to others. I think there may

[1] Evans Wentz, ed. cit., pp. 85–6.   [2] Ibid., p. 113.   [3] Ibid., pp. 129–30.

be an intermediate stage between life on earth and heavenly life, and it may be in this that spirits and fairies live.'[1]

This seems to be rather a mixed testimony; but here, as in Man, the suggestion is that fairies are no better than devils, though this last witness went on to say that there are both good and bad among them. It is more generally said that the fairies are not good enough for Heaven and are too good for Hell. But the belief that fairies are no more than devils, which was so widely held among the Puritans, still has its modern supporters. A particularly valuable witness among those interviewed by Evans Wentz was John Davies, a herb-seller of Balsalla. He showed clearly the blending of beliefs about the fairies, by which some were supposed to be spirits of the dead, and some devils or fallen angels. We have a trace, too, of the Manx belief that the fairies inhabited the lowest Heaven, for which reason they were called 'People of the Middle World'. Again and again this middle position of the fairies is suggested. They are too bad for Heaven, but too good for Hell; they are in the middle way between men and angels; they are the old heathen, not fit for salvation but too good for Hell, and so on. John Davies located Fairyland, as Drayton did, in the air.

'Before education came into the island,' he said, 'more people could see the fairies; now very few people can see them. But *they* are as thick on the Isle of Man as ever *they* were. *They* throng the air, and darken Heaven, and rule this lower world. It is only twenty-one miles from this world up to the first heaven. There are as many kinds of fairies as populations in our world. I have seen some who were about two and a half feet high; and some who were as big as we are. I think very many such fairies as these last are the lost souls of people who died before the Flood. At the Flood all the world was drowned; but the Spirit which God breathed into Adam will never be drowned, or burned, and it is as much in the sea as on the land. Others of the fairies are evil spirits; our Saviour drove a legion of devils into a herd of swine; the swine were choked, but not the devils. You can't drown devils; it is spirits they are, and just like a shadow on the wall.'[2]

A somewhat similar testimony came from Wales, sent by a clergyman.

[1] Evans Wentz, ed. cit., p. 154.   [2] Ibid., p. 123.

'After Mr. Wentz visited me on Thursday, September 30th, 1909, I went to see Mr. Shem Morgan, the occupier of Cwm-castellfach farm, an old man about seventy five years old. He told me that in his childhood days a great dread of the fairies occupied the heart of every child. They were considered to be evil spirits who visited our world at night, and dangerous to come in contact with; there were no good spirits among them.'[1]

This gloomy view, however, was by no means the only one taken by the Welsh people. The testimony given by David Williams of Carmarthen, a J.P., reads very differently.

'The general idea, as I remember it, was that the *Tylwyth Teg* were only visitors to this world, and had no terrestrial habitations. They were as small in stature as dwarfs, and always appeared in white. Often at night they danced in rings amid green fields. Most of them were females, though they had a king, and, as their name suggests, they were very beautiful in appearance. The king of the Tylwyth Teg was called *Gwydion ab Don*, *Gwyd* referring to a temperament in man's nature. His residence was among the stones and was called *Caer Gwydion*. His queen was *Gwenhidw*. I have heard my mother call the small, fleece-like clouds which appear in fine weather the *Sheep of Gwenhidw*. . . . As aerial beings the *Tylwyth Teg* could fly and move about in the air at will. They were a special order of creation. I never heard that they grew old; and whether they multiplied or not I cannot tell. In character they were almost always good.'[2]

In this account the Tylwyth Teg seem to be thought of as sylphs, those of the elementals which inhabit the air. In Ireland, too, they are occasionally thought to be elementals, not only by the more educated and sophisticated believers, who tend to describe the fairies as 'astral beings' or the like, but among the true peasants. An old Donegal man of seventy-three, for instance, said:

'The *gentle folk* are not earthly people; they are a people with a nature of their own. Even in the water there are men and women of the same character. Others have caves in the rocks, and in them rooms and apartments. These races were terribly plentiful a hundred years ago, and they'll come back again. My father lived two miles from here, where there were plenty of the *gentle folk*. In

---

[1] Evans Wentz, ed. cit., p. 150. [2] Ibid., p. 151.

olden times they used to take young folks and keep them and draw all the life out of their bodies. Nobody could ever tell their nature exactly.'[1]

An Irish mystic interviewed by Evans Wentz described two orders of the Sidhe that he had often seen, the shining and the opalescent. He believed that the lower orders of the Sidhe were the same as the creatures called elementals by the medieval mystics.[2] These fairies are of more than human size, perhaps fourteen feet in height; but some of the Irish fairies are supposed to be tiny. In one rather freakish account they took the form of flies, like some of the witches' familiars in the seventeenth century. This was in County Mayo, at an old Abbey, where a tremendous battle was held between the tribes of the fairies, who came from all quarters in great swarms. They fought for a day and a night, and at the end of the battle basketfuls of dead flies floated on the river.[3]

It is curious to find in Wales one stray example of the Scandinavian account of the origin of the Huldre-folk, or Hidden People. This comes from Carmarthenshire.

'Our Lord, in the days when He walked the Earth, chanced one day to approach a cottage in which lived a woman with twenty children. Feeling ashamed of the size of her family, she hid half of them from the sight of her divine visitor. On His departure she sought for the hidden children in vain; they had become fairies and had disappeared.'[4]

The Scandinavian tale is more detailed. The mother had only washed half the children, and she was ashamed of the others being seen dirty, so she sent them to hide among rocks and woods, and by streams. And God said: 'What you have hidden from me shall be hidden from Mankind.' And henceforth these children and their descendants became huldre-folk, and lurked in caves or woods or streams.[5] Hans Sachs the German cobbler playwright, used the same legend in *Eve's Children* to account for the different social orders among men.

These beliefs are still alive among the old people in Eire and even in Ulster. Instances of them have been collected by Michael Murphy of Clontifleece and by T. G. F. Paterson of

[1] Evans Wentz, ed. cit., p. 73.   [2] Ibid., p. 60.   [3] Ibid., p. 39.
[4] Ibid., p. 153.   [5] T. Keightley, ed. cit., p. 159, note.

147

the Armagh Museum. In his *Miscellanea* he notes that the traditions are collected from people between seventy and ninety years of age and he noted, besides listing some legends about them, that many tales show the belief that fairies were fallen angels; that they put out the eyes of people who could see them, kidnapped mothers in childbirth and their babies, took men, but could not take priests, were propitiated by libations of milk. Another point he mentions was the use of eggshells as boats. 'The raison people would up-end the eggs when they picked the mate from it, and drive the spoon through its bottom, was that the wee people wouldn't be able till sail away in it. Me grandfather did it, and his grandfather afore him. But there are some that didn't, and that's why there are no wee people now.' Evidently it was considered a good thing to prevent the wee people from leaving. John Davies of Wales would have been only too glad to speed their departure.

So various, even in comparatively recent times, are the opinions about the fairies among the Celtic people. As usual, it is the old people who are vocal on the subject, and it is generally said that the belief in the fairies will soon be a thing of the past. In the English-speaking parts of the country the belief has long been less explicit and less generally held.

In England the small flower fairies—possibly one form of elemental—perhaps dominate, but the prettiness of these fairies and their lack of power makes it difficult to test the belief in them; it is apt to evaporate into whimsy. In a television programme in the Woman's Hour in 1963 there were four people who said that they believed in fairies, but with some of them it seemed more fancy than actual belief. One of the team regarded the fairies as supplying the principle of growth in plant life, another was psychic, and had seen fairies as a child. To both these the fairies were more or less of the English type. In the central counties of England the meagre fairy practices that survived into the present century would seem to show them as agricultural spirits—whether natural forces or the souls of those who once possessed the land is doubtful. In Devon and Somerset there seem certainly to be some nature spirits, though no doubt the dead races dispute the land with them. It may be that the pixies represent the dead, and the saying that the pixies drove out the fairies, and that the last fairies were seen at

148

Buckland St. Mary may be accounted for by a different theory of origin.[1] In the North of England and Lowland Scotland the dead tend to preponderate, though there is some trace of the belief that the fairies were fallen angels in the notion that they have to pay a tithe to Hell. In Hugh Miller's account of the passing of the fairies they say that they are not of the race of Adam, and call themselves the People of Peace.[2] It is clear that these fairies were not the dead. In England at any rate visions and descriptions of the fairies are much commoner than any theorizing about their origin.

Those who do not believe in the fairies, but who wish to account for the belief of others have nearly as many theories to put forward as the believers. Perhaps the strongest case is made out by those that believe that the fairy faith is a result of the cult of the dead, and, as we have seen, these can draw support from the believers themselves. The small size of one class of fairies can be plausibly accounted for by the primitive conception of the soul as a miniature man. The dead very often take up their habitation in rocks and trees, they inhabit green mounds and are powerful over the fruits of the earth. The anthropological theory, first put forward by Mac Ritchie, has received recent support from the researches into the distribution and cults of neolithic man. According to this the fairies were a conquered race, or the memory of the people who took refuge in rocks and caves. Many of the fairy traditions lend colour to this. A fairly late theory is that which regards the fairies as the chief witches, or the gods of the witches. This theory is made more convincing by the undoubted association of fairies and witches in popular belief. Other theories advanced are not necessarily supposed to cover the whole ground. These suggest that some of the fairies are dwindled gods or nature spirits. It has been seen that all these theories can procure witnesses from among the believers. Another cause to be reckoned with is psychic manifestations, poltergeist phenomena, dreams, and so on. Whatever their explanation, they have been an undeniable cause of some fairy beliefs. The psychological foundation of fairy tales, so profoundly explored by Jung, cannot be ignored by folklorists. The fallibility of human memory

---

[1] R. L. Tongue, ed. cit., p. 111.
[2] Hugh Miller, *Old Red Sandstone* (Edinburgh, 1887), pp. 221–3, note.

has also its contribution to make to the whole. Most of the people telling of fairy beliefs and happenings are old, and this is not peculiar to the present age. There is a tendency among the old to confuse what they have heard with what they have actually experienced. There is an incremental power in reminiscence; and what has been surmised or suggested at first tends, on the tenth telling, to have hardened into fact. No single hypothesis seems quite to stand upon its own feet; and all these factors must be taken into account.

Part Three

SOME LITERARY FAIRIES

Eighteen

THE POETS: EIGHTEENTH CENTURY

SHAKESPEARE'S age was the great time of fairy poetry in English literature; and right on into the seventeenth century the tradition was maintained, though the treatment became more trivial. In the next century the climate changed, and if it had not been for Blake we should have little to say about fairies at that time; and yet there was no sudden cleavage; the thread is spun thinner, but it is not broken. In their first appearance in English literature a certain amount of humour and scepticism appeared in the treatment of fairies, and in Herrick and Drayton they were satirically treated. In Thomas Tickell's *Kensington Gardens*, published in 1722, the mock-heroic, humorous tradition is continued. There is no apparent satire here, the treatment is light and decorative. In the course of the poem Tickell says that he had the story from his nurse, but the whole inspiration might well have been purely literary; and since he was born in Cumberland it is perhaps unlikely that his nurse had any traditional lore about Kensington Gardens, though she would probably tell him stories about fairy changelings. At any rate, Tickell's fairies have the usual characteristics of the literary fairies of the seventeenth century. They are very small— ten inches to be precise—not so minute as the Duchess of Newcastle's midgets, and larger than those who could hide in acorn-cup or cowslip. There are some echoes of *A Midsummer Night's Dream* which could almost be called quotations,

> May the keen east-wind blight my favourite flowers,
> And snakes and spotted adders haunt my bowers,

153

and

> Through bush, through brake, through groves and gloomy
> dales,
> Through dank and dry, o'er streams and flowery vales.[1]

The poem also seems to owe something to Drayton's *Polyolbion*. The action is set in the remote past, in the reign of King Albion of Britain, but the fairy characteristics remain constant.

> When Albion ruled the land, whose lineage came
> From Neptune mingling with a mortal dame,
> Their midnight pranks the sprightly fairies play'd
> On every hill, and danc'd in every shade.
> But, foes to sun-shine, most they took delight
> In dells and dales concealed from human sight:
> There hew'd their houses in the arching rock;
> Or scoop'd the bosom of the blasted oak;
> Or heard, o'er-shadow'd by some shelving hill,
> The distant murmurs of the fading rill.
> They, rich in pilfer'd spoils, indulg'd their mirth,
> And pity'd the huge wretched sons of earth.
> Ev'n now, 'tis said, the hinds o'erhear their strain,
> And strive to view their airy forms in vain;
> They to their cells at man's approach repair,
> Like the shy leveret, or the mother-hare,
> The whilst poor mortals startle at the sound
> Of unseen footsteps on the haunted ground.[2]

Here we have the usual traits of the fairies, their midnight dances, their pranks and their pilfering. Oberon, as in *A Midsummer Night's Dream*, is the King of the Fairies; and, like all the fairies in these islands, they steal human changelings. Albion, the hero, is the stolen son of the King of Britain, dosed with ground elder and the juice of daisy roots to reduce him to elfin stature. In this tale Oberon had a daughter, Kenna, and her love for Albion caused the catastrophe of the story. Albion, though he had become outwardly a fairy, did not share the fairy immortality; when he fought with a fairy rival the wounds he gave could not kill his adversary, but those that he received

---

[1] Thomas Tickell, *Kensington Gardens. The Works of the English Poets*, edited by S. Johnson (1779), Vol. 26, pp. 207–15.

[2] Ibid., pp. 201–2.

proved mortal; the most that his true love could do was to turn him into a snowdrop. Not all Tickell's contemporaries would have agreed with him in this. Kirk, for instance, who was the greatest authority of his time on fairy lore, said that they passed out of this life after a long time and at something the same age; and there are scattered stories of fairy funerals. Supernatural creatures, too, who would not die naturally, can often be killed. The general consensus of opinion, however, would be with Tickell.

Another fairy trait mentioned by Tickell is that of giving rewards for cleanliness.

> When cleanly servants, if we trust old tales,
> Besides their wages had good fairy vails,
> Whole heaps of silver tokens, nightly paid
> The careful wife, or the neat dairy maid,
> Sunk not his stores.[1]

But the pleasantest embroidery is on the fairy hatred of daylight, which is several times elaborated, as, for instance, when Albion holds his secret meeting with Kenna.

> All things are hush'd. The sun's meridian rays
> Veil the horizon in one mighty blaze:
> Nor moon nor star in heaven's blue arch is seen
> With kindly rays to silver o'er the green,
> Grateful to fairy eyes; they secret take
> Their rest, and only wretched mortals wake.
> This dead of day I fly to thee alone,
> A world to me, a multitude in one.[2]

'Dead of day' is a pleasing notion, reminding one of Oberon's 'moon-burned lip' in Steward's poem. The towering tulip under whose lofty shade the lovers met became a popular flower with eighteenth-century painters of fairy themes. As we have seen, it is a fairy flower according to folk tradition.

As Persephone played her part in Drayton's *Nymphidia*, so Neptune here avenged his slaughtered descendant by rooting up the fairy palace and city with one stroke of his trident, and forcing the fairies into dispersal and flight. Only Kenna remained, cultivating her snowdrops; and it was a dream

---

[1] Thomas Tickell, ed. cit., p. 208.
[2] Ibid., pp. 206–7.

inspired by her that suggested to Wise the design of Kensington Gardens.

Eight years or so before the publication of Tickell's poem, Pope chose sylphs rather than fairies for the machinery of *The Rape of the Lock*. Even the Neo-Platonists, however, on whom Pope relies for his spirits, confuse the elementals and fairies, holding, for instance, that the gnomes are the earthy spirits; and Pope's sylphs are clearly fairies of a kind. Ariel, speaking in a dream to Belinda, says:

> 'If e'er one Vision touch'd thy infant Thought,
> Of all the Nurse and all the Priest have taught,
> Of airy Elves by Moonlight Shadows seen,
> The silver Token, and the circled Green,
> Or Virgins visited by Angel-Pow'rs,
> With Golden Crowns and Wreaths of heav'nly Flow'rs,
> Hear and believe! thy own Importance know,
> Nor bound thy narrow Views to Things below.'[1]

Ariel seems to claim here some kinship with both fairies and angels. Ariel was not only the name given by Shakespeare to Prospero's attendant spirit, it was also supposed both by magicians and neo-Platonists to be that of one of the sylphs, sometimes said to be the ruler of Africa. Pope even makes the elementals, like some of the fairies, spirits of the dead, apparently resolved to their dominant humour.

> Think not, when Woman's transient Breath is fled,
> That all her Vanities at once are dead:
> Succeeding Vanities she still regards,
> And tho' she plays no more, o'erlooks the Cards.
> Her Joy in gilded Chariots, when alive,
> And Love of *Ombre*, after Death survive.
> For when the Fair in all their Pride expire,
> To their first Elements their Souls retire;
> The Sprights of fiery Termagants in Flame
> Mount up, and take a *Salamander's* Name.
> Soft yielding Minds to Water glide away,
> And sip with *Nymphs* their Elemental Tea.

[1] *The Poems of Alexander Pope*, edited by John Butt (1963), p. 219, Canto I, ll. 29–36.

The graver Prude sinks downward to a *Gnome*,
In search of Mischief still on Earth to roam.
The light Coquettes in *Sylphs* aloft repair,
And sport and flutter in the Fields of Air.[1]

He goes on to speak of the Fairy Lover, or Incubus as a sylph, though he does not press that theme. If the sylphs are fairies, here is a clear case of the fairies being given wings, perhaps the first, though Branston, in *The Lost Gods of England*, interprets an illustration in the Utrecht Psalter as a ninth-century picture of an elf-shot man, surrounded by winged elves.[2] It is true that they look very like the angels in the other pictures, but they seem to be an illustration of the 'illusiones' of the Psalm, and may have been either elves or devils. If we disallow them, De Lancre's butterfly-winged devils might rank as the first;[3] but here at last in the eighteenth century we have them indubitably.

> Some to the Sun their Insect-Wings unfold,
> Waft on the Breeze, or sink in Clouds of Gold,
> Transparent Forms, too fine for mortal Sight,
> Their fluid Bodies half dissolv'd in Light.
> Loose to the Wind their airy Garments flew,
> Thin glitt'ring Textures of the filmy Dew;
> Dipt in the richest Tincture of the Skies,
> Where Light disports in ever-mingling Dies,
> While ev'ry Beam new transient Colours flings,
> Colours that change whene'er they wave their Wings.[4]

These ethereal creatures are addressed by Ariel as '*Sylphs* and *Sylphids*, *Fays*, *Fairies*, *Genii*, *Elves* and *Daemons*'.[5] All, however, who are under his control have the most trivial office, the care of Belinda's toilet; the hoop alone takes fifty of them. These tiny creatures hover round Belinda, assiduous to avoid a disaster that they can only vaguely foresee, but powerless to prevent the clipping of the shears, though one sylph heroically allows herself to be cut in two in the attempt. The power of the evil spirit Umbriel to raise strife seems to be rather greater, but

---

[1] *The Rape of the Lock*, Canto I, ll. 51–66.
[2] Brian Branston, ed. cit. For the Utrecht Psalter see E. T. Dewald, *The Illustrations of the Utrecht Psalter*, Princeton University Press (1933). Psalm XXXVII, p. 19.
[4] Reproduced in *The World of Witches*, Julius Caro Baroja, ed. cit.
[4] *The Rape of the Lock*, Canto II, ll. 59–67.
[5] Ibid., Canto II, ll. 73–4.

the last word is not with the sylphs; as usual the gods intervene, and the lock is raised to the heavens to form a new constellation.

All these treatments are alike trivial and satiric, following the literary tradition set in the previous century. Rather earlier than these there is one fairy reference that seems almost to hark back to the spirit of the sixteenth century. It is in *The Jovial Crew*, an adaptation of an earlier play by Richard Brome. Here, as in *Round Our Coal Fire*, we have a mention of the old people as believers in the fairies.

> *Rachel:* I remember an old Song of my Nurse's, every Word of which she believed as much as her *Psalter*, that used to make me long when I was a Girl, to be abroad in a Moon-light Night.

> At Night by Moon-light on the Plain,
> With Rapture, how I've seen,
> Attended by her harmless Train,
> The little *Fairy Queen*
> Her midnight *Revels* sweetly keep
> While Mortals are involved in Sleep
> They tript it o'er the Green.

> And where they danced their cheerful Round
> The Morning would disclose,
> For where their nimble Feet do bound,
> Each Flow'r unbidden grows;
> The *Daisy* (fair as Maids in May),
> The *Cowslip* in his gold Array,
> And blushing *Violet* 'rose.[1]

This is so much in the earlier style that it may have been a real quotation, though it is not in Brome's version of 1641. It is at any rate quite different in spirit from the other writings of the century.

Through the greater part of the eighteenth century the classics were the chief inspiration of the poets. If they turned to country themes they generally treated them as classical pastorals, though sometimes at a second remove, with a side-

---

[1] *The Jovial Crew, A Comic Opera* (1760). (Adapted from *A Joviall Crew, or The Merry Beggars*, Richard Brome, acted 1641.) Act I, Sc. I, p. 12.

glance at Spenser, as in Ambrose Phillips' *Pastorals* (1709).
In the twenties James Thomson looked directly at Nature,
but his verse was cast in a classical mould and was full of
classical mannerisms. As the century went on, however, the
Romantic Revival cast a shadow before it. It might be called a
monstrous and distorted shadow, for the fashion for the Gothick
produced strange grotesqueries. It was enough for a line to be
portentous, without its actually portending anything, like the
enormous and unexplained helmet in *The Castle of Otranto*,
which descended from the sky and crushed the unlucky heir.
The popular ballad was never quite forgotten, and the attempts
to reproduce it sometimes caught its spirit, but often the
desire to heighten the horror and dress the pathos produced
such absurdities as *Alonso the Brave and the Fair Imogene*.

> All present then uttered a terrified shout;
>   All turned with disgust from the scene.
> The worms they crept in, and the worms they crept out,
> And sported his eyes and his temples about
>   While the spectre addressed Imogene.[1]

It is fair to say that the Broadside Ballads were sometimes
equally unfortunate in their style. Nevertheless the love of the
ballads runs like a fresh stream through the literature of the
period, and, however Bishop Percy refurbished them, he did
almost more than anyone to help forward the Romantic
Revival when he published his *Reliques* in 1765.

Before his time, however, poets were turning to native
sources, and particularly to the North for inspiration, and
native folklore began to assume importance. An example is
Collins' *Ode on the Popular Superstitions of the Highlands of Scotland*.

> There must thou wake perforce thy Doric quill;
> 'Tis Fancy's land to which thou sett'st thy feet;
> Where still, 'tis said, the Fairy people meet
> Beneath each birken shade, on mead or hill.
> There, each trim lass, that skims the milky store,
>   To the swart tribes their creamy bowls allots;
> By night they sip it round the cottage-door,
>   While airy minstrels warble jocund notes.

---

[1] M. G. Lewis, *The Monk* (1796), Vol. III, p. 65.

There, every herd, by sad experience, knows
How, wing'd with Fate, their elf-shot arrows fly,
When the sick ewe her summer food foregoes,
Or, stretch'd on earth, the heart-smit heifers lie.[1]

This might seem to be borrowed from the English poetry
of the seventeenth century, from Milton's swart goblin and
milk-bowl, but the elf-shot cattle strike a note native to Scotland, and a few verses further on we have the Water Kelpie,
which here makes its first appearance in English poetry.

Very different in style, a verse which might have been
borrowed from some of the light fairy poetry of the previous
century, is Horace Walpole's poem on Anne Cavendish. It
purports to be a proclamation made by King Oberon.

By these presents be it known,
To all who bend before our throne,
Fays and fairies, elves and sprites,
Beauteous dames and gallant knights,
That we, Oberon the grand,
Emperor of Fairyland,
King of moonshine, prince of dreams,
Lord of Aganippe's streams,
Baron of the dimpled isles
That lie in pretty maidens' smiles,
Arch-treasurer of all the graces
Dispers'd through fifty lovely faces;
Sovereign of the slipper's order,
With all the rites thereon that border,
Defender of the sylphic faith;
Declare—and thus your monarch saith:
Whereas there is a noble dame,
Whom mortals countess Temple name,
To whom ourself did first impart
The choicest secrets of our art,
Taught her to tune th' harmonious line
To our own harmony divine,
Taught her the graceful negligence,
Which, scorning art and veiling sense,
Achieves that conquest o'er the heart
Sense seldom gains, and never art:
This lady, 'tis our royal will
Our laureate's vacant seat should fill;

---

[1] *The Poems of William Collins*, edited by Edmund Blunden (1929), p. 124.

A chaplet of immortal bays
Shall crown her brows, and guard her lays;
Of nectar-sack, an acorn cup
Be at her board each year fill'd up;
And, as each quarter feast comes round
A silver penny shall be found
Within the compass of her shoe—
And so we bid you all adieu:[1]

Given at our palace of Cowslip Castle, the shortest night of the year.
Oberon.

Here we see substantially the same erotic tradition about
the fairies as we find in Pope, and earlier in Herrick and
Steward, treated with the same graceful lightness.

At the first dawn of the Romantic Revival the treatment of
the fairies deepened, yet it is at this time that Thomas Stothard
set the fashion for the butterfly-winged fairies which illustrators
followed so long. John Adlard has written a short but important
paper on William Blake's Fairies which appeared in the
Bulletin of *Modern Language Studies* in 1964.[2] He traces the
various strands of belief and allegorical treatment in Blake's
work, from the first fairy caught like a butterfly under a hat in
1784 to the return to folklore and simplicity in the illustrations
to Milton in 1816. Blake generally treated his fairies as elementals, but his symbolic use of them nearly always seems to
have erotic significance, connected as a rule with the awakening
of male desire by feminine vanity and caprice. The fairies
seem at once to arouse desire and deny it, as Pope's sylphs do in
The Rape of the Lock. One passage seems, as John Adlard points
out, to be directly inspired by the toilet-haunting sylphs.

A FAIRY leapt upon my knee
Singing & dancing merrily;
I said, 'Thou thing of patches, rings,
Pins, Necklaces, & such like things,
Disguiser of the Female Form,
Thou paltry, gilded, poisonous worm!'[3]

[1] *Horace Walpole's Fugitive Verses*, edited by W. S. Lewis (1930), pp. 54–5.
[2] John Adlard, *Mr. Blake's Fairies*, Bulletin of the Modern Language Society,
2 LXV (1964), Helsinki, pp. 144–60.
[3] *The Poetry and Prose of William Blake*, edited by Geoffrey Keynes (Nonesuch
Press, 1946), p. 104.

The fairy is conquered by this harsh treatment, weeps, confesses that the Poet is the lord of the fairies, and defends himself, though rather incomprehensibly. Here perhaps Blake continues in the tradition set by the magicians and followed by Prospero, that which advises harsh, peremptory treatment of spirits to keep them under subjection. Blake's constant advice is to catch and cage the fairies, by which he seems to signify female dominion.

So sang a Fairy, mocking, as he sat on a streak'd Tulip,
Thinking none saw him; when he ceas'd I started from the trees
And caught him in my hat, as boys knock down a butterfly.
'How know you this,' said I, 'small Sir? Where did you learn this song?'
Seeing himself in my possession, thus he answer'd me:
'My master, I am yours! Command me, for I must obey.'[1]

And again:

> The Good are attracted by Men's perceptions,
> And think not for themselves;
> Till Experience teaches them to catch
> And to cage the Fairies and Elves.[2]

In Blake's private letters and conversation he treated fairies more simply, as a countryman might do, and seemed to believe that he actually saw them. John Adlard quotes two examples.
'Did you ever see a fairy's funeral, madam?' said Blake to a lady who happened to sit next to him. 'Never, Sir!' said the lady. 'I have,' said Blake, 'but not before last night.' And he went on to tell how, in his garden, he had seen 'a procession of creatures of the size and colour of green and grey grasshoppers, bearing a body laid out on a rose-leaf, which they buried with songs, and then disappeared'.[3] Here we have the insect fairies of his period, smaller than those seen in *The Fairy Funeral* in Hunt, where the body on the hearse was the size of a small doll.[4]
There are, too, the fairies seen by Bruno, his pony, and in a

[1] *William Blake*, p. 212.
[2] Ibid., p. 101.
[3] John Adlard, ed. cit., quoting from Alan Cunningham, *Lives of Eminent British Painters*, Scott Library (1876), pp. 228–9.
[4] R. Hunt, ed. cit., p. 102.

letter to Thomas Butts, also cited by John Adlard, is a verse
which suggests fairies more naturalistic and less erotic or
symbolical than most of Blake's fairies.

> With happiness stretch'd across the hills
> In a cloud that dewy sweetness distills,
> With a blue sky spread over with wings
> And a mild sun that mounts & sings,
> With trees & fields full of Fairy elves
> And little devils who fight for themselves.[1]

In the bawdy poem of *Long John Brown and Little Mary Bell*,
the fairy is clearly taken to mean the cold flirtatiousness which
stimulates and repels love, and the devil is lust. The poem is
full of erotic folk-symbols.

> LITTLE Mary Bell had a Fairy in a Nut,
> Long John Brown had the Devil in his Gut;
> Long John Brown lov'd little Mary Bell,
> And the Fairy drew the Devil into the Nut-Shell.
>
> Her Fairy Skip'd out and her Fairy Skip'd in;
> He laugh'd at the Devil saying, 'Love is a Sin.'
> The Devil he raged & the Devil he was wroth,
> And the Devil enter'd into the Young Man's broth.
>
> He was soon in the Gut of the loving Young Swain,
> For John eat & drank to drive away Love's pain;
> But all he could do he grew thinner & thinner,
> Tho' he eat & drank as much as ten Men for his Dinner.
>
> Some said he had a wolf in his stomach day & night,
> Some said he had the Devil & they guess'd right;
> The Fairy skip'd about in his Glory, Joy & Pride,
> And he laugh'd at the Devil till poor John Brown died.
>
> Then the Fairy skip'd out of the old Nut-Shell,
> And woe and alack for Pretty Mary Bell!
> For the Devil crept in when the Fairy skip'd out,
> And there goes Miss Bell with her fusty old Nut.[2]

In the more serious poem of *William Bond*[3] the fairies seem
to symbolize natural erotic impulses while the angels represent
the restraints of morality or of consideration for others. In the
poem the gentler, more unselfish love is victorious, and the

---

[1] *William Blake*, p. 859.   [2] Ibid., pp. 121–2.   [3] Ibid., p. 122.

fairies come over to the side of the angels. It can be seen that Blake's conception of the fairies is a complex one, but the darker side has plainly revived with him, and the same tendency is to be traced in the paintings of Fuseli, more strongly even than in Blake's. In Fuseli's work there is a Surrealist play of imagination which would almost be at home among the strange nightmares of Bosch. In the illustrations to *A Midsummer Night's Dream* there are ladies-in-waiting as sophisticated as those who waited on Queen Mab in *Nymphidia*, or as Pope's sylphs, but there are also strange and sinister groups, such as that in 'Titania with Bottom', the nymph who has a tiny, wizened bearded figure on a lead. Gert Schiff, in a small monograph on Fuseli,[1] ingeniously suggests that this represents a Nimue figure, with an enslaved and dwindled Merlin. Again, in 'Titania's Awakening' there is a witchcraft group, a half-naked woman suckling her imp, a child-witch making her profession, and between them the buttocks of a small, obscene demon, while between the ankles of the sleeping Bottom there is a crouching devil who might well have been conceived by Bosch. The tradition did not entirely die even in the next century. Amidst the riot of prettinesses in Noel Paton's *Quarrel of Oberon and Titania* there is a strange circle of kneeling demons obsequious to the commands of a winged nightmare, groups of malicious spirits are torturing an owl, and there are other birds on the ground swarmed over by little sprites. There is also an ancient bearded figure, very like that in the Fuseli picture, being pulled down into a pool by a couple of tiny nymphs. Even in the reconciliation scene the fairy world is little kinder. The owl is on the ground and is being despatched; a satyr-like devil is peering into a hollow tree where two lovers are embracing, and hideous faces peep out of odd crannies. In spite of their butterfly wings the prettification of the fairies is not yet quite complete.

[1] Girt Schiff, *Johan Heinrich Füssli. Ein Sommernachtstraum* (Stuttgart, 1961).

Nineteen

THE POETS: THE NINETEENTH CENTURY AND AFTER

THE full romantic treatment of the fairy tradition is to be found in Walter Scott's verse. In Scott we have a folklorist of authority, a collector of folk traditions at first hand and from his earliest days. The essay on the fairies which prefaces his *Minstrelsy of the Scottish Border* is still a source work, and his *Essay on Demonology and Witchcraft* is full of good material. Where he is unique among folklorists is in the tremendous vigour of his creative impulse, which surged out into thirty novels, as well as histories, poems, translations and essays. It is his poems that concern us here. They are not equal to his prose works and they are very much of his period, but they are not to be despised. *The Lay of the Last Minstrel*, the first of his verse-romances, was founded on a particular tradition, the tale of a boggart-like spirit called Gilpin Horner who for some time haunted one of the Border farms. His cry, 'Lost! Lost! Lost!' is borrowed from the Ettrick tale of Shellycoat which Scott himself tells in *Minstrelsy of the Scottish Border*,[1] but Shelly-coat used the cry to decoy travellers, while the Goblin Page was a spirit who had escaped from Michael Scot's conjurations, to whose ghost he at last surrendered with a cry of, 'Found! Found! Found!' Like changelings and evil spirits in general

---

[1] Walter Scott, ed. cit., Vol. I, p. 150, footnote.

he was forced to return to his natural form when he crossed running water.

There are many references to fairies as well as to wizards scattered through Scott's poems, but the most complete fairy story is *Alice Brand*, the ballad sung by Allan-Bane in *The Lady of the Lake*. There are turns in the poem which mark it as belonging to its period, for no man can walk abroad save on his own shadow, but it is the work of someone steeped in the fairy traditions of the Border Country. The human who was unconscious at the dangerous hour of twilight, and so was carried off into fairyland—only to be rescued by a holy sign, the cross, the bible or cold iron—the danger of wearing green, and the shifting glamour of fairyland, these themes are common to Scottish lore at all periods.

> 'Tis merry, 'tis merry in Fairy-land,
>   When fairy birds are singing,
> When the court doth ride by their monarch's side,
>   With bit and bridle ringing;
>
> And gaily shines the Fairy-land—
>   But all is glistening show,
> Like the idle gleam that December's beam
>   Can dart on ice and snow.
>
> And fading, like that varied gleam,
>   Is our inconstant shape,
> Who now like knight and lady seem,
>   And now like dwarf and ape.[1]

Such were the fairies that St. Collen saw on Glastonbury Tor, or the grotesque rade described by Dunbar, all translated into Scott's pleasant, ringing rhetoric.

Robert Burns gave us no fairy poetry, though he made a notable addition to witchcraft poetry in *Tam o' Shanter*. James Hogg, however, not only retold fairy legends in prose but also wrote one of the most evocative of our fairy poems, with its strange mystical passages. Kilmeny had vanished into fairyland, but its fairies were the dead, and the blessed dead. It is the story, familiar to us in so many tellings, of the man who

---

[1] *The Poetical Works of Sir Walter Scott*, Author's Edition (Edinburgh, n.d.), pp. 299–300.

6 'Oberon and Titania: The Quarrel.' Joseph Noel
Paton, Scottish National Gallery, 1847 (*see* chapter 18)

7 'Oberon and Titania Reconciled.' Joseph Noel
Paton (*see* chapter 18)

disappears into a timeless and beautiful land, who returns after many years and, in many versions of the story, crumbles into dust. This did not happen to Kilmeny, nor did she lose her youth and beauty, but after a short time, in which she told the message she had come to deliver, she vanished into Paradise again. Her return follows a familiar pattern:

> When seven lang years had come and fled;
> When grief was calm, and hope was dead;
> When scarce was remembered Kilmeny's name,
> Late, late in a gloamin Kilmeny came hame![1]

The land she visited is in some ways like St. Martin's Land as described by the Green Girl, but it is more Heavenly.

> For Kilmeny had been she knew not where,
> And Kilmeny had seen what she could not declare;
> Kilmeny had been where the cock never crew,
> Where the rain never fell, and the wind never blew.[2]

There is a touch of medieval feeling about the whole poem. One short passage has an air and turn of thought that reminds one of the lovely medieval lyric, *The Faucon hath Borne my Make Away*.[3]

> In yon green-wood there is a waik,
> And in that waik there is a wene,
> And in that wene there is a maike,
> That neither has flesh, blood, nor bane,
> And down in yon green-wood he walks his lane.[4]

Like Scott, Hogg was nurtured on the Border Ballads, and the turns and catch phrases of the ballads are scattered through his poetry. At first reading *The Mermaid* might strike one as almost a repetition of Clerk Colvil, but Hogg is trying to say something rather different, and is aiming at a subtler effect. There is an interaction here between the long-lived supernatural creature, and the immortal mortal. The mermaid is not tempting or evil, only dangerous to mortal men, and she warns her lover of the danger. After a hundred years his grave is a green mound and she is as young and fair as ever, but she begins to look

---

[1] *Selected Poems of James Hogg*, edited by J. W. Oliver (Edinburgh, 1940), p. 15.
[2] Ibid., p. 8.
[3] *Early English Lyrics*, E. K. Chambers and F. Sidgwick (1907), p. 148.
[4] *Kilmeny*, ed. cit., p. 8. A 'waik' is a clearing or glade, a 'wene' is a dwelling.

to the Eternal Day when her lake will dry and his soul will rise again. The lyric folk-song note sounds again, but with deeper overtones.

> For beauty's like the daisy's vest
> That shrinks from the early dew,
> But soon it opes its bonnie breast,
> An' sae may it fare wi' you.
>
> . . . .
>
> For passion's like the burning beal
> Upon the mountain's brow,
> That wastes itself to ashes pale,
> An' sae will it fare wi' you.[1]

The rhythm and turn of this irresistibly reminds one of *The Gardener*, but the message of it is different.

There are other supernatural tales, the *Witch's Chant* and *The Witch of Fife*, a re-telling of the well-known Blue-cap tale, which is sometimes told of fairies but as often of witches. In this poem Hogg makes the witches and the fairies meet together, as they did in both Irish and Scottish beliefs, but these were Lapland fairies.

In Ireland the fairy tradition needed no reviving, for it was alive all the time, but it was made known outside Ireland by Crofton Croker and Patrick Kennedy at the same time that Cunningham and Cromek were popularizing Scottish traditions. The great time of Irish fairy poetry was yet to come, however.

The English poets of the Romantic Revival showed comparatively little knowledge of fairies or interest in them. The pixies of Coleridge's early poems seem to have been sylphs, and have no resemblance at all to the pixies of Somerset, though he might have happened across them while he stayed there. Their filmy wings and silent-sandalled feet and rainbow-hued gauzes have nothing to do with the red-headed, earthy pixies. Wordsworth's eyes were intent on piercing to the truth of Nature, and Man's relationship with it; he had little attention to spare for fairies, and the Northern traditions, of which he must have known many. Southey, the least poetic of the three, was the

---

[1] *The Mermaid*, ed. cit., pp. 17–20.

best folklorist, and many tales and traditions are revived in the course of his poems. It was to him that Mrs. Bray addressed her letters on West Country Folk Beliefs, and it was he who recorded one of the best-known of our Nursery Tales, *The Three Bears*. Yet the fairies themselves make little appearance in his work. Shelley's early and immature poem, *Queen Mab*, has a so-called fairy queen as its genius, but she is an abstraction. She is chosen as the Queen of Dreams, for it is in a dream that the vision appears to Ianthe, but in the partial revision of the poem she is changed to the Daemon of the World. In appearance she is most like those ethereal beings described by some of the Irish seers.

> The Fairy's frame was slight; yon fibrous cloud,
> That catches but the palest tinge of even,
> And which the straining eye can hardly seize
> When melting into eastern twilight's shadow,
> Were scarce so thin, so slight; but the fair star
> That gems the glittering coronet of morn,
> Sheds not a light so mild, so powerful,
> As that which, bursting from the Fairy's form,
> Spread a purpureal halo round the scene,
> Yet with an undulating motion,
> Swayed to her outline gracefully.[1]

There seems rather a hangover from the eighteenth century here, but it is fair to say that votaries of the occult describe fairies of rather this kind, though they seem a long way from the folk fairies.

The fairy tradition was much nearer to Keats' heart. In *La Belle Dame Sans Merci* he took the evocative title of a rather dull medieval poem, treated it as a Melusine story and made one of the most beautiful fairy poems in the English language. This theme seems to have had an attraction for Keats, for he used it at full length in *Lamia*, the well-known tale of the serpent wife. About the same time Thomas Hood departed from his usual style to write the fairy-tale poem of *The Two Swans*, a curiously brilliant and touching poem, full of pictures. The fairy theme is taken up again in a short lyric, *The Water Lady*.

[1] *The Complete Works of Percy Bysshe Shelley*, edited by R. I., The Julian Edition (1927), Vol. I, pp. 69–70.

It is the haunting metre used by Keats in *La Belle Dame Sans Merci*, with its singing last line.

> Alas, the moon should ever beam
> To show what man should never see!—
> I saw a maiden on a stream,
> And fair was she![1]

Even more relevant to our subject is a long poem, *The Plea of the Midsummer Fairies*,[2] in which the spirit of Shakespeare saves the fairies from Time's scythe. The conceit is very pleasantly treated, and, light as it is, it is somehow moving. If we consider these poems with his love lyrics, his poems of social protest and his humorous verse, it gives us a pleasing view of Hood's rounded personality.

As the century went on the knowledge of fairy tradition spread, partly through the collections of the folklorists, but chiefly perhaps from the growing knowledge of the Irish and Highland traditions. The works of the Irish poets are scattered with fairy poems. At the beginning of the century George Darley's unequal but brilliant work drew the attention of literary circles. Miss Mitford said of his *Sylvia, or The May Queen*[3]—'It is exquisite—something between *The Faithful Shepherdess* and the *Midsummer Night's Dream*.' We should not now rate it so highly, but Darley is happiest in his fairy lyrics. The Dirge from the unpublished *Sea Bride* which was included in Sharp's *Lyra Celtica* is one of his best.

> Prayer unsaid, and mass unsung,
> Deadman's dirge must still be rung;
> Dingle-dong, the dead-bells sound!
> Mermen chant his dirge around![4]

Nora Hopper's *The Dark Man* and *The Wind among the Reeds* are two fairy lyrics, the last a lament for the absence of the Shee:

[1] *The Works of Thomas Hood, edited by his Son and Daughter* (1871), Vol. V, p. 154.

[2] Ibid., p. 243. An extract from this poem will be found in Appendix III.

[3] George Darley, *Sylvia or The May Queen* (London, 1827). An extract from this poem will be found in Appendix III.

[4] *Lyra Celtica*, edited by E. A. Sharp and J. Matthay (Edinburgh, 1932) (1st Edition, 1896), p. 104.

Dance in your rings again: the yellow weeds
You used to ride so far, mount as of old—
Play hide-and-seek with wind among the reeds,
And pay your scores again with fairy gold.[1]

This is the age-old lament for the departing fairies.
In the Highlands we have Robert Buchanan's *The Faëry
Foster-Mother*, on the theme of the stolen mother.

Bright Eyes, Light Eyes! Daughter of a Fay!
I had not been a wedded wife a twelvemonth and a day,
I had not nurs'd my little one a month upon my knee,
When down among the blue-bell banks rose elfins three times
   three,
They gripp'd me by the raven hair, I could not cry for fear,
They put a hempen rope around my waist and dragg'd me here,
They made me sit and give thee suck as mortal mothers can,
Bright Eyes, Light Eyes! strange and weak and wan![2]

In all these examples, and they are a few chosen from many,
we see an entire change in the attitude to the fairies. There is
nothing satirical here, some of the treatment is entirely decorative, much of it springs from a delight in strangeness, distance,
otherness, 'The horns of Elfland faintly blowing'. But the
situations are often accepted seriously, and seriously imagined.
This is not only among the Irish poets, the *Faëry Foster-Mother*
is matched by Charlotte Mew's *Changeling*,[3] which gives the
fairy, not the human standpoint. In Christina Rossetti's
Goblin Market the fairies are more grotesque, half-animal in
form, but the old prohibition holds good, pining and death
follows the eating of their fruits; for all their comical looks
they are dangerous and the situation is again seriously treated.

Backwards up the mossy glen
Turned and trooped the goblin men,
With their shrill repeated cry,
'Come buy, come buy.'
When they reached where Laura was
They stood stock still upon the moss,

[1] *Lyra Celtica*, p. 125.
[2] Ibid., p. 235. Robert Buchanan, b. 1841.
[3] *Collected Poems of Charlotte Mew* (1953) (First published in 1916. Charlotte Mew b. 1869).

Leering at each other,
Brother with queer brother;
Signalling each other,
Brother with sly brother.
One set his basket down,
One reared his plate;
One began to weave a crown
Of tendrils, leaves, and rough nuts brown
(Men sell not such in any town);
One heaved the golden weight
Of dish and fruit to offer her:
'Come buy, come buy,' was still their cry.[1]

Here, queerly enough, the effect of ominousness is given by those two identical rhymes—'other, brother, other, brother', and the short-lined, almost doggerel verse, which could be used for comic effect, here gives the thing urgency. William Allingham's fairy poems, *The Fairies*, *The Leprecaun*, *The Fairy King was Old* and *The Elf*[2] are different from the rest, direct, uncomplicated, practical, they strike again the lyric note of the sixteenth century. A longer poem cast in dramatic form is less successful. It was accompanied by pictures by Richard Doyle, with something of the intricacy and complication of the Noel Paton illustrations, purged of their sinister implications. Doyle's fairies are mischievous but innocent. Andrew Lang evidently felt that the pictures and poem did not match each other, for he wrote the short fairy story *Princess Nobody*[3] round the illustrations, a tale which lacks something of drive because each picture has somehow to be fitted into it.

With Yeats' poetry a different note came into our literature, for he believed in the fairies. From Chaucer onwards the poets wrote of other people's beliefs, of things they had only believed in childhood. Some were near to the country traditions, like Shakespeare, some far from them like Horace Walpole; but all treated them as rustic notions, not to be held by educated men. To Yeats fairies were a real danger, and a real delight.

---

[1] *The Poetical Works of Christina Rossetti*, edited by W. M. Macmillan (1904). *Goblin Market* (1852), p. 2.

[2] William Allingham, *Rhymes for the Young Folk*, (London, n.d.).

[3] *In Fairyland. A Series of Pictures from the Elf-World by Richard Doyle with a Poem by William Allingham* (London, 1870). *Princess Nobody* has been reprinted in *Modern Fairy Stories*, Dent's Children's Illustrated Classics.

'They had 'um out and thumped 'um; and that's not the sort of thing that a man wants to imagine,' he cried once,[1] and he tells of an old man who, asked if he believed in the fairies, said, 'Amn't I annoyed with them.'[2] Here is real, practical, matter-of-fact belief, and yet at the same time the glamour of fairyland drummed through his blood; it was he who popularized the phrase, 'the Celtic Twilight', and his fairy poems are full of escape and strangeness.

> Though I am old with wandering
> Through hollow lands and hilly lands,
> I will find out where she has gone,
> And kiss her lips and take her hands;
> And walk among long dappled grass,
> And pluck till time and times are done
> The silver apples of the moon,
> The golden apples of the sun.[3]

It is impossible not to think of Walter de la Mare when one talks of fairies. The air of Fairyland blows through his poems, though there are not many poems explicitly about fairies, and those are mostly among his children's verses, such poems as *The Mocking Fairy* and *Peak and Puke*. These are mocking, homely fairies.[4] Those that sidle and jape and mutter in *Crossings* are dangerous without being quite inimical. The play has been and can be acted, but it is better fitted for reading, for the fantasy is apt to evaporate on the stage. The fairies, 'fantastically disguised as earth-children', are better imagined than they are perceived. The stage directions about them are the cream of the play. But de la Mare's prose treatment of the fairies must be kept for a later chapter. C. S. Lewis and J. R. Tolkien both write fairy poetry, but both are chiefly notable for their prose. They have not, and neither has de la Mare, the factual belief that inspired Yeats, but the imaginative integrity is there, their fairies are full of meaning.

---

[1] G. K. Chesterton, *Autobiography* (1937), p. 147.
[2] *Irish Fairy and Folk Tales*, edited by W. B. Yeats, Scott Publishing Library, p. lx.
[3] *The Collected Poems of W. B. Yeats* (London, 1950), pp. 66–7.
[4] Walter de la Mare, *Peacock Pie*, n.d. (*circa* 1916), pp. 149–50, 140 and 69–71.

Twenty

THE FOREIGN INVASION

THE first and greatest wave of the invaders who came to bring a literary influence to bear on our native fairies were the lesser deities of the classical poets. It is possible that some fairies come directly to us from Roman mythology, and not from classical literature. The Brownie and the Lar, at any rate, seem very close to each other, and Puck is in many ways, and particularly in outward appearance, very like a satyr.

The fairy ladies of the Romances made the first entrance into literature of our Celtic fairies, just as Grendel and his Mother were the first literary treatment of the Scandinavian monsters and hags. After the Norman Conquest the Celtic tradition crossed and recrossed between England and France, promoted by the migration of the Cornishmen to Brittany, until one shining web was woven, and the Normans carried the Arthurian Legends down into Italy and up into Scotland.

The tales that seem native to these Islands are those of the Daoine O Sidhe, of fairy brides and changelings, of prankish bogey-beasts and helpful hobgoblins, and of the dangerous spirits of rivers and lakes. Among them, too, are the tiny fairies, sometimes only a few inches high.

At the time of the Renaissance the classical nymphs and naiads, fauns and satyrs mixed with these, so that in the writings of the sixteenth- and seventeenth-century poets it is difficult to distinguish between fairies and nymphs, mermaids and sirens. The nymphs dance their nightly heydegies, and satyrs peep out of the brake and crack jokes with fairies. In the chap-books of these times we have the re-telling of classical tales, and beside them the native stories complained of by Herrick:

> The *farting Tanner*, and *familiar King*;
> The *dancing Frier*, tatter'd in the bush;
> Those monstrous lies of little *Robin Rush*.[1]

We have Tom Thumb and Robin Goodfellow, and the prophecies of Sibylla and Merlin and Mother Shipton, all mixed with the re-telling of classical stories. Even the uneducated could not escape some classical knowledge, and every schoolboy knew his Ovid. In *Love's Labours Lost* it was the village schoolmaster who made up the pageant of *The Seven Worthies*, but it was the rustics who acted in it. The Seven Worthies themselves are a good example of the extraordinary medley of Classical, Biblical and Romance tradition on which the literature of that time was founded.

In the ninety-fifth number of *The Tatler* (1709) Steele describes the reading of his godson, who had abandoned Aesop's *Fables* as improbable, and was concentrating on the Adventures of Don Bellianis of Greece, Guy of Warwick, the Seven Champions, 'and other historians of that age'. His sister Betty, however, who, her mother said, was a better scholar than he, 'deals chiefly in fairies and sprites; and sometimes in a winters night will terrify the maids with her accounts until they are afraid to go up to bed'.[2] It seems likely that these fairies and sprites were of native origin, of the same kind as those heard of by Reginald Scot from his grandmother's maids. But a few years later her studies might have been of another kind of fairy, for a second wave of foreign invasion was soon to come that altered the whole type and texture of children's fairy tales in England. The fairies became a fashion in the Court of France about a hundred years later than in England. Just as the small fairies of Shakespeare and Lyly and Drayton were imported into the fashionable world from the country, so the French fairies were borrowed from nurses and governesses, who told cradle tales to the children of the nobility. The first

---

[1] *The Poetical Works of Robert Herrick*, edited by F. W. Moorman (1925), p. 155.
[2] R. Steele, *The Lucubrations of Isaac Bickerstaff Esq.*, *The Tatler*, No. 95 (1709, Nov. 15th–17th).

person who started the fashion was the Comtesse d'Aulnoy, whose first fairy tale was printed in 1690. An English translation of her tales was printed in 1707, so Steele's little Betty might just have read it. The stories nearest to the folk tradition, however, were those of Pierre Perrault d'Armancour, the son of Charles Perrault, well-known as a savant, and a writer on his own account.[1] Of these stories *Cinderella, Puss in Boots, Sleeping Beauty* and *Hop o' my Thumb* made an immediate conquest of the English children. Well they might, for they were told with a demure humour unlike anything that came before them. Though they were a re-telling of tales told to children they were not written for children, and were therefore not tuned to edification. Even Perrault's *Tales* seem in the details and the style strangely unlike folk-tales, although their plots are unmistakably folk themes. It may well be, however, that they were nearer to their originals than one would be inclined to imagine, for the modern oral French folk-tales have an urbanity which distinguishes them from our own. Those retold by Henri Pourrat may have been a little re-polished,[2] but those published by Paul de la Rue[3] were taken down verbatim from the mouths of peasants, and though they have more of the folk-tale terseness than Perrault they have a comparable touch of style.

In the *Tales* of Madame d'Aulnoy, however, the atmosphere of the Court is unmistakable, and as her successors worked over the themes in the voluminous *Cabinet des Fées*[4] the fairies became more and more sophisticated, as sentiment, sentimentality and edification burgeoned over their works. The more elaborate tales were not often reproduced, but those nearest to folk-tales captured the hearts of English children at once; and with Perrault the Fairy Godmother entered England. The Fairy Godmother was a new character among the Personae of Fairyland, but she soon began to play a leading part.

The English fairies had indeed a code of behaviour which

[1] See Percy Muir (*English Children's Books*, 1954, p. 39) for the ascription to the son rather than to the father.

[2] Henri Pourrat, *A Treasury of French Tales* (1953), translated from *Le Trésor des Contes* (1951).

[3] *The Borzoi Book of French Folk Tales*, edited by Paul de la Rue (New York, 1956).

[4] *Le Cabinet des Fées*. Published in Amsterdam and Geneva, 1785 and 1789, 41 volumes.

they exacted from the humans whom they happened to meet. Kindliness, courtesy, openhandedness and orderly ways, these were essential to gaining their favour. They had no patience with misers or sluts; but these were qualities demanded in intercourse between humans and fairies, they were not generally a deliberate educational effort. It is true that the fairies felt themselves to be in a kind of partnership with humans in increasing the fertility of the land—it was this that made them intolerant of prudes. Fecundity and merriment were dear to them. It was important, too, to speak the truth in dealing with them and to keep contracts; but, in spite of Elidor, this was perhaps not so much because they were honourable as because they were spirits, and dangerous; to tell lies to devils, ghosts or fairies was to put oneself into their power, and it is as well not to be in the power of even the best-disposed fairy.

In the French fairy tales, however, the fairies seem to have made human morals their chief concern. We have, for instance, in one of the Comte de Caylus' tales the story of a series of princesses who were brought up by a fairy in a kind of boarding school, to each of whom was given at the end of her stay a fairy gift of her own choosing—beauty, wit and so on. The youngest of the girls was sent round on a tour of inspection before she made her choice, and as the result of her researches asked only for a contented spirit.[1] The fairies were indeed goddesses of fortune, who could bestow not only such trinkets as rings of invisibility and bottomless purses, but qualities of beauty and wit and even virtue. Princess Cabbage-Stalk in *The Golden Branch*,[2] for instance, was offered by the fairy the choice between beauty and virtue, strangely to be determined by whether she breathed on one side or the other of a fur muff. She chose goodness, but no noticeable change of character resulted from it, though she would have deteriorated if she had made the other choice. She had her cake as well as eating it, for she became strikingly beautiful; presumably her goodness needed no augmentation. At any rate, these fairies took the first step to becoming those moral instructors indignantly described by

[1] A translation of this tale appears in Andrew Lang's *Green Fairy Book*, under the title 'Fairy Gifts'.
[2] *Le Rameau d'Or*, Madame d'Aulnoy, published in Andrew Lang's *Red Fairy Book*.

Puck of Pook's Hill as 'that sugar-and-shake-your-head set of impostors'.[1]

The next wave of invaders was from the East. *The Arabian Nights Entertainment* was introduced into France late in the seventeenth century, and was an immediate success there. Three of the stories, *Sinbad the Sailor*, *Ali Baba* and *Aladdin*, were soon naturalized into English nurseries, and reproduced in chap-books. When the Commedia dell'Arte developed into the Pantomime two of these were among the most popular plots used; but the djinns and afrits and peris of the Arabian tales had no influence on the English fairies, and in no way modified them as the French fairies had done; the tradition was too alien.

In the beginning of the nineteenth century a tremendous impetus was given to the love of fairy tales by the appearance of *The Household Tales* of the Brothers Grimm in 1823 and 1826. The first impulse towards the collection and publication of *Haus-und-Kinder-Märchen* was the patriotic desire to preserve German traditions during the French occupation of Germany; but the stories burst the bounds of nationality and were eagerly welcomed all over Europe. They even modified some of the folk-tale traditions in Japan.[2] The tales themselves belonged to International Tale Types, and many stories with the same plots or general themes had already been told in England, though they had been overlaid by the utilitarian ideal of education in the eighteenth century, and buried by the cleavage between the classes, the uprooting of the poor from the land, and the laborious lives which almost starved folk culture out of existence. There can be no culture without a leisure; the life in the Highlands and Islands of Scotland was hard, and poverty was as great there as anywhere, but winter brought enforced leisure to the crofters and fishermen, there was time for stories and songs, and the folk culture survived. Among the English poor in the time of the Industrial Revolution there was no holiday, the machines claimed men through winter and summer. In countless homes the chain of tradition was broken and could not be mended. Nevertheless, some memory survived;

[1] Rudyard Kipling, *Puck of Pook's Hill* (New York, 1906), p. 14.
[2] Hiroko Ikeda, *The Introduction of Foreign Influences on Japanese Children's Literature through Grimm's Household Tales. Brüder Grimm Gedenken* (Marburg, 1963), pp. 575–83.

the Grimm tales came home to the English mind as something native. There were differences in style and character—the witchcraft persecutions and the Thirty Years War had left a black legacy, and the revenges inflicted on bad characters are more ruthless than is usual in English tales, but that the tales aroused interest in the collection of English fairy tales is one sign of their relationship. The Grimm Brothers' method of working was an inspiration to collectors, and after their time the conscientious reproduction of tales as they were told began in England. Most of the *Märchen* are more tales of enchantment and strange happenings than of real fairies, but where fairies occur, as in *Rumpelstiltschen, The Cobbler and the Elves, Snowdrop and the Seven Dwarfs* and so on, they are very much after the English pattern. As far as the German fairies altered the English tradition it was to strengthen the image of the hobgoblins, pixies and hags and rather to overlay the memory of the fairy ladies of the Romances. From the time of the Grimms onward our own stories began to be collected; but their numbers were sparse, and they never attained to the Nursery popularity of the French and German tales. *The Three Bears, Jack and the Beanstalk, Jack the Giantkiller* and *Dick Whittington* are known to all English children, but are not so well loved as *Cinderella, Red Riding Hood, Sleeping Beauty, Snowdrop* or *The Twelve Dancing Princesses.*

The Scandinavian tradition was the next to invade us in two different forms, the true folk-tales of Dasent and Thorpe,[1] and the Hans Andersen *Tales*, first introduced into this country by Mary Howitt, who was doubly distinguished, for she was the author of one of our best-known Nursery Rhymes. Hans Andersen's fairy tales are as much a work of art and as carefully polished as those of Perrault and Madame d'Aulnoy. The earliest of them were free renderings of real folk-tales, but as time went on Andersen invented more, and related his plots only loosely to folk themes. The same may be said of the Cabinet des Fées, except that Andersen was a great artist and the later French story-tellers were not.

Hans Andersen was immensely admired and very much imitated in England. Oscar Wilde reproduced almost exactly his

[1] George Dasent, *Popular Tales from the Norse* (1859) and Benjamin Thorpe, *Yuletide Stories* (1884).

179

mixture of satire and sentiment, something at once sweet and bitter.[1] Tales like those of Mary de Morgan and Laurence Housman owe a good deal to him. It is perhaps unfair to say it, but it seems to me that with Hans Andersen whimsy crept into our treatment of the elves and fairies. Perhaps some of the Irish writers must bear a little of the blame, perhaps we can cast back to Horace Walpole and Tickell and their predecessors, and say that the germ of whimsy was always there, but it certainly flourished in the first quarter of this century; and the style and flavour and taste of it is Hans Andersen and water.

[1] Oscar Wilde, *The Happy Prince and Other Tales*, (1888).

Twenty-one

THE MORALISTS

In the eighteenth century the publication of books for children first became a really profitable trade. Before then educational works had been produced, indeed, Caxton's *Babees Book* was one of the first to be printed, and grammars and lesson books had been published from the sixteenth century, some of them dreary and some lively and entertaining, like Hollyband's *French Schoolemaister*;[1] but for amusement children had to rely on the books which pleased the more simple-minded of the grown-up people, stories retold in chapbooks or ballads. These were intended to amuse and were not twisted to edification; indeed some of them, like *The Witch of the Woodlands*,[2] were very unedifying indeed. But when authors began expressly to write for children the moral effect of their books and their educational quality became a primary consideration, as indeed it often is to this day. The psychology of childhood was little understood, and educationalists were impatient for quick results and wished to turn children into little grown-up people as early as possible. Where the value of entertainment was admitted it was generally as a means of sugaring the pill. It was a bad time on the whole for the fairies. In 1709 Steele had vainly pointed out the moral value of popular tales, but as the century went on Mrs. Trimmer and her school triumphed, and they condemned fairy tales as meaningless fictions. The greater part of the stories written for

[1] Claudius Hollyband, *The French Schoolemaister* (1573).
[2] *The Witch of the Woodlands or The Cobler's New Translation*, by L. P. (1655).

181

children in the eighteenth and early nineteenth centuries are rigorously matter-of-fact in their machinery, though their plots are often those of fairy tales. The stories of The Good-Natured and the Ill-Natured Boys told by Mr. Barlow in Day's *Sandford and Merton* are the plot of Tale Type 403, *Kind and Unkind*, and are as neat in their retribution as any fairy tale could be.[1] Where fairies were admitted they were generally more like the later French fairies than the true fairies of folklore, and often the fairy tales are no more than allegories. *Prince Life*, for instance, by G. P. R. James, is frankly an allegory, while Uncle David's Nonsensical Story in *Holiday House*[2] is something between an allegory and a parody, with its Giant Snap-em-Up and Fairy Teach-All. *The Giant Hands* is another, rather later allegorical fairy story, with an ogress in it and a pair of fairy hands, quite ingeniously illustrated, 'the Hands of Industry'. The story, because of its positive attitude, is a more pleasing one than many.[3] The play of fancy at this time was chiefly reserved for such trifles as Roscoe's *Butterfly's Ball* and its imitations, *The Peacock at Home*, *The Rose's Breakfast*, *Flora's Gala*, and so on. Their popularity shows how people hungered for anything fantastic. We see the moralists at work on a chap-book version of *Jack and the Beanstalk*,[4] in which a fairy lady appears to Jack and tells him that the Giant has stolen his treasures from Jack's father, and that therefore there is no dishonesty in stealing them back. Those people who felt a real interest in fairies and in the supernatural were still conscientiously anxious to screw a moral out of them. Cruikshank reduced the matter to an absurdity by turning *Hop o' my Thumb*, *Cinderella* and *Jack and the Beanstalk* into temperance tracts.[5] He took the already over-moralized chap-book version of *Jack and the Beanstalk*, and, as well as the tutelary flower fairy, turned the harp and hen into fairies, and introduced a sort of hobgoblin into the tale. The

[1] Thomas Day, *The History of Sandford and Merton* (4th edition, corrected, 1787), Vol. I, pp. 181–203.

[2] Catherine Sinclair, *Holiday House* (Edinburgh, 1831), Chapter IX. 'Uncle David's Nonsensical Story about Giants and Fairies', pp. 147–209.

[3] *The Giant Hands, or The Reward of Industry*, Mother Goose's Fairy Tales (*circa* 1880), pp. 97–116.

[4] Reproduced in *English Fairy and Folk Tales*, S. Hartland. Scott Publishing Library.

[5] George Cruikshank's Fairy Library. *Hop o' my Thumb, Cinderella, Jack and the Beanstalk* (n.d., *circa* 1853).

8   Richard Doyle's Elves. From *Fairyland. A Series of Pictures from the Elf-World*, 1870 (*see* chapter 19)

9   From Doyle: *Fairyland. A series of Pictures from the Elf-World*

10 From Doyle: *Fairyland. A Series of Pictures from the Elf-World*

11 From Doyle: *Fairyland. A Series of Pictures from the Elf-World*

Giant's bad conduct he attributed to his drunken habits, and in the end he was not killed but reproved, mended his ways and learnt to be an affectionate husband to his ill-used wife. It was drink that led Hop o' my Thumb's father astray and caused his unnatural conduct, and Cinderella's godmother easily persuaded the Prince's father to have all the drink in his kingdom destroyed. Dickens was rightly indignant at this tampering, and protested against it in *Household Words*.

In an utilitarian age, of all other times, it is a matter of grave importance that Fairy tales should be respected. Our English red tape is too magnificently red ever to be employed in the tying up of such trifles, but every one who has considered the subject knows full well that a nation without fancy, without some romance, never did, never can, never will, hold a great place under the sun. The theatre, having done its worst to destroy these admirable fictions— and having in a most exemplary manner destroyed itself, its artists, and its audiences, in that perversion of its duty—it becomes doubly important that the little books themselves, nurseries of fancy as they are, should be preserved. To preserve them in their usefulness, they must be as much preserved in their simplicity, and purity, and innocent extravagance, as if they were actual fact. Whosoever alters them to suit his own opinions, whatever they are, is guilty, to our thinking, of an act of presumption, and appropriates to himself what does not belong to him.[1]

He would probably have felt much the same about Charlotte M. Yonge's retelling of the chap-book *Tom Thumb*.[2] A good deal of erudition has gone into the little book, and in her notes she quotes many of the Elizabethan fairy poems. The tale is ornamented with Arthurian legends and references, the Marriage of Sir Gawain, the drawing of Excalibur and King Arthur's combat with the Giant Ryence. Charlotte Yonge knows, too, the dangers of eating or drinking in fairyland. The danger of the unsained fairies is present to her, so that she neither makes the fairies the instruments of edification nor prettifies them, as some of her successors were to do. Yet the whole spirit breathed by the book is so unlike the rather matter-of-fact humour of the original as to make it a completely different thing. It is im-

---

[1] Charles Dickens, *Frauds on the Fairies, Household Words*, Vol. VIII (October 1st, 1853), pp. 97–100.
[2] Charlotte M. Yonge, *The History of Thomas Thumb* (1855).

pregnated with the nineteenth-century notion of Christian chivalry. Tom Thumb is a serious character, tempted by the fairies to forsake his Christian faith and his allegiance to the King. He is as much a hero of romance as if he had been six-foot high, but he is not Tom Thumb.

George Macdonald was born and brought up in Aberdeen-shire, a part of Scotland which has preserved folk tale and ballad in its greatest purity. He had a keen eye for the super-natural and an understanding nourished on folklore; but he was a moralist, of Puritan stock, and the fairies were a favourite instrument of his. The moral fairies of the later French tradition, the arbitresses of Destiny, were dear to him. In *Curdie and the Goblins* we have the evil goblins of the mines, but the fairy godmother is raised to almost angelic stature in Princess Irene's Great-Grandmother. In *The Lost Princess, or The Wise Woman*,[1] she is even higher, and may be regarded as a personi-fication of God's Providence, or at least as Wordsworth's 'Stern Daughter of the Voice of God'. Only divine status could excuse that forcible intermeddling with the very roots of Agnes's soul. No creature could rightly assume such powers, only omniscience could know whether that torture of solitude would push the child over the edge of madness, or give her a last chance of redemption.

In the short fairy tales George Macdonald often followed the regular French pattern in which there is an evil fairy and one that acts as a tutelary genius. Sometimes he uses a different theme, as in *The Giant's Heart*,[2] and the poetical and allegorical *Mossy's Key*.[3] The family fairy in *Little Daylight*[4] is much in the same style as that introduced into the moral chap-book version of *Jack and the Beanstalk*. The treatment of this fairy in Cruik-shank's elaborated version is not unlike something of George Macdonald's, though it has not his poetic vision.

> As Jack was hastening along to the village, he saw a little old woman, in a cloak and hood, sitting by the roadside, who appeared to be bent down with age and illness. Now, although Jack was in a great hurry, his heart was too good to pass by any one who

[1] George Macdonald, *The Lost Princess* (1895).
[2] George Macdonald, *Dealings with the Fairies* (1867), pp. 1–99.
[3] Ibid., pp. 100–40.
[4] Ibid., pp. 248–308.

seemed in distress, so he went to the old woman and asked her if he could do anything to help her. At first she only answered by a low, moaning sort of sound, and kept rocking herself backwards and forwards; but Jack stooped down, and, speaking kindly to her, took her hand, in order to raise her from the ground.

Her cloak and dress were of a dark, dingy brown; but as she got up it seemed to change to green, mixed with red, and blue, and yellow; and her aged, wrinkled face seemed also to be changing from a pale yellow to pink; and the half-shut grey eyes seemed to open into two bright, glistening, little blue ones, that fixed their gaze upon him. And then, slowly, the hood, the cloak, and gown, with the old pale face, and brown wrinkled hands and arms, all disappeared or melted away into the air; and there stood before him a most charming and graceful little lady, with light flaxen hair, encircled by a wreath of little tiny flowers. She had a pair of wings like those of some beautiful butterfly, to which her dress corresponded. In one hand she held a thin light wand, and in her other a Bean, speckled with bright purple and gold.[1]

The old woman befriended might belong to any folk fairy story, but the description of the fairy is a typically nineteenth-century one. One rather like it appears in the story *Patty and her Pitcher* which can be found in a collection of tales put together by Routledge in the 1880s.[2] From the varying set-up it would appear to be a binding together of a number of cheap individual tales. Some of the tales in that excellent series of penny pamphlets called 'Stead's Books for the Bairns' have similar moral fairies, like one in *The Legend of the Birch Tree*, which exemplifies the Biblical proverb, so popular in earlier times— 'Spare the rod and spoil the child.' The allegories and moral tales continued till at least the twentieth century in such books as *Sylvia's Travels*,[3] but from 1850 onwards tricksier, more irresponsible fairies began to appear. The fairies who stole Amelia in Mrs. Ewing's *Amelia and the Dwarfs* were bent at first on her moral improvement; but when she was reformed they tried to keep her like any folk fairies, and the description of the fairies and the stock in that tale are hardly to be bettered.

'Here is Amelia!' shouted the dwarf when they reached the first haycock.

[1] George Cruikshank's Fairy Library, ed. cit., *Jack and the Beanstalk*, p. 9.
[2] *Patty and her Pitcher*, *Mother Goose's Fairy Tales*, ed. cit., pp. 157–76.
[3] Constance Armfield, *Sylvia's Travels* (1911).

'Ho, ho, ho!' laughed all the others, as they poked out here and there from the hay.

'Bring a stock,' said the dwarf; on which the hay was lifted, and out ran six or seven dwarfs, carrying what seemed to Amelia to be a little girl like herself. And when she looked closer, to her horror and surprise, the figure was exactly like her—it was her own face, clothes and everything.

'Shall we kick it into the house?' asked the goblins.

'No,' said the dwarf; 'lay it down by the haycock. The father and mother are coming to seek her now.'

When Amelia heard this she began to shriek for help; but she was pushed into the haycock, where her loudest cries sounded like the chirruping of a grasshopper. . . .

'Rub her eyes,' said the dwarf; on which Amelia's eyes were rubbed with some ointment, and when she took a last peep she could see that the stock was nothing but a hairy imp, with a face like the oldest and most grotesque of apes—'and send her below,' added the dwarf. On which the field opened, and Amelia was pushed underground.

She found herself on a sort of open heath, where no houses were to be seen. Of course there was no moonshine, and yet it was neither daylight nor dark. There was as the light of early dawn, and every sound was at once clear and dreamy, like the first sounds of day coming through the fresh air before sunrise.[1]

We are here in a different world from that of the sophisticated, moralizing fairies, and the morals in these stories are not much more obtrusive than they are in many of the folk-tales, though it cannot be denied that the tales are written around them. We have returned to the morality of the folk fairies. The Industrious Apprentice is no longer the hero; generosity and a merry heart are the prime virtues, and a miser is the greatest of villains. The morals implicit in *Granny's Wonderful Chair* are in the same way unforced.[2] Even the King of the Golden River, though Ruskin was born didactic, follows a true folk pattern. In *Mopsa the Fairy*, written as early as 1869,[3] one travels through a tricksy, irresponsible fairy world, where anything can happen

---

[1] J. H. Ewing, *Amelia and the Dwarfs*, *The Brownies and Other Tales* (1871), pp. 82–91.

[2] Frances Browne, *Granny's Wonderful Chair* (1st edition, 1857), Dent's Children's Illustrated Classics No. 55.

[3] Jean Ingelow, *Mopsa the Fairy* (1st edition, 1869), Dent's Children's Illustrated Classics No. 62.

and where one may do whatever one can do. At the bottom of it there is a kind of wild reality that reminds one of the best of the Surrealist paintings. It is a complete break with the rational moralists of the eighteenth century. We are launched on to a wilder sea, and its very unreason brings it nearer to reality.

Twenty-two

FOLKLORISTS AND COLLECTORS

O<small>RAL</small> tradition has been the subject of continuous study from the sixteenth century onwards. The three great periods were those of the seventeenth-century antiquaries, of the Romantic Revival at the end of the eighteenth century and of the folklorists at the turn of the nineteenth. The earlier stress was on antiquities and customs; in the nineteenth century, however, folktales began to be collected, and, what is of even more importance to our present purpose, traditions about fairies, elves and other supernatural beings were systematically written down. In 1831 Joseph Ritson made a collection of native fairy tales, prefaced by a short essay on the Pigmies of Antiquity and their like in more modern times. There is no new matter in the book, it is a useful reprint of fairy anecdotes from the medieval chronicles down to those from Waldron's *Isle of Man*. Halliwell-Phillipps followed the same plan in 1845 in his *Illustrations of the Fairy Mythology of A Midsummer Night's Dream*, and in 1874 Carew Hazlitt combined the two books in his *Fairy Mythology of Shakespeare*. Thomas Keightley used the same method in his *Fairy Mythology*, but spread his net wider, for he collected fairy anecdotes from all over Europe, arranging them according to nationality. All these are learned works, and most valuable, as assembling a great deal of the printed matter available. We owe their authors a great debt of gratitude for their work, as we do to those popularizers who have made obscure folk-tales available to children. Lang and Jacobs come specially to mind and James Stephens, whose delightful books breathe the very spirit of Irish tradition. There are later popularizers too, Amabel Williams-Ellis and Roger Lancelyn Green and the Montgomeries, who all deserve to be mentioned. There were other works, however, which were the fruit of first-hand research, and provided the material used by Keightley. The earliest in the field was Allan Cunningham in 1822, for Scotland, and Crofton Croker was hard on his heels in 1825, with his *Fairy Legends of the South of Ireland*. England was not much behind, for in 1836 Mrs. Bray published her account of *Traditions of the Borders of the Tamar and Tavy* in a series of letters addressed to Robert Southey. She did not attempt to reproduce the stories exactly as they were told, but they were reliable in substance and we owe to her much knowledge about the fairy faith in that part of Devon, as well as some good pixy tales, such as that of the lazy maid who was struck with lameness, and the well-known fairy midwife story. An even greater wealth of material was produced by Robert Hunt in his *Popular Romances of the West of England*. Hunt travelled the country, and met the last of the travelling droll-tellers of Cornwall, who kept long rambling stories, such as *Duffy and Terrytop*,[1] going for several nights on end. Hunt's style is rather high-flown, but he preserved many traditions and tales that would otherwise have been lost. The whole book gives a picture of the life, atmosphere and beliefs of the old Cornish countryside which could ill be spared. A little later Bottrell's *Traditions*[2] supplemented and confirmed Hunt's findings. In the North Henderson collected beliefs about Dunnie, Shag, the Picktree Brag, Dunters, Redcaps and Powries and other strange creatures of the Borders, Wag at the Wa' and Kilmoulis and many another.[3] The *Denham Tracts* covered Durham and Westmorland.[4] Parkinson[5] and Atkinson[6] collected traditions of Yorkshire and Roby—though in almost unreadable diction—of Lancashire.[7] Addy, another Northerner, was one of the first to

[1] R. Hunt, ed. cit., pp. 239–47.
[2] William Bottrell, *Traditions and Hearthside Stories of West Cornwall*, ed. cit.
[3] William Henderson, *Folk-Lore of the Northern Counties and the Borders*, ed. cit.
[4] *The Denham Tracts*. Reprinted from the Tracts Published by *M. A. Denham between 1846 and 1849* (F.L.S., 1892).
[5] Thomas Parkinson, *Yorkshire Legends and Traditions* (London, 1888).
[6] J. C. Atkinson, *Forty Years in a Moorland Parish* (1891).
[7] John Roby, *Traditions of Lancashire*, 2 vols. (1829).

try to reproduce the stories in the exact language in which they were told.[1] As the Folk-Lore Society got under weigh tales and fairy beliefs were collected from various quarters. Mrs. Balfour's *Legends of the Cars*[2] were particularly notable, and introduced one to a stark Paganish world of fairy beliefs and practices. Tales were contributed by Lang, Clodd, Burne, Hartland, Newell, Gregor, and many other well-known folklorists. Many notable books were published, one of the most complete was Campbell's *Popular Tales of the Western Highlands*,[3] still an example of faithful presentation. Wirt Sikes collected stories and beliefs from Wales,[4] and later John Rhys did the same with more accuracy and deeper knowledge.[5] Burne and Jackson's *Shropshire Folk Lore* did the same for that part of the Western Midlands, Jabez Allies included some fairy beliefs in his *Folk-Lore of Worcestershire*,[6] and in the beginning of this century Mary Leather produced the latest of the books of this particular stamp in *Hereford Folklore*, published in 1913.

From the eighteenth century onwards *The Gentleman's Magazine* had been the repository of much curious matter, and in 1885 G. L. Gomme collected the articles of folklore interest into a single volume, *English Traditional Lore*. In 1847 Thoms had contributed a series of folklore notes to the *Athenaeum*, and later he began to publish *Notes and Queries* which at first had a strong folklore interest, though later it veered to history. In the nineteenth century most counties had archaeological or field societies, and the periodicals of some of these contain articles of folklore interest, though more often about customs than about fairylore.

The Highlands and Lowlands of Scotland, and Aberdeen were well covered, and Patrick Kennedy, Douglas Hyde, Lady Wilde and many other admirable collectors dealt faithfully with the rich material to be found all over Ireland. Orkney, Shetland and the Isle of Man were well served by their collectors. The methods employed, however, depended on

---

[1] S. O. Addy, *Household Tales and Traditional Remains* (1895).

[2] Mrs. Balfour, *Legends of the Cars*, Folk-Lore, Vol. II (1891).

[3] J. F. Campbell, *Popular Tales of the Western Highlands*, 4 vols. (1890).

[4] Wirt Sikes, *British Goblins* (London, 1880).

[5] John Rhys, *Celtic Folklore, Welsh and Manx*, 2 vols. (Oxford, 1901).

[6] Jabez Allies, *On the Ancient British, Roman and Saxon Antiquities and Folk-Lore of Worcestershire* (1840).

having someone resident on the spot. There is no doubt that more deep and accurate information can be gained by someone who has always lived in a place and has known the inhabitants from childhood than from a passer-by, however acute. Alexander Carmichael or Campbell of Islay would not have had the immense success they enjoyed if they had not been Highlanders and fluent Gaelic speakers. But this is not always necessary. Some collectors can establish a rapport very quickly, and inspire confidence in people who are ordinarily shy and loath to betray their hidden beliefs to strangers. One has only to instance the remarkable results that Evans Wentz obtained in his travels through the Celtic Countries. Wirt Sikes, too, was an American who succeeded in collecting some good and authentic material from Wales. The Isle of Man also owes to Waldron the preservation of some of its best stories.[1] Therefore when resident folklorists are not to be found it is worth while for travelling ones to try what they can do. There are many counties of England which are inadequately represented in our tale collections and other folklore material. Warwickshire, Wiltshire, Gloucestershire, Oxfordshire, Bedfordshire and Hertfordshire have very little to show. The songs and dances collected in some of these counties would seem to indicate that other material is awaiting the collector if he is not too late.

In spite of gaps and deficiencies, however, a great deal of information about fairy beliefs was available by the end of the nineteenth century for anybody who cared to read it. Those who wrote stories for children had only themselves to thank if they handed round and round among them a small bundle of pretty fancies which became successively more thread-bare.

[1] George Waldron, *A Description of the Isle of Man* (London, 1744).

Twenty-three

THE HUMORISTS

T HERE were humorists even among the earliest of our writers
on fairies. Chaucer's sly reference to the limitors and holy
friars who have taken the place of the elves will occur to everyone. Drayton's treatment of the Fairy King and the little
Court ladies of Fairyland is frankly farcical.

> From thence he ran into a Hive,
> Amongst the Bees hee letteth drive
> And downe their Coombes begins to rive,
>   All likely to have spoyled:
> Which with their Waxe his face besmeard,
> And with their Honey daub'd his Beard,
> It would have made a man afeard
>   To see how he was moyled.[1]

And of the Ladies in Waiting:

> When like an uprore in a Towne,
> Before them every thing went downe,
> Some tore a Ruffe, and some a Gowne,
>   Gainst one another justling;
> They flewe about like Chaffe i' th' winde,
> For hast some left their Maskes behinde;
> Some could not stay their Gloves to finde,
>   There never was such bustling.[2]

[1] *The Works of Michael Drayton*, edited by J. W. Hebel (Oxford, 1932), Vol. III,
p. 132.
[2] Ibid., Vol. III, p. 135.

As we have seen, the eighteenth century followed the same
fashion, though not quite so broadly, until the Moralists took
control, and the fairies became mentors instead of butts. When
the humorous treatment revived it was canalized along the
grooves cut by the French fairy tales. The Fairy Blackstick in
The Rose and the Ring was one of the French tutelary fairies who
discovered the practical difficulties of fairy gifts:

> Fairy roses, fairy rings,
> Turn out sometimes troublesome things.[1]

The farcical element in this story is in the shifting fortunes
caused by the transfers of the magical talismans. Plain, carroty-
haired Angelica is considered a beauty until she parts with the
ring; hideous Countess Gruffanuff becomes desirable when
she puts it on. The Fairy Blackstick is in the end the *dea ex
machina*. In fact, this is a tale of magic rather than fairy lore,
as so many folk-tales are. This particular theme was to be used
many times again in humorous fairy tales, not all of them
meant for children. A magic ring which gives mastery to the
wearer is the subject of *The One Before* by Barry Pain.[2] Andrew
Lang's *Prince Prigio* depends for its humour on much the same
device. It is the story, used again and again in sophisticated
fairy stories, of the fairies at a christening and the curse of the
uninvited fairy. The Prince is cursed by being too clever, and
grows up much too intellectual to believe in the magical wonders
that surround him. There is a touch of satire in the story, but
the satire is directed against intellectual self-conceit; the
humour, for the story is two-pronged, depends on an implicit
reference to folk-tales, generally those of French origin.

> Then the king went to Prigio, and said that his country was in
> danger, and that he was determined to leave the crown to which-
> ever of them would bring him the horns (for it has horns) and tail
> of the Firedrake.
> 'It is an awkward brute to tackle,' the king said, 'but you are the
> oldest, my lad; go where glory waits you! Put on your armour and
> be off with you!'
> This the king said, hoping that either the Firedrake would
> roast Prince Prigio alive (which he could easily do, as I have said;

---

[1] *The Oxford Thackeray*, edited by G. Saintsbury, Vol. X (1909).
[2] Barry Pain, *The One Before* (London, 1902).

for he is all over as hot as a red-hot poker), or that, if the prince succeeded, at least his country would be freed from the monster.

But the prince, who was lying on the sofa doing sums in compound division, for fun, said in the politest way:

'Thanks to the education your majesty has given me, I have learned that the Firedrake, like the siren, the fairy, and so forth, is a fabulous animal which does not exist. But even granting, for the sake of argument, that there is a Firedrake, your majesty is well aware that there is no kind of use in sending *me*. It is always the eldest son who goes out first, and comes to grief on these occasions, and it is always the third son that succeeds. Send Alphonso' (this was the youngest brother), 'and *he* will do the trick at once. At least, if he fails, it will be most unusual, and Enrico can try his luck!' [1]

The sequel to *Prince Prigio* is about King Prigio's son, Ricardo, a lovable but unlettered boy with a strong taste for adventures, who places all his reliance upon the magic talismans given to his father. There is a wider range of reference here—Cornelius Agrippa, Kenelm Digby's *Powder of Sympathy*, *Orlando Furioso*, and an excursion into history in a meeting with Prince Charles Edward Stuart—but the background is still the world of fairy stories; Prince Ricardo fights the Yellow Dwarf and The Giant Who Does not Know when he has had Enough, and Jacqueline, the rescued Princess, has had lessons in magic from the Fairy Paribanou. This story is mellower and less farcical in tone than the earlier one; lacking a little in unity, but full of pleasant turns. The third tale in the same book is not comic at all, it is squarely founded on Scottish fairylore.

Lewis Carroll's *Alice* books have nothing to do with Fairyland, and his attempt at the fairies in *Sylvie and Bruno* is not completely successful. Where Bruno is funny it is as a small boy, not as a fairy. There are some funny moments with the Sub-Warden and Sub-Wardeness, as in the mishandled attempt at a revolution and in their earnest study of the town directory as an alibi,[2] but they are not fairies and their kingdom is only on the outskirts of Fairyland. The book suffers from being a kind of hold-all into which Lewis Carroll stuffed all the mis-

[1] Andrew Lang, *My Own Fairy Book*, pp. 16–18.
[2] Lewis Carroll, *Sylvie and Bruno* (1889), pp. 125–6. *Sylvie and Bruno Concluded* (1894).

cellaneous jokes, stories and general reflections that had been hovering in his mind for years. The fairy parts of it cannot quite be acquitted of whimsy.

Mrs. Nesbit's full-length magical stories have no real fairies in them, though the Psammead claims to be a sand fairy. In *Nine Unlikely Tales for Children*, however, in which there are three tales about fairies, she relied on the same device of the fantastication of the fairy story for her humour. The fairies at the christening occur in two of the nine stories. In *Melisande* the King and Queen, to be on the safe side, had refrained from inviting any of the fairies. The result was unfortunate.

> The Queen nearly fainted as Malevola drew back, and another fairy, in a smart bonnet with snakes in it, stepped forward with a rustle of bats' wings. But the King stepped forward too.
> 'No you don't!' he said. 'I wonder at you, ladies, I do indeed. How can you be so unfairylike? Have none of you been to school? —have none of you studied the history of your own race? Surely you don't need a poor, ignorant King like me to tell you that this is *no go*?'
> 'How dare you?' cried the fairy in the bonnet, and the snakes in it quivered as she tossed her head. 'It is my turn and I say the Princess shall be——' The King actually put his hand over her mouth.
> 'Look here,' he said; 'I won't have it. Listen to reason—or you'll be sorry afterwards. A fairy who breaks the tradition of fairy history goes out—you know she does—like the flame of a candle. And all traditions show that only *one* bad fairy is ever forgotten at a christening party and the good ones are always invited; so either this is not a christening party, or else you are all invited except one, and, by her own showing, that was Malevola. It nearly always is. Do I make myself clear?'
> Several of the better-class fairies who had been led away by Malevola's influence, murmured that there was something in what His Majesty said.[1]

It is unnecessary to say that the rule about the fairies, going out like a snuffed candle was invented to suit the story. The device used here is to assume that all fairy stories belong to one world. It is common to most parodies, and is employed, for instance, in Elnovia, a parody of the novel world.

[1] E. Nesbit, *Nine Unlikely Tales for Children* (1901), *Melisande*, pp. 163–4.

A. A. Milne uses the same kind of device with a lighter touch in *Once on a Time*[1] and the play, *Make Believe*. There is no fairy in *Make Believe*, and only three are introduced incidentally in *Once on a Time*, the fairy who had an unsuccessful bout with King Merriwig, the little fairy whom Wiggs rescued from a wizard and the old woman who lodged Udo and Coronel for the night. The main humour is concerned with magical implements—a wishing ring, a cloak of darkness, seven-league boots and so on. There is some very amusing foolery in the story, though there is no denying that a touch of rather tiresome whimsy steals into it occasionally.

In some of the stories we get a parody not of folk-tales but of the moralizing tales of the eighteenth century. There is a touch of this in *The Sums that Came Right* by E. Nesbit. The fairy in this story is an Arithmetic Fairy.

"Did no one ever tell you," the fairy went on, shaking out her dress, which was woven of the integral calculus, and trimmed with a dazzling fringe of logarithms,' and 'The fairy drew herself up, and her graceful garland of simple equations trembled as Edwin breathed heavily.'[2]

A clearer case is Anstey's story of the priggish little girl who met a fairy, and was given the traditional gift of rubies and pearls dropping out of her lips. These only appeared when she had made a particularly virtuous remark, but since her virtues were all affectations the jewels were invariably false.[3]

A rather different type of humour is that of the fairies in *Iolanthe*. The skit is on the Pantomime fairy, a large, bouncing young woman in tights and gauzes, who claims to feed on dew-drops and dance on a spider's web. This is unusual in turning on fairylore rather than fairy tales. The jokes are on the perpetual youth and beauty of fairies and their tendency to become amorous of mortals. In fact, we find a revival here of real fairy traditions, however sophisticated.

[1] A. A. Milne, *Once on a Time* (*circa* 1916).
[2] E. Nesbit, ed. cit., p. 227.
[3] F. Anstey, *The Good Little Girl*. *Modern Fairy Tales*, edited by R. Lancelyn Green (1955), pp. 152–77.

Twenty-four

WHIMSY

THE literary treatment of fairies has been beset with the dangers of whimsicality ever since the poets ceased to believe in them. There are still many serious believers in ghosts; and many who would not describe themselves as believers have yet a store of anecdotes, curious happenings which come within the circle of their acquaintance. The belief in witchcraft had such tragic accompaniments that, even when incredulity set in, it was not at first to be treated lightly. The tide of credulity is rising again; a sufficient number of people have built up a witchcraft ritual, founded on the theories of Margaret Murray, to give the subject fresh publicity. But in the early twentieth century—at the low-water mark of witchcraft belief—several humorous and whimsical books about witchcraft were written, of which *Lolly Willows*[1] and Stella Benson's *Living Alone*[2] were the best and best-known. A coven of witches provide the villains in Masefield's *The Midnight Folk*.[3] There are still, as we have seen, real believers in fairies—if anything they are perhaps on the increase—but the general incredulity among poets and writers dates from early times, and the accompaniments of fairy beliefs are so picturesque as to make the temptation to use them as a pretty trimming almost irresistible. This is particularly so with the small fairies. The passion for the miniature which is

[1] Sylvia Townsend Warner, *Lolly Willows* (1926).
[2] Stella Benson, *Living Alone* (1919).
[3] John Masefield, *The Midnight Folk* (1927).

so strong in England rendered them less and less formidable. When they were given butterfly and dragonfly wings they were reduced to almost the status of insects, and in the sheltered days of the early twentieth century every care was taken to render them unalarming.

Judge Parry's *Katawampus*, evidently told to his children before it was written, is an early example of the kind of thing. There is a good deal of archness about the story generally, and the fairies who appear in it incidentally are perhaps more straightforward than most of the book.

> But the most delightful and enchanting thing of all was that every now and then, in and out among the gulls, came delicate light tripping fairies, dancing on the top of the waves, their light gossamer wings spotted with stars of gold and bright colours all sparkling in the sun; and Pater thought them to be the most beautiful creatures he had ever beheld. Some of them joined hands and danced in a ring on the top of the surf as the waves broke, singing a lovely song, while others hung in the air with their wings outstretched, playing sweet music upon hollow shells, or beating two little pebbles together to keep time.[1]

At his date Parry is not to be blamed for the gossamer wings, which had held their place in illustration and literary tradition for nearly two hundred years. The golden spangles mark a step down, but there is worse whimsy in other parts of the book than this description.

The children's annuals and magazines displayed this whimsy at its worst, and of published books which had any vogue perhaps Rose Fyleman's fairies are as weak and lacking in meat as any we are likely to have the ill luck to come across. But before her day rock-bottom was probably reached in *The Little Grey Rabbit*, a verse which insulted the intelligence of the young some time about 1910.

> 'Oh dear, oh dear,' said a tiny mole,
> 'A fairy's fallen into a hole.
> It's full of water and slimy things,
> And she can't get out 'cos she's hurt her wings.'

Enid Blyton's *Noddy* stories are almost as bad. The kind of

---

[1] E. A. Parry, *Katawampus and The First Book of Krab* (1927), p. 10.

12 'The Fairies are Out.' James Nasmyth, 1808-
1890. (Wingless Lilliputian fairies in the 19th century)

Jack gets the Golden Hen, away from the Giant.

13 'Jack the Giantkiller.' George Cruikshank. From
The Fairy Library, c. 1853 (*see* chapter 21)

thing is amusingly parodied by Angela Thirkell in *Wild Strawberries*:

'Look, Emmy, there is a picture of Hobo-Gobo trying to snatch the poor little fairy Joybell's golden doll away. Wasn't he a *naughty* Hobo-Gobo?'[1]

It is an amusing but unprofitable business to beat the coverts of bad literature for the sake of starting such feeble game. There are many accomplished and gifted writers who slip occasionally into whimsies that are unworthy of them. James Barrie will occur to most people at once. He was reared in Angus, which has not the rich traditional heritage of Aberdeen or the Border Country, but he knew quite enough of fairy beliefs to have been saved from the quirks in which he often indulged.

'I thought all the fairies were dead,' Mrs. Darling said.

'There are always a lot of young ones,' explained Wendy, who was now quite an authority, 'because you see when a new baby laughs for the first time a new fairy is born, and as there are always new babies there are always new fairies. They live in nests on the tops of trees; and the mauve ones are boys, and the white ones are girls, and the blue ones are just little sillies who are not quite sure what they are.'[2]

This is pretty poor stuff; but in *Mary Rose* Barrie worked on a real folk legend, and treated with some subtlety the theme that he had already used in *Peter Pan*, of a child who had been in contact with Fairyland and had been checked in her growth, so that she could never come to womanhood. It is apparent by his prose treatment of a kindred theme in *Sentimental Tommy* that Fairyland is a symbol of creative imagination and the dangers of a flight from reality.

The fairy chapters of *The Little White Bird* are the best part of the book. They have a good many twists and inventions about them, and yet on the whole they give a convincing picture of fairy character. Lob in *Dear Brutus* is perhaps the best conceived and carried out of Barrie's fairy people. He has the great age of the fairy changelings, who have seen the acorn before the oak. He is more convincing than Peter Pan in having an old age that has never been manhood. He has the fairy

---

[1] Angela Thirkell, *Wild Strawberries*, Penguin Edition, p. 49.
[2] J. M. Barrie, *Peter and Wendy* (1911), p. 252.

tricksiness and the fairy insights. The appearing and disappearing wood is true enough to folk tradition, and so is the granted wish, and the way in which destiny conforms to character. Like all Barrie's work the play has a hidden unsoundness in it. Excellent craftsman though Barrie was, he was yet like his own Peter Pan; he could not master nor come to terms with adult life.

Something of the same streak—a tinge of the bitterness of sentimentality, as we taste it in Hans Andersen and Oscar Wilde—is to be found in Laurence Housman's works, good though they are. We are concerned here with his fairy stories. Many of them are variations of the fairy tale themes, often with a family fairy after the French style. Occasionally, however, real fairies are introduced, though sometimes they belong to the literary tradition. In *Moon-Struck*[1] there is a tiny fairy, the size of a dragonfly, with a fairy wand. In this, as in many of the stories and many modern fairy stories, the culmination is escape out of a world too cruel to be bearable. Yeats' lines might be the motto of many of them:

> Come away, O, human child!
> To the woods and waters wild,
> With a fairy hand in hand,
> For the world's more full of weeping than you can
> understand.[2]

There is no sentimentalizing of the fairies in *A Cupful of Moonshine*; they are to the full as dangerous and deceptive as in any folk traditions. In this story, as in many folk-tales, a handicapped man—often only a fool, though in this story he is a mute and an innocent—is the one who can break the fairy enchantment. The silence to be preserved in order to see the fairies safely is in the true folk tradition. The capful of moonshine and double handful of courage strike a slightly false note, but are not too off the track. The sophisticated turn to the story is given at the end, when the dumb boy has rescued his father from the fairies.

[1] Laurence Housman, *Moonshine and Clover* (1922) (containing stories dating between 1894–1904), pp. 153–63.

[2] *Irish Fairy and Folk Tales*, edited by W. B. Yeats, Scott Publishing Library, p. 59.

As father and son went down the hill together, the old man whistled and piped like a bird. 'Why, why!' he said; 'you are a lad of strength and inches: with you to work and look after me, I can keep on to a merry old age! Ay, ay, I have had long to wait for it; but wisdom is justified in her children.'[1]

Many of Eleanor Farjeon's stories are fairy stories, but they happen to have few fairies in them. They are without the touch of sentimental bitterness that marks some of Laurence Housman's, and they are full of charm, but we cannot always quite acquit them of whimsy. The story which deals most directly with a fairy is a retelling of *The Old Woman Who Lived in a Vinegar Bottle*. In it, however, caprice and not ambition is the fault which causes the loss of the gift. The fairy is a tiny one.

'Oh dear!' sighed the Lady.
'What's the matter with *you*, Lady?' said a tiny voice at the window, and there, sitting on the sill, was a Fairy no bigger than your finger, and on her feet she wore two little shoes as green as grass in April.

The fairy's shoes change with the seasons, and so do the lady's wishes, until in the end she wishes for a black room.

'The matter with *you*, Lady,' said the fairy, 'is that you don't know *what* you want!' And she jumped on the bed, and lay on her back, and kicked away with her two little feet. And the wall fell through, and the ceiling fell up, and the floor fell down, and the Lady was left standing in the black starry night without any room at all.[2]

It is impossible even to name all the sophisticated fairy stories that were written in the hundred years between 1865 and 1965. Among them were those of Mary de Morgan. In most of them enchantments and the courtship of princes was the commonest theme, but occasionally we have also the fairies. In *The Toy Princess*[3] there is a fairy shopman, who makes a mechanical princess to take the place of the real one whom the benevolent fairy carries away—a highly civilized version of the changeling

[1] Laurence Housman, ed. cit., p. 46.
[2] Eleanor Farjeon, *The Little Bookroom* (Oxford, 1955), *The Lady's Room*, pp. 138–41.
[3] Mary de Morgan (1850–1907), reprinted in *The Enchanted Land*, edited by Louey Chisholm (1906).

or stock. Something of the same theme of a clockwork child provided by a fairy is used by Judge Parry at about the same time in *Tales of Krab*.[1] Between the two World Wars Mrs. Baldwin produced a collection of tales, *The Pedlar's Pack*,[2] some of them novelle, some variants on folk-tales. *The Giant's Baby* may have been inspired by *Tom Hickathrift*, *Hubert the Shepherd* combines the Rumpelstiltzkin type with the motif of the gift of animal speech. *Conrad of the Red Town* uses a number of the true fairy motifs—the danger of spying on the fairies, elf locks, the fatal eating of fairy food and the theft of a mortal into fairyland. The only thing rather unconvincing about it is the elaboration of the Fairy Rade by which Conrad is decoyed away. It is a kind of pageant of fairy tales, reminding one somewhat of the wedding festivities in the ballet of *Sleeping Beauty*. But for this the story should rather belong to the next chapter, where, again *Hubert the Shepherd* might be placed, were it not for a little embroidery about the Butterflies' Ball with which it is adorned.

[1] E. A. Parry, ed. cit., pp. 155–74.
[2] Mrs. Alfred Baldwin, *The Pedlar's Pack*, n.d., Chambers, Edinburgh.

Twenty-five

SOMETHING TO BITE ON

THE people who knew what tradition was and were impatient of the airy-fairies on which young intelligences had been fed, began at last to get a hearing. Kipling, writing as early as 1905, was one of the most explicit of them.

> 'Besides, what you call *them* are made-up things the People of the Hills have never heard of—little buzzflies with butterfly wings and gauze petticoats, and shiny stars in their hair and a wand like a schoolteacher's cane for punishing bad boys and rewarding good ones! *I* know 'em!'
>
> 'We don't mean that sort,' said Dan. 'We hate 'em too.'
>
> 'Exactly,' said Puck. 'Can you wonder that the People of the Hills don't care to be confused with that painty-winged, wand-waving, sugar-and-shake-your-head set of impostors? Butterfly wings indeed! I've seen Sir Huon and a troop of his people setting off from Tintagel Castle for Hy-Brasil in the teeth of a sou'westerly gale, with the spray flying all over the castle, and the Horses of the Hill wild with fright. Out they'd go in a lull, screaming like gulls, and back they'd be driven five good miles inland before they could come head to wind again. Butterfly-wings! It was Magic— Magic as black as Merlin could make it, and the whole sea was green fire and white foam, with singing mermaids in it. And the Horses of the Hill picked their way from one wave to another by lightning flashes! *That* was how it was in the old days!' [1]

[1] Rudyard Kipling, ed. cit., p. 14.

203

The Puck insisted on through Kipling's two books is at once earthy and spiritual, like the hobgoblin of folklore, able to eat human food, yet ageless, and able to appear and disappear as he wished. The character is convincing, though the diction is perhaps a little precise. It might have been tiresome to keep up the Sussex dialect throughout the book, but a suggestion of it would have added conviction. The word 'exactly' in the passage I have just quoted strikes a falsely didactic note. But the diction of the fairies is always difficult. The three stories in the books which deal with fairylore and not with human history are *Weland's Sword*, about the descent of the gods into fairies, *Cold Iron*, the first story since *A Midsummer Night's Dream* to treat the changeling traffic from the fairies' point of view, and *Dymchurch Flit*, which is a retelling of a real folk tradition about the departure of the fairies.

If Kipling's fairies are earthy, Walter de la Mare's are at the other extreme of the folk tradition, rarefied and etherialized like all his creations so that one seems to be looking at life in a mirror, or staring into a crystal globe; yet the stuff of it is nevertheless true. One can hardly get a better picture of the pixyish type of fairies than in *The Dutch Cheese*:

> Now these were a tribe of fairies, sly, small, gay-hearted and mischievous, and not of the race of fairies noble, silent, beautiful and remote from man. They were a sort of gipsy fairies, very nimble and of aery and prankish company, and partly for mischief and partly for the love of her were always striving to charm John's dear sister Griselda away, with their music and fruits and dancing.[1]

More successful still, instinct with a power which makes every word used significant, is the picture of the evil and beautiful fairies in *Miss Jemima*.

> In the midst of the faint singing of the wild birds, out of the light that lay beyond the stone church wall I spied her come stealing. My heart almost stopped beating, nor did I turn my head one inch, so that my eyes soon ached because they were almost asquint with watching. If you can imagine a figure—even now I cannot tell you how tall she was—that seems to be made of the light of rainbows, and yet with every feature in its flaxen-framed face as clearly marked as a cherub's cut in stone; and if

[1] Walter de la Mare, *Broomsticks* (1925), p. 33.

you can imagine a voice coming to you, close into your ear, without your being able to say exactly where it is coming *from*—*that* was what I saw and heard beneath that grey roof down there on that distant morning, seventy-five years ago.[1]

There is no whimsy here, but the careful building up, touch by touch, of what almost becomes a personal experience.

Something the same effect of inhuman creatures is given in that strange book, *The Lore of Proserpine*[2] by Maurice Hewlett. It is a spoof book—the carefully given references are all false, and yet the beautiful, ruthless, non-human creatures described in it are curiously convincing. The birch-tree wife with her savage sisters, the beautiful fairy boy who sat idly squeezing a rabbit to death as a child might squeeze a snap-dragon flower, the little wounded fairy who decoyed away the child of its rescuer, these all have an air of verisimilitude. They are inventions, but they almost compel our belief, like the tales told by William of Newburgh and Ralph of Coggeshall in medieval times.

Descendants of these medieval fairies are treated of in a strange book, *The Moon is Feminine*, by Clemence Dane.[3] It is set in Brighton in the Regency Period. The Hero is a Mr. Cope, descendant of Ralph of Coggeshall's Green Girl. The girl who loves him has an artist's eye and heart, a kind of second sight.

She is destroyed by his other love, a half-human creature who descended from the sea man, Nicholas Pipe, described by William of Newburgh. After all these years the fairy blood is still in them, and they are unable to make terms with ordinary humanity. The Green Man was an actual person, an eccentric of the Cope family who always wore green because he was crossed in love. His ghost haunted Bramshill, and he was seen in childhood by little Joan Cope.[4]

I have already mentioned two earlier books which have the quality of fairyland. One of them is George Macdonald's *Phantastes* and the other is Jean Ingelow's *Mopsa the Fairy*.

[1] Walter de la Mare, ed. cit., p. 66.

[2] Maurice Hewlett, *The Lore of Proserpine* (1913).

[3] Clemence Dane, *The Moon is Feminine* (1937; reprinted in Evergreen Books, 1941).

[4] *Bramshill: Being the Memoirs of Joan Penelope Cope* (1938), pp. 17–18.

Phantastes is one of the first books that George Macdonald wrote. It is a young man's book, full of a dewy poetry, but there is a stern morality implicit in it as in all George Macdonald's writings. The arbitrary taboos and seemingly irrational adventures have an ethical reality behind them, and yet they are of the true stuff of Fairyland. No one will easily forget the scene when Anados looks into the cupboard against which the ogress warned him—well knowing that the warning was in itself a temptation—hears footfalls and sees a dark silhouette approaching from a distance; watches without power to shut the cupboard, until it shoots past him and lies on the floor behind him as the evil shadow which will henceforth dog him through Fairyland.[1] The fairies in this book can be large or small at will, and this is true of some folk fairies, though not by any means of all.

In *The Princess and the Goblin* the goblins are wicked, earthy creatures, as material as men, grotesque and comical; Irene's Grandmother is as powerful and beneficent as the Wise Woman in *The Lost Princess*, but a little more human because of her personal love for Irene. She is an ancestress, a tutelary fairy attached to one family, like many in folklore.[2]

Mopsa the Fairy is less of an allegory than *Phantastes* and more of a pure fairy tale. The little nest of fairies which Jack finds is a curious conception; but that one of them should gain a kind of soul when a mortal kisses her is true to folk tradition, and so is the relative solidity of mortal money and the mortal contribution to fairy life. The Kingdom of the one-foot-one fairies gives a good impression of this.

> So he walked up that beautiful garden till he came to the great tent. A banquet was going on inside. All the one-foot-one fairies sat down the sides of the table, and at the top sat the Queen on a larger chair; and there were two empty chairs, one on each side of her.
>
> Jack blushed; but the hound whispering again: 'Master, whatever you can do you may do,' he came slowly up the table towards the Queen, who was saying as he drew near: 'Where is our trusty and well-beloved the apple-woman?'

[1] George Macdonald, *Phantastes* (First published, 1858), Everyman Library, pp. 68–71.

[2] George Macdonald, *The Princess and the Goblin* (1872).

And she took no notice of Jack; so, though he could not help feeling rather red and ashamed, he went and sat in the chair beside her with Mopsa still on his shoulder. Mopsa laughed for joy when she saw the feast. The Queen said: 'Oh Jack, I am so glad to see you!' and some of the one-foot-one fairies cried out: 'What a delightful little creature that is! She can laugh! Perhaps she can also cry.' . . .

In the meantime there was a noise outside, and in stumped an elderly woman. She had very thick boots on, a short gown of red print, an orange cotton handkerchief over her shoulders and a black silk bonnet. She was exactly the same height as the Queen —for of course nobody in Fairyland is allowed to be any bigger than the Queen; so, if they are not children when they arrive, they are obliged to shrink.

'How are you, dear?' said the Queen.

'I am as well as can be expected,' answered the apple-woman, sitting down in the empty chair. 'Now, then, where's my tea? They're never ready with my cup of tea.'

Two attendants immediately brought a cup of tea and set it down before the apple-woman, with a plate of bread-and-butter; and she proceeded to pour it into the saucer, and blow it because it was hot. In doing so her wandering eyes caught sight of Jack and little Mopsa, and she set down the saucer and looked at them with attention. . . .

'Pretty lamb!' said the apple-woman; 'it's just like a child.' And then she burst into tears, and exclaimed, sobbing: 'It's many a long day since I've seen a child. Oh dear! Oh deary me!'

Upon this, to the astonishment of Jack, every one of the guests began to cry and sob too.

'Oh dear! Oh dear!' they said to one another, 'we're crying; we can cry just as well as men and women. Isn't it delightful? What a luxury it is to cry, to be sure!'[1]

This passage reminds one a little of the *Fairy Dwellings on Selena Moor*,[2] where it is said that the fairies have no real emotions, only the faint memory of those they knew when they were alive. In the same way the Irish fairies need human strength to help them in games and war. Kirk, too, says that the fairy people have no real pleasure, only simulated fits of mirth, like 'the constrained grinning of a Mort head'.[3]

[1] Jean Ingelow, ed. cit., pp. 68–70.
[2] See Part I, Chapter II.pp. 15–18
[3] R. Kirk, ed. cit., p. 75.

The apple-woman is a mortal carried into Fairyland, free to go if she can wish it with her whole heart, but unable to do so. There is a subtle psychological truth in this. Few people are capable of a whole-hearted wish. In this book Fate is the Old Mother of the fairies. It is possible that Jean Ingelow knew that the word fairy originally came from *Fatae*.

A modern book which is intended for fairly young children but which displays a good knowledge of Celtic folk tradition is *Borrobil* by William Croft Dickinson.[1] It owes something to *Puck of Pook's Hill*, but it illuminates folk-lore rather than history. On Beltane Eve two modern children go between the Beltane fires and dance round nine standing stones at the top of the hill, and so make their way into the remote past, in the Early Stone Age, the time of the Pictish earthhouses and the Fenian brochs. Borrobil, the good magician who conducts them, leads them safely through various magic experiences, in the course of which they enter a fairy hill. The tradition of the danger of accepting fairy gifts or eating fairy food is faithfully followed, but the fairies are presented as benevolent creatures, whose only fault is that they are too fond of human children. The danger and the strangeness is a little lost, but the whole treatment is honest and straightforward.

In *The Little Grey Men* by B.B. we have fairies without magical powers, tiny creatures, only different from animals in their longevity, which is curiously intensified by the way in which a short time is long to them, so that they seem to exist in two dimensions. B.B. firmly rejects all airy-fairy stuff. 'This is a story about the last gnomes in Britain. They are honest-to-goodness gnomes, none of your baby, fairy-book, tinsel stuff, and they live by hunting and fishing, like the animals and birds, which is only proper and right.'[2]

The invisibility of the gnomes is a matter of skill in hiding, like the Hobbits', and the world they live in is one of natural, everyday happenings.

> You may wonder that they now chose the dusk and evening to do most of their travelling, but like rabbits and hedgehogs, gnomes prefer this time of day to all others, and they were in strange country. One reason was that they were less likely to be

---

[1] William Croft Dickinson, *Borrobil* (1944).
[2] B.B., *The Little Grey Men* (1942), Introduction, p. vi.

seen, and another that their eyes were like those of cats and owls, they could see better then than at any other time. Perhaps this accounts for the fact that our Great-Grandparents so seldom caught sight of the Little People, and even on those very rare occasions when they did, they put it down to some trick of the imagination; it is so easy to imagine things in the shadows under the bushes.[1]

It is refreshing to have fairies so free from all traces of whimsy, but it has been so resolutely excluded that B.B.'s gnomes are more like Mary Norton's Borrowers, Carroll Kendal's Minnipins or the Liliputians in T. H. White's *Mistress Masham's Repose* than any fairies. Indeed, they are more matter-of-fact than any of these.

C. S. Lewis, who uses all mythology with respect, peoples his Narnia with supernatural creatures as well as talking beasts. Most of these are classical, Bacchus, fauns, centaurs and dryads, but there are giants, gnomes, mermaids and hags as well, and a few creatures of his own invention like the Marsh-Tiggers and the Earthlings. The Narnia books are as serious as George Macdonald's. They are marred by a few pieces of carelessness and an occasional lapse of full attention, often very short, where the author has allowed himself to write below his best; but they are full of varied delights, and rise to passages of great poetic power. They are rich food for young minds.

The best of all the modern writings on fairy people are J. H. Tolkien's Hobbit books. The Hobbits are inventions of his own, something between hobs and humans; beside them are wizards, dwarves, elves, goblins, trolls, men, and heroes like Elrond, the Elf-Friend, whose span of life is longer than that of ordinary humans. The first book, *The Hobbit*, is meant for children, based evidently upon an imaginary game. It is splendid reading for children with strong nerves, though some of it has a nightmarish quality.

Deep down here by the dark water lived old Gollum. I don't know where he came from, nor who or what he was. He was Gollum—as dark as darkness, except for two big round pale eyes. He had a boat, and he rowed about quite quietly on the lake; for lake it was, wide and deep and deadly cold. He paddled it with large feet dangling over the side, but never a ripple did he make.

[1] B.B. ed. cit., p. 57.

Not he. He was looking out of his pale lamp-like eyes for blind fish, which he gripped with his long fingers as quick as thinking. He liked meat too. . . . Gollum got into his boat and shot off from the island, while Bilbo was sitting on the brink altogether flummoxed and at the end of his way and wits. Suddenly up came Gollum and whispered and hissed: 'Bless us and splash us, my precioussss! I guess it's a choice feast; at least a tasty morsel it'd make us, gollum!' And when he said *gollum* he made a horrible swallowing noise in his throat. That is how he got his name, though he always called himself 'my precious'.[1]

The riddle contest which follows is a minor epic. In the trilogy, *The Lord of the Rings*, the story has been lifted into adult status. To those who yield to the spell of the books they have a compelling atmosphere, and on first reading them no friend is felt to be a companion who is not able to discuss them. It is admission into a world which has objective quality. The distinctive flavour of the elves, dwarves and other creatures is truly preserved without loss of individual characterization. Fairy lore in literature has here reached its highwater mark.

Even in these books, where the elves are in full power and activity the end is one of diminishment and vanishing. After the fatal ring has been destroyed something of elfin power seemed to go with it, and the elves began to cross the sea to the Western Lands, and to leave the world increasingly to the dominance of men. In nearly all the fairy stories of this century that note is struck, the fairies are everywhere fugitive and in hiding. But this is not, as we have seen, peculiar to this century. In the earliest mentions of them in literature the fairies are already spoken of as departed or departing. The tradition of them burns up and flickers like a candle that is going out, and then perhaps for a time burns up again, but always the fairies are to be seen only between two twinklings of an eye; their gifts must be secret if they are to be enjoyed; they are, and always have been, the Hidden People.

[1] J. R. Tolkien, *The Hobbit* (1937), pp. 83–4.

APPENDICES
LIST OF BOOKS CITED
INDEX

Appendix I

FAIRY TYPES AND INDIVIDUALS

(This list does not claim to be exhaustive.)

It is difficult sometimes to distinguish between these two categories. For instance, *The Apple-Tree Man* might be treated as an individual except that there is one in each orchard.

The Apple-Tree Man. (Somerset) The spirit of the oldest tree in the orchard. R. L. Tongue, *Somerset Folklore*, p. 28.

Asrai. (N.W.) Water Fairies. R. L. Tongue recollects a tale, probably from Shropshire. The name is mentioned in Robert Buchanan's verses.

Athach. (Highland) A general name for a monster or giant. Mackenzie, *Scottish Folk-Lore and Folk Life*, p. 251.

Aughisky. Irish form of water kelpie which preys on cattle.

Banshee. (Irish) A death spirit who wails only for members of the old families. When several keen together it foretells the death of someone very great or holy. The banshee has long streaming hair and a grey cloak over a green dress. Her eyes are fiery red with continual weeping. In the Scottish Highlands the Banshee is called 'Little Washer by the Ford', and she washes the grave-clothes of those about to die. Lady Wilde; J. F. Campbell.

Baobhan Sith. (Highland) The word is the same as Banshee, and means 'Fairy Woman', but it is generally employed to mean a kind of Succubus, very dangerous and evil. Mackenzie, p. 236.

Barguest. (North and East) A kind of bogey-beast. It has horns, teeth

213

and claws and fiery eyes. *County Folk-Lore; North Riding*, p. 126; *County Folk-Lore Lincolnshire*, p. 53; Henderson, pp. 274–5.

Bauchan, or Bocan. A hobgoblinish spirit, often tricksy, sometimes dangerous, and sometimes helpful. J. F. Campbell gives a story of one who followed his master when he emigrated to America. *Popular Tales of the Western Highlands*, Vol. II, p. 103.

Bean-nighe. (Highland and Irish) The washer. A form of Banshee. L. Spence, *Fairy Tradition*, pp. 54–5.

Beithir. (Highland) A destructive demon haunting caves and corries. Mackenzie, p. 247.

Bendith y Mamau. (The Mother's Blessing) The Glamorganshire name for the Fairies. They steal children, elf-ride horses and visit houses. Bowls of milk were put out for them. Rhys, *Celtic Folk-Lore*; Sikes, *British Goblins*.

Black Dogs. (General) Stories of Black Dogs are to be found all over the country. They are generally dangerous, but sometimes helpful. An account is given in Hartland's *English Fairy and Folk Tales*, pp. 234–44, but the fullest treatment is by T. Brown in *Folklore*, Vol. 69, p. 175.

The Blue Men of the Minch. (Highland) The Blue Men used particularly to haunt the strait between Long Island and the Shiant Islands. They swam out to wreck passing ships, and could be baulked by captains who were ready at rhyming and could keep the last word. They were supposed to be fallen angels. Mackenzie, pp. 88–90.

Bodach. The Scottish form of bugbear, or bug-a-boo. He comes down the chimney to fetch naughty children. The Bodach Glas is a death token. Henderson, p. 344.

Bodachan Sabhaill. (Highland) The little old man of the Barn. A Barn Brownie, who takes pity on old men, and threshes for them. Mackenzie, p. 230.

Boggart. (North Country) A mischievous Brownie, almost exactly like a poltergeist in its habits. Keightley, Henderson, etc.

Bogey Beast. (General) A mischievous hobgoblin.

Bogles. (Scottish, North Country and Lincolnshire) Evil Goblins. Henderson, p. 247; Mrs. Balfour, *Legends of the Cars, Folklore II*, 1891.

The Boobrie. A gigantic water-bird, which inhabits the lochs of Argyllshire. It has a loud harsh voice and webbed feet, and gobbles up sheep and cattle. J. F. Campbell, Vol. IV, p. 308.

Booman. (Shetland and Orkney) A Brownie-like hobgoblin. Its name is preserved elsewhere in singing games, 'Shoot, Booman, shoot,' and 'Booman is dead and gone.' Alice Gomme, *Dictionary of British Folk-Lore*, Part I, *Traditional Games*, Vol. I, p. 43.

Brag. (Northern Counties) A mischievous hobgoblin, a shape-shifter, often in the form of a horse. Henderson, p. 270.

Brollachan. (Highland) Brollachan is the Gaelic for a shapeless thing. There is a Nemo story told of one by J. F. Campbell, Vol. II, p. 203. L. Spence.

Browney. (Cornish) Guardian of the bees.

Brownie. The best-known of the industrious hobgoblins. His country is from the Northern Counties of England right up to the fringe of the Scottish Highlands. His habits have been sufficiently described in the course of the book.

Bucca. (Cornish) There are Bucca-dhu, the black bucca, and Bucca-gwidden, the white bucca. Margaret Courtney; Wentz, p. 165.

Buckie. (Scottish) A mischievous Scottish fairy, probably invoked in the folk-rhyme, 'Buckie, Buckie, biddy bene!' Also known in Ireland. *Denham Tracts*, Vol. II, p. 78.

Bug-a-boo, Boggle-bo, bugbear, etc. Nursery goblins.

Buggane. (Manx) A particularly noxious bogle. Gill, S. Morrison, D. Broome.

Buggan. (Cheshire) A form of Bogie. Burne & Jackson, *Shropshire Folk-Lore*, p. 45, note.

Bullbeggar. Mentioned by Reginald Scot. The Bullbeggar of Creech Hill, R. L. Tongue, *Somerset Folk-Lore*, pp. 121–2. From Mrs. Aitken I have a note, Bullbeggar Lane in Surrey.

The Bwbachod. The Welsh Brownies. They were friendly and industrious, but they disliked dissenters and teetotallers. Sikes, p. 31; Rhys, p. 81.

Bwca. The Welsh Boggart or Brownie. See Bwca'r Trwyn, The Brownie who Became a Boggart. Rhys, pp. 596–7.

Bwganod. The Welsh bogies. Rhys, Sikes.

Cait Shith. (Highland) The Fairy Cat. A large black cat with one white spot on its breast which belongs to the fairies. Mackenzie, p. 204.

Caoidheag (The Weeper). (Highland) A Highland Banshee. Mackenzie, p. 239.

Caval Ushteg. (Manx) Water Horse.

Cearb (The killing one). (Highland) A demon. Mackenzie, p. 244.

Ceasg. Highland mermaid, half woman, half grilse. Mackenzie, p. 251.

Church Grim. (Yorkshire) An inhabitant of the church, from which it does not stir except in very dark, stormy weather. It tolls the bell sometimes at midnight; and the clergyman, reading a funeral service, would sometimes see it at the Tower window, and could tell from its looks whether the buried man was saved or lost. *County Folk-Lore; North Riding*, pp. 127–8.

Cipenapers. (Welsh) The Welsh version of the word 'kidnappers' applied to fairies. (Kidnappers is given in the *Denham Tracts*, Vol. II, p. 78, in the list of fairy names.) G. M. Hopkins Journal, p. 263.

Clurican. (Irish) Nearly allied to a leprechaun, though Keightley gives a tale of one very like an abbey lubber.

Coblynau. Welsh mining fairies. They are ugly but friendly. About half a yard high and dressed like miners. They bring good luck to the mine. Sikes, p. 24.

Colt-Pixy. (Hampshire) Orchard guardian. Spence, p. 18.

Cowlug-sprites. (Border) Sprites with cows' ears that haunt the villages of Bowden and Gateside on Cowlug Night. Henderson, p. 262.

Crodh Mara. (Highland) These are hornless cattle belonging to the sea fairies, which are sometimes given to human favourites. Mackenzie, p. 204.

Cu sith. (Highland) This is a great dog, as large as a bullock with a dark green coat. Mackenzie, p. 204.

Cughtach. (Manx) Cave-haunting spirit. Gill, *A Second Manx Scrapbook*, p. 252.

Cwn Annwn. The Welsh Hellhounds. Sikes, p. 233.

Cyhyraeth. (Welsh) The crying spirit, who wails before disasters. Sikes, p. 219.

Dando and his Dogs. (Cornish) The Wild Hunt. Hunt, pp. 220–3.

Danes. A Somerset name for the fairies. The Dane Hills in Leicestershire have probably the same origin. Tongue, *Somerset Folklore*, pp. 110–11.

Daoine Sidhe (Deenee shee). (Irish) The fairy people. Supposed by some to be Fallen Angels and by some the dwindled remnant of the Tuatha De Danann, the ancient gods of Ireland. Yeats, *Irish Fairy and Folk Tales*, pp. 1–2.

Derrick. (Devon and Hants) Ill-natured in Devon but more friendly in Hampshire. Hampshire reference in Part II, Chapter 6.

The Devil's Dandy Dogs. (Cornish) A pack of fire-breathing hounds led by the Devil who hunt over lonely moors by night. They will tear any man to pieces, but can be kept off by prayer. Hunt, pp. 223–4.

Dinny Mara. (Manx) The sea man. J. F. Campbell, Vol. I, p. xlvi.

Direach (or Fachan). (Highland) A dwarfish monster with one hand, one leg, one eye. J. F. Campbell, Vol. IV, p. 298.

Dobie. (Yorkshire) A rather clownish and foolish Brownie. He was

216

often invoked to guard treasure, but those who could get one preferred a Brownie as more astute. *County Folk-Lore; North Riding,* p. 95 (Henderson, p. 247).

Duergar. (Northumberland) The worst and most malicious of the Border goblins. *County Folk-Lore; Northumberland,* p. 15.

Dunnie. (Northumberland) A mischievous bogey-beast, who most frequently takes the form of a horse, and spills the rider in the mud. Henderson, p. 263.

Dunters (or Powries). (Scottish Border) Spirits which inhabit old deserted peel towers. They make a loud, constant noise like the beating of flax. If it gets louder it foretells disaster. Henderson, p. 255.

Each Uisge (Water horse). (Highland) Like land horses to look at, but treacherous and dangerous. Sometimes took the form of young men, to be detected by the weed in their hair. J. F. Campbell, iv, pp. 304–7. Water horses are also common in Ireland.

Elf. Originally the Anglo-Saxon name for fairies. Later applied in England to small fairy boys, retained in Scotland for some time for all fairies. Elfame, Scottish name for Fairyland.

Ellylldan. Welsh Will o' the Wisp. Sikes, p. 18.

The Ellyllon. Welsh Elves. Tiny creatures living on fairy butter and fairy food. Their Queen is Mab. Sikes, pp. 13–17.

Fachan. (Highland) An evil goblin. See also *Direach.* Mackenzie, p. 251.

Fairy. Late, though general, name for the whole race. Originally Fay, from *Fatae,* the Fates. Faërie was first used for enchantment. Name considered unlucky to use.

Fane. The Ayrshire word for fairy. Spence, *Fairy Tradition;* Jamieson, *Scottish Dictionary.*

Farisees. Suffolk name for fairies. Spence, *Fairy Tradition,* Keightley, p. 306.

Fear Sidhean (fear-sheen). (Highland) Fairy Men.

Feeorin. (Lancashire) Bowker, p. 29.

Fenoderee (or Phynoderee). The Manx Brownies. Waldron, Gill, S. Morrison, etc.

Feriers (or Ferishers). Suffolk name for Fairies. *County Folk-Lore; Suffolk,* p. 36.

The Ferries. Orcadian name for Fairies. Gentler, more friendly and beautiful than Trows. *County Folk-Lore; Orkney,* p. 28.

Ferrishyn. (Manx) Probably English Gallicized. Gill, *A Second Manx Scrapbook,* p. 25.

Fetch. (England) A common name for a double or wraith. Seen at night it is a death portent.

The Fideal. (Highland) A malignant water spirit, like a girl in appearance, who drags swimmers down and drowns them. Mackenzie, p. 235.

Fir Bolgs. (Irish) Primitive fairies, conquered by the Tuatha De Danann. Wentz, p. 32.

Fir Darrig (or Fear Dearg). (Irish) A red man, generally helpful to mortals caught in Fairyland. Crofton Croker, pp. 153–217; Lady Wilde.

Fir Chlis. (Highland) The Merry Dancers. Gaelic for Northern Lights. Mackenzie, p. 222.

The Formorians (or Formors). (Scottish) They were great stone-throwers and quarrelled among themselves, but were not as often accused of a liking for human blood as the English Giants.

The Fridean. (Highland) Supernatural beings that dwelt under rocks, to whom offerings of milk and bread used to be made. *Mackenzie*, p. 244.

Fuath (Foo-a). (Highland) The name of a whole class of malignant fairies or demons, Shellycoat, the Urisk, Each Uisge and others. J. F. Campbell, Vol. II, pp. 109–111.

Gabriel Hounds, or Ratchets. (Northern England) Like the Wisht Hounds, except that they hunt high in the air. To hear them is a presage of death. They are said to be the souls of unchristened children. *County Folk-Lore; Northumberland*, p. 17.

Galley-Beggar. (Somerset) A headless ghost. Tongue, *Somerset Folklore*, pp. 122–3.

Gally-Trot. (N. Country and Suffolk) A white dog the size of a bullock who pursues any who run from it. E. M. Wright, *Rustic Speech and Folk-Lore*, p. 194.

Cancanagh (or Ganconer). (Irish) The Love-Talker. A fairy who appears in lonely valleys with a pipe in his mouth and makes love to maidens, who pine and die for him. In a tale quoted by Yeats, *Irish Fairy and Folk Tales*, they appear more like ordinary fairies. Wright, p. 207.

The Gentry. The polite Irish name for the fairies, equivalent to the Highland 'People of Peace', for it is not lucky to call them Fairies.

The Glaistig. (Highland) A female fairy, often half-woman, half-goat. Generally hostile and dangerous, but occasionally she plays a Brownie's part. Often supposed to be a water spirit. Classed by Campbell with the Fuaths.

The Glashtyn. (Manx) Something between Lob-Lie-by-the-Fire and a Fuath. Some of the Fuath stories are told of him. Gill, *A Second Manx Scrapbook*, p. 253.

Gnomes. The earth-spirits according to the Neo-Platonists, but also to

218

be found in Folk tradition. Wentz, p. 242, for Gnomes seen in Ireland by a percipient.

Goblins. (General) Mischievous or evil spirits, generally small and grotesque.

Grig. (West Country) A small fairy. 'Merry as a grig.'

Greenies. (Lancashire) Bowker, p. 29.

Grogan. The Ulster Brownie. Nearly related to Gruagach. Wood-Martin, *Elder Faiths of Ireland*, Vol. II, p. 3.

Gruagach. (Highland) A spirit with long fair hair, who would often come drenched to the door and beg for shelter. She was lucky about the house. A male Gruagach is sometimes known. J. F. Campbell; Mackenzie, p. 241.

The Gwyllion. The Hill Fairies of Wales. Generally forbidding and malignant. They are close friends of the goats. Sometimes they visit houses and must be hospitably received. Sikes, pp. 49–54.

Gwragedd Annwn. (Welsh) The water maidens who live below the lakes. Beautiful and not dangerous like mermaids or nixies. They have often wedded mortals. Sikes, 34 ff; Rhys.

Gwrach y Rhibyn. The Welsh Banshee. Rhys, p. 453.

Henkies. (Orkney and Shetland) Trooping Fairies who limped as they danced. Their hills are called 'henkie knowes'. Wright, p. 207.

Hinky-Punk. (Somerset, Devon Border) Will o' the Wisp. 'One leg and a light, and lead you into bogs.' R. L. Tongue, from four members of Dulverton Women's Institute.

Hob (or Hobthrush). (North Country) Friendly spirits attached to particular localities. Henderson, p. 264; *County Folk-Lore; North Riding,* also *E. Riding.*

Hobmen. (N. Country) General name for Brownie-like spirits. Henderson.

Hobyah. Malignant and dangerous goblins. Jacobs, *More English Fairy Tales*, p. 118.

Hogmen. (Manx) Hillmen, or fairies. Spence, p. 83; W. Harrison, *Mona Miscellany*, pp. 148 ff.

Hookeys. (Lincolnshire) Said to be another name for fairies. *County Folk-Lore; Lincolnshire*, p. 57.

Hoopers. (Cornish) Beneficent spirits who warned fishermen of storms. Shrouded in thick mist. Bottrell, Vol. II, p. 28.

Hyter Sprites. (Lincolnshire, E. Anglia) Good but stern. Returned lost children from the Fens. R. L. Tongue.

Imps, Impets. Small devils, not properly fairies.

Incubus. A spirit vaguely coupled with the Brownie by Reginald

Scot as having milk set for him, but more properly a devil who lay with women.

The Kelpie. (Scottish) A malignant water spirit who generally took the form of a horse; the subject of many tales.

Killmoulis. (Border) The Mill spirit, deeply attached to the miller's family, but often very mischievous and tiresome. Henderson, pp. 252–3.

Klippes. (Forfar) Trooping fairies. Simpson, *Folklore in Lowland Scotland*, p. 93.

Knockers (Cornish) Mine spirits, said to be the ghosts of the Jews who worked in the Cornish mines. Often helpful. Hunt, Bottrell.

Leanan-Sidhe. (Irish) The life-giving fairy, who inspires poets and singers, as opposed to the Ban-Sidhe who foretells death. Lady Wilde, Vol. I. p. 257.

Leprechaun. (Irish) The fairy shoemaker. One of the best-known of the Irish fairies.

Llamhigyn y Dwr. (The Water Leaper). (Welsh) A demon who troubles fishermen, breaking their lines and dragging them into the water. It drags down sheep and eats them. It is rather like a gigantic toad, with wings and a tail instead of legs. Rhys, p. 79.

Lhiannan Shee. (Manx) The Fairy Sweetheart. Gill, *A Second Manx Scrapbook*, pp. 238–44.

Lil Fellas, the Crowd, the Mob, Themselves. Manx euphemisms for the fairies. Gill, *A Second Manx Scrapbook*, p. 217.

Lob-Lie-by-the-Fire. Called the Lubbar Fend by Milton. A hairy spirit with a long tail, who labours about his farm in the early part of the night, and then rests by the fire. Exacts his bowl of milk like a Brownie.

The Loireag. (Highland) A water fairy connected with fulling and weaving. Fond of music, and angry if any of the weavers sang out of tune. J. F. Campbell; Mackenzie, p. 206.

Lubberkin. An Elizabethan diminutive of Lob, used for a Puck-like spirit.

Lunantishee. (Irish) Tribes that guard the blackthorn bushes. Wentz, p. 53.

The Mermaid. The best-known of all the sea-fairies. Very variable in character, but on the whole hostile. They haunt streams and pools as well as the sea. A. Waugh and G. Benwell have made an exhaustive study of the mermaid in *Sea Enchantress*.

The Merman. The mermaid's husband is uglier and even fiercer than she is and generally haunts the sea, not rivers. Many Mermen tales are told in Orkney and Shetland. *County Folk-Lore; Orkney and Shetland*, pp. 179 ff.

Merrows. (Irish) The Merrows are the Irish mer-people. Like the Roane they live on dry land under water, but they use red caps, not sealskins, to pass through the sea. The females are beautiful but the males hideous. They are not so ill-disposed as other mer-people. Crofton Croker, Vol. II, pp. 30–52.

The Merry Dancers (or Na Fir Chlis). Spence, p. 58; A. A. Mac-Gregor, *The Peat-Fire Flame*, p. 121.

Moddey Dhoo. (Manx) The Black Dog. Gill, *A Second Manx Scrapbook*, p. 254.

Mooringer Veggey. (Manx) The Little People. Gill, *A Second Manx Scrapbook.*

Morgan. (Welsh) A lake spirit. Rhys, pp. 372–4.

Neagle, Noggle, Nuggle or Nyaggle. The Shetland Water Kelpie. *County Folk-Lore; Orkney and Shetland*, p. 189.

Ouph. An Elizabethan variant of Elf; now literary.

Padfoot. (North Country) A bogey-beast, often in the shape of a huge black dog, but sometimes white. It drags a clattering chain and has fiery eyes. Its name comes from the padding of its feet. Henderson, p. 273.

Peallaidh (pyaw-le). (Highland) The Shaggy One. A Perthshire urisk, from which the name Aberfeldy is said to be taken. Mac-kenzie, p. 234.

Pechs, Pechts or Picts. Scottish mound fairies, dwarfish and red-haired like the Somerset Pixies. MacRitchie: Spence, etc.

Pellings. (Welsh) A half-fairy tribe living near Snowdon. Supposed to be children of Penelope, a fairy bride. Rhys, pp. 46–8.

People of Peace, or the Daoine Sidhe. One of the Highland names for the fairies.

Perry Dancers. The Suffolk name for the Northern Lights.

The Pharisees or Frairies. Sussex, Suffolk, Hereford, Warwick and Worcestershire name for the Fairies.

Phooka, Pouka. The Irish Puck. Often takes animal form, more especially that of a horse. Crofton Croker, Lady Wilde.

Phynoderee. See Fenoderee.

Pinket. The Worcestershire name for a Will o' the Wisp. Jabez Allies. *Ignis Fatuus.*

Pisgies. Cornish metathesis of the word 'pixies'.

Pixies. Somerset, Devon and Cornish trooping fairies. See Hunt, Mrs. Bray, R. L. Tongue, etc.

Plant Annwn. (Welsh) The Tribe of underwater fairies, who came out to hunt and possessed great wealth of cattle. Their King was Arawn. Rhys, pp. 143–5.

Plant Rhys Dwfn. (Welsh) A race of fairies (perhaps half human) on whose land there grows a plant that makes it invisible. They came to market in Cardigan and raised the price of corn and goods. Rhys, pp. 158–62.

Plentyn-Newid. The Welsh changeling. Sikes, p. 56.

Portunes. (English) Medieval. Gervase of Tilbury.

Powries. See Dunters.

Redcap, or Redcomb. (Border) Bloodthirsty spirits which haunted old peel towers. Henderson, pp. 253–5.

Redshanks. (Somerset) Treasure-owning fairies of Dolbury Camp. Supposed by some to be ghosts of the old Danes. Said to smoke little pipes. R. L. Tongue, *Somerset Folklore*, p. 111.

Roane. (Highland) Seals or Mer-people. They take off their skins on land, but need them for going through the water. They are the gentlest of the sea people. *Scottish Fairy and Folk Tales.*

The Seelie Court. (Scottish) The kindly fairy host. 'Seelie' is 'blessed'. The malignant fairies were sometimes called 'the unseelie Court'. Macpherson, *Primitive Beliefs in the North-East of Scotland*, p. 98.

Selkies. (Orcadian) The Seal men of the Orkneys. *County Folk-Lore; Orkney and Shetland*, pp. 170 ff.

Shefro. (Irish) Gregarious fairy who wears foxglove flower as cap. Henderson, p. 228.

The Sidhe (Shee). The general Celtic name for fairies.

Silkies. (North Country) Ladies wearing white or grey silk, something between ghosts and Brownies, who haunt certain Border houses. Henderson, pp. 268–70.

Skriker. (Yorkshire and Lancashire) Sometimes called Trash from the padding of its feet. A death portent. Sometimes it wanders invisibly in the woods, giving fearful screams. Sometimes it takes a form like Padfoot, a huge dog with large feet and saucer eyes. Wright, pp. 194–5.

Sleih Beggey. (Manx) 'Little Folk'. Gill, *A Second Manx Scrapbook*, p. 217.

The Sluagh. (Highland) The Host (of the Dead). Wentz, p. 108.

Spriggans. (Cornish) Some say the Spriggans are ghosts of the Giants. They guard old cairns and cromlechs, and hidden treasure. They are grotesquely ugly, and can alter their size at will. Storms, the fall of buildings and the loss of children are put down to them. Hunt; Bottrell.

Sprites. A general name for fairies and other supernatural creatures.

Spunkies. Scottish Will o' the Wisps. Also known in Somerset. Kittredge, *Friar's Lantern; County Folk-Lore; Fife*, p. 34.

Spoorne. A spirit mentioned by Reginald Scot.

Swarth. (Cumberland) A wraith or double. Henderson, p. 46.

Tangie. (Orkney) A water kelpie who gains his name from the seaweed that covers him. He appears sometimes as a man, sometimes as a horse. Wright, p. 195.

Tankerabogus. (Devon and Somerset) A bogie who comes after bad children. Wright, p. 198.

Tarans. (Scottish) The spirits of unbaptized children. Macpherson, *Primitive Beliefs in the North-East of Scotland*, p. 114.

Tatterfoal. (Lincolnshire) A goblin horse. *County Folk-Lore; Lincolnshire*, p. 53.

Thrummy-cap. (North Country) A spirit who haunted the cellars of old houses; he wore a cap of weavers' thrums. *Denham Tracts*, Vol. II, p. 79.

Thrumpin. (Border) A kind of attendant demon, believed to haunt every man with the power of taking his life. Henderson, p. 262.

The Tiddy Ones. (Lincolnshire) Name for the Fen fairies. The Tiddy Mun controls the floods. Balfour, *Legends of the Cars.*

Trows. The Hill Fairies of Shetland and Orkney. Have most of the usual fairy characteristics and some others, such as that of being 'day-bound', which they seem to have caught from the Scandinavian Trolls. *County Folk-Lore; Orkney and Shetland.*

Tuatha De Danann. (Irish) The People of the Goddess Danu. Spence, Lady Wilde, Yeats, etc.

Tylwyth Teg. (Welsh) The Fair Family. General name for the 'Seelie Court' of Wales. All the usual fairy characteristics. Rhys, Sikes, etc.

Urchins. A popular name for a hedgehog, used in the sixteenth century for a kind of pixy; still used for small boys, but for fairies only in literary use.

The Urisk, or uruisg. (Highland) A kind of rough Brownie, half human, half goat, very lucky to have about the house, who herded cattle and did farm-work. He haunted lonely pools, but would sometimes crave company and follow terrified travellers all night. Urisks lived solitary, but met at stated times. A corrie near Loch Katrine was their favourite meeting place. Grahame, *Picturesque Sketches of Perthshire*; Mackenzie, pp. 185–7.

Vough. (Highland) A form of fuath. J. F. Campbell; Spence, p. 60.

Waff. (Yorkshire) Wraith, fetch or double. Henderson, pp. 46–8.

Water Wraith. (Scottish) A female water spirit. Dressed in green, withered, meagre and scowling. Macpherson, p. 63.

Wee Folk. Scottish and Ulster euphemism for the fairies.

Wight. A vague term for a supernatural spirit or fairy. 'The Seelie wicht' or 'the evil wicht'. Spence, p. 122.

The Wisht Hounds, or Yeth Hounds. (Somerset, Devon and Cornwall) The Spectral Pack which hunts for souls. Hunt.

Yarthkins. (Lincolnshire) Earth spirits. Balfour, *Legends of the Cars.*

FAIRY INDIVIDUALS

It is difficult sometimes to distinguish between individuals and types. Some may be listed as individuals merely because the references to them are uncommon.

Aengus. One of the Tuatha De Danann, or god-fairies of Ireland. Wentz, p. 292.

The Afanc. (Welsh) A water demon who haunted the river Conway and dragged all living things he could catch into its depths. He was captured through the treachery of a maiden whom he loved. Rhys, p. 130.

Aillan Mac Midhna. The fairy musician, one of the Tuatha De Danann. Wentz, p. 298.

Aiken-Drum. (Scottish) Name given to the Brownie of Blednoch in William Nicholson's Poetical Works, pp. 78–81.

Aine. (Ireland) A fairy goddess or lake spirit, the mother of Earl Fitzgerald by the Earl of Desmond. Wentz, p. 79.

Ainsel. (Northumberland) The little fairy girl in the Border version of Motif K 622 'Noman'. Keightley, p. 313.

Awd Goggie. (E. Yorkshire) A demon who guards unripe fruit in orchards. *County Folk-Lore; East Riding*, p. 40.

Biasd Bealach Odail. A Skye monster. Mackenzie, p. 250.

Billy Blind. (Border) A friendly domestic spirit who gives good advice. Child, *Young Beichan.*

Billy Winker. (Lancashire) The bedtime spirit. Wright, p. 202.

Black Annis. (Leicestershire) A malignant hag with a blue face and only one eye, very like the Highland Cailleach Bheur in character. Her cave was in the Dane Hills; she devoured lambs and young children. Billson; Mackenzie.

Blue Burches. (Somerset) A domestic spirit haunting a cobbler's house on the Blackdown Hills. Tongue, *Somerset Folklore*, p. 121.

Blue Cap. (Border) A colliery hobgoblin who worked for wages as a putter. *Denham Tracts*, Vol. II, p. 363.

Bodca-an-Dun. (Highland) Spectre of the Rothmurchus family, death token. Henderson, p. 344.

Brother Mike. (Suffolk) The name of a captured fairy. *County Folk-Lore; Suffolk*, p. 34.

The Brown Man of the Muirs. (Border) A dangerous spirit, protector of wild game. Henderson, p. 251.

Burlow Beanie. The name of a hobgoblinish spirit in the ballad *King Arthur and the King of Cornwall.* Child, Vol. I, pp. 274–88.

Cailleach Bheur. The Blue Hag of the Highlands. Personification of the spirit of winter. J. F. Campbell; Mackenzie.

Caillagh ny Groagmagh (Old Woman of Gloominess). (Manx) A weather hag who was often reputed to have fallen into clefts in the rocks, but was otherwise very like the Highland *Cailleach Bheur.* Gill, *A Manx Scrapbook,* p. 347.

The Cauld Lad of Hilton. (Border) A ghost or brownie, laid by a gift of clothes. W. Henderson, pp. 266–7. There was also a Cauld Lad of Gilsland who was more definitely a ghost.

Churn-Milk Peg. (W. Yorkshire) A wood spirit who protects unripe nuts from children. She smokes a pipe.

Colman Gray. (Cornish) The name of a little pisky boy adopted by a human. Hunt, p. 95, from T. Quiller Couch in *Notes and Queries.*

Coluinn Gun Cheann. (The Headless Trunk). A Bauchan attached to the Macdonals of Morar. Though friendly to them he was dangerous in the neighbourhood, as he would attack and kill any single man who passed by the river Morar after dark. He was at length overcome by one of the Macleods of Raasay. J. F. Campbell, Vol. II, p. 101.

The Cowie. A spirit something like a Brownie who haunted Goranberry Tower. Scott, *Border Minstrelsy,* Vol. IV, p. 248.

Crackerbones. (Somerset) A Goblin. Tongue, *Somerset Folklore,* J. O. Halliwell-Phillipps.

Cuachag. (Highland) The river spirit who haunts Clen Quaich. Mackenzie, p. 233.

Cutty Soams. (Border) A colliery bogie who used to cut the ropes by which the trucks were hauled. *Denham Tracts,* Vol. II, p. 362.

Dagda. (Irish) High King of the Tuatha De Danann, the greatest of the Sidh of Ireland.

Dathera Dad. Name of Fairy child in pudding. Addy, *Household Tales,* p. 9.

Dobby. (Yorkshire), or *Master Dobbs* (Sussex) A Brownie-like hob who joins workmen and helps them with their task. Wright, p. 202.

Dooinney-Oie. (Manx) The Night Man who warns of storms. Gill, *A Second Manx Scrapbook,* p. 246.

The Dun Cow of Mac Brandy's Thicket. (Highland) A mischievous fairy cow. Macdougall, *Folk Tales and Fairy Lore,* p. 281.

The Dun Cow of Kirkham. (Lancashire) A monster cow whose yield was destroyed by the greed of witches. (There is an Irish parallel.) Harland and Wilkinson, p. 16.

Etain. (Irish) The second wife of the fairy King, Midir, who, in human form, married Eochaid, High King of Ireland. Lady Gregory, *Gods and Fighting Men*; Evans Wentz, pp. 369, 374–6, 395.

Farvann. (Ayrshire) The green fairy hound as large as a two-year-old stirk. Bays three times when hunting, with a pause between each bay. Pursued Macleod of Raasay. Simpson's *Folk Lore in Lowland Scotland*, p. 108.

Fear Dearg (The Red Man) (See Fir Darig). (Irish, Munster) A little man, about two and a half feet in height, wearing a scarlet sugar-loaf hat and a long scarlet coat, with long grey hair and a wrinkled face. He would come in and ask to warm himself by the fire. It was very unlucky to refuse him. Crofton Croker.

Finvarra. (Fin Bheara) The King of the Connaught Fairies. Lady Wilde, I, p. 147; Wentz, p. 42.

Foul Weather. (Cornish) A variant of Tom Tit Tot. *Old Cornwall*, Vol. II, pp. 21, 27.

Friar Rush. A tricksy hobgoblinish devil. Chap-book.

Gentle Annie. (Cromarty Firth) A hag who raises and governs storms. Of mild address and appearance but treacherous and evil nature. Mackenzie, p. 160.

Ghillie Dhu. (Highland) A harmless spirit, kind to children, but wild and shy. Dressed in leaves and green moss. J. F. Campbell; Osgood Mackenzie, *A Hundred Years in the Highlands*, p. 186.

The Gooseberry Wife. (Isle of Wight) Looks after green gooseberries in the form of a large hairy caterpillar. Wright, p. 198.

The Grant. (Medieval English) A demon. Like a yearling foal, but goes on hind legs and has fiery eyes. A death portent. Gervase of Tilbury, Vol. I, p. 980.

Greensleeves. (Aberdeen) The name of a fairy wizard. Peter Buchan, *Ancient Scottish Tales*, pp. 170–7.

Grindylow. (Yorkshire) A malignant water demon. Wright, p. 198.

Grim. (English) Fairy Grim in *The Life of Robin Goodfellow* (1628). Grim's Dyke, Church Grim, etc.

Gull. (English) The name of one of the elves in *The Life of Robin Goodfellow* (1628). See Jabez Allies. These names may merely express the activities of the elves.

Gunna. (Highland) A fairy lad banished from Fairyland. Dressed in fox-skins. L. Spence; Mackenzie, p. 230.

Gwydion. The wizard king of the fairies of North Wales. Sikes, p. 5.

Gwynn ap Nudd. The Welsh King of the Fairies. Sikes, p. 6; Wentz, pp. 319–20.

Gyl Burnt Tayle. Name for Will o' the Wisp. Gayton, Festivious Notes (1654).

The Gyre-Carling. The Name of the Fairy Queen in Fife. Simpkins, *County Folk-Lore; Fife.* F.L.S., p. 33.

Habetrot. (Scottish Border) The spinning-wheel fairy. A shirt made by Habetrot was considered efficacious against many illnesses. W. Henderson, pp. 258–62.

Hairy Jack. (Lincolnshire) Name of a goblin dog haunting a barn at Willoughton Cliff. Gutch, *County Folk-Lore,* Vol. V, p. 53.

Half-Hannikin. (Somerset) Information collected by R. L. Tongue, 1958. Counting-out rhyme,

'Kinnekin-kannikin and a Half-Hannekin,
Kinnekin-kannekin kout.
Kinnekin-kannekin and a Half-Hannekin,
Kinnekin-kannekin—OUT.'

Half-Hannikin described as 'the little man who cleaned the house at night'. Earlier mention 1912.

The Hedley Kow. (Northumbrian) A shape-shifting bogey-beast who haunted Hedley. Balfour, *County Folk-Lore; Northumberland,* p. 17.

Hobbledy. (Midland) 'Hobbledy's Lantern' a name for Will o' the Wisp. Wright, p. 200.

Howlaa. (Manx) A spirit who howls before storms. *A Vocabulary of the Manx Dialect.* A. W. Moore and S. Morrison.

Jack-in-Irons. (Yorkshire) A gigantic spectre with clattering chains. E. M. Wright, p. 194.

Jack o' Lantern. (English) Another name for Will o' the Wisp. Jabez Allies; Kittredge, *Friar's Lantern.*

Jeanie of Biggersdale. (Yorkshire) A murderous spirit. Gutch, *County Folk-Lore; N. Riding,* p. 130.

Jenny Greenteeth. (Lancashire) A malignant water fairy. Her presence known by the green scum on the water. Henderson, p. 265.

Jimmy Squarefoot. (Manx) Sometimes a pig, sometimes a pig-like man. Ridden by a stone-throwing giant. Gill, *A Manx Scrapbook,* p. 356.

Joan the Wad. (Cornish) A Variant of Will o' the Wisp. Quiller Couch, *History of Polperro,* p. 144. Kittredge, *Friar's Lantern.*

John Tucker. (Devon) Household spirit. R. L. Tongue.

Kit-with-the-Canstick. Will o' the Wisp in Scot and Harsnet.

Knocky Boh. (Yorkshire) A goblin who taps behind wainscots. Wright, p. 198.

The Lady of the Lake. The fairy lady of Arthurian legend. Wentz, p. 316.

Lambton Worm. (Border) Monster slain by the Heir of Lambton. Henderson, pp. 287–92.

Lazy Lawrence. (Somerset) Orchard guardian; gives cramps to thieves. R. L. Tongue, *Somerset Folklore*, pp. 119–20.

Licke. One of the female fairies in *The Life of Robin Goodfellow.*

Linton Worm. (Scottish Border) Henderson, pp. 295–7.

Luideag. (Skye) A female demon in rags who haunted Lochan nan Dubh Breac. Mackenzie, p. 251.

Lull. One of the female fairies in *The Life of Robin Goodfellow.*

Luridan. (Orkney) A kind of Brownie who inhabited the Isle of Pomona for seven years. Black, *County Folk-Lore; Orkney and Shetland Islands*, p. 46.

Mab. A dual character. The Queen of the Fairies, in which form she may have some connection with Queen Maeve of Ireland, and the prankish fairy of Shakespeare and Ben Jonson. In the British Museum MS Sloane 1727 she is mentioned as 'Lady to the Queen'.

Mara. An old English name for a demon, which survives in Nightmare and Mare's Nest.

Mauthe Doog. (Manx) The local name for the Black Dog which haunted the guardroom of Peel Castle.

Meg Moulach, or *Hairy Meg.* (Highland) A female Brownie who haunted the Grants of Strathspey (Aubrey, *Miscellanies*), but later became dangerous. Still in oral tradition.

Melsh Dick. (Lancashire) A wood spirit who protects unripe nuts. Wright, p. 198.

Micol. The Fairy Queen invoked in the British Museum MS Sloane 1727, p. 28.

Midir. (Irish) The Fairy Husband of Etain. Lady Gregory, Wentz, pp. 374–5.

Morgan le Fay. The fairy enchantress of Arthurian Legend. Wentz, p. 311.

Morrigan, or *Morrigu.* (Irish) A War Goddess. Often appears as a raven or crow. Another name for Badb. Wentz, pp. 302–5.

The Muileartach. (Highland) A giant hag with one eye, so like the Cailleach Bheur as probably to be no more than another name for her. She is closely connected with the sea, however. Mackenzie, p. 233.

Mumpoker. (Isle of Wight) A Nursery goblin. Wright, p. 198.

Nanny Buttoncap. (Yorkshire) Wright gives a rhyme about her, p. 207.

Nelly Longarms. (North-West) A water spirit who drags children into ponds. Wright, p. 198.

Nicneven. Another name for the Gyre-Carlin. Named by Montgomerie in his *Flyting with Polwart:* 'Nicnivin with hir nymphis in nomber anew.' Scott, *Letters on Demonology and Witchcraft*, pp. 128–9.

Nuala. (Irish) Finvarra's Fairy Queen. Wentz, p. 28.

Nuckelavee. (Scottish) A monster that came out of the sea, but could not cross running water. Douglas, *Scottish Fairy and Folk Tales*, p. 160.

Oberon. The name of the Fairy King according to Shakespeare, *Huon of Bordeaux* and some popular traditions. Auberon or Oberycom were names of familiar spirits in early Renaissance times.

Oonagh. (Irish) Finvarra's Fairy Queen, according to Lady Wilde.

Old Bloody Bones. (Cornish) *Old Cornwall*, Vol. II, pp. 2, 17.

Old Lady of the Elder Tree. (Lincolnshire) The tree spirit, whose leave must be asked before a limb is cut off. Mrs. Gutch, *County Folk-Lore; Lincolnshire*, pp. 20–1.

Old Man Crook. (Devon) A helpful spirit, Bideford area. R. L. Tongue.

Pach. The name of one of the elves in *The Life of Robin Goodfellow*.

Peerifool. Orcadian Tom Tit Tot. His tale is a combination of Tale Type 500 with 311, IV. Black, *County Folk-Lore; Orkney and Shetland Islands*, pp. 222–6.

Peg o' Nell. (Lancashire of the Ribble) The ghost of a servant girl who demands a life every seven years. Henderson, p. 265.

Peg Powler. The spirit of the Tees. Has long green hair and is insatiable for human life. The frothy foam on the higher reaches of the Tees is called 'Peg Powler's suds'. Henderson, pp. 265–6.

The Picktree Brag. (Durham) A shape-shifting bogey-beast. Henderson, p. 270.

Pinch. The name of one of the elves in *The Life of Robin Goodfellow*.

Pokey-Hokey. (E. Anglia) A Nursery goblin. Wright, p. 198.

Puck. A half-domestic fairy of the hobgoblin type. Shakespeare has given him an individual character, but the word is occasionally used in the plural.

Pwca. The Welsh Puck. In character very like the English one. Rhys, Sikes, p. 20.

The Radiant Boy. Perhaps a ghost rather than a fairy. Henderson, pp. 267–8.

Raw-head-and-Bloody-Bones, or sometimes Tommy Rawhead. A widely distributed Nursery goblin, who dragged children down into marlpits or lurked in dark cupboards. Wright, p. 199; R. L. Tongue, S.F.L., p. 123.

Robin Goodfellow. The best-known of all the hobgoblins. Mentions of him in Elizabethan literature are frequent.

Robin Round-cap. A Yorkshire Brownie. Gutch, *County Folk-Lore; Yorkshire, East Riding*, p. 54.

Scantlie Mab. (Scottish Border) A spinning fairy, servant to Habetrot. Henderson, pp. 259, 261.

Shag, Shagfoal or Tatterfoal, Gutch, *County Folk-Lore; Lincolnshire*, pp. 53, 55.

Shellycoat. (Scottish) A mischievous water spirit. Scott, *Minstrelsy of the Scottish Border*, Vol, I. p. 151.

The Shock. (Suffolk) Gurdon, *County Folk-Lore; Suffolk*, p. 91.

Shony. The spirit of the sea on the West Coast of Scotland, to whom libations were poured. Mackenzie, pp. 252, 253; Wentz.

Shorthoggers of Whittinghame. (Scottish) An un-named ghost child, very near to a spunky. Chambers, *Popular Rhymes*, p. 334.

Sib. Name of female fairy in *The Life of Robin Goodfellow.*

Sili-go-Dwt, or Sili Ffrit. Names of little Welsh fairies, something like Whuppity Stoorie. Rhys.

Skillywidden. Name of a little fairy caught by a farmer at Treridge. Hunt.

The Skriker. (Lancashire) A Death portent. Wright, p. 194; Bowker.

Spotloggin. Ghost of a murdered man that haunts a ditch near Evesham. Wright, p. 192.

Tankerabogus, or Tantarabobus. (Somerset and Devon) A wicked bogey. Wright, p. 198.

Terrytop. The Tom Tit Tot of the Cornish drolls. Hunt, Bottrell.

Tib. A female fairy in *The Life of Robin Goodfellow.*

Titania. Oberon's consort in Shakespeare. Her name is one of the epithets of Diana. It is doubtful if there is folk tradition behind her, though the Sloane MS 1727 mentions Tytan, with Florella and Mabb, as 'the treasures of the earth'.

Tom Dockin. (Yorkshire) A bogey with iron teeth who devours bad children. Wright, p. 198.

Tom Poker. (East Anglia) A bogey who inhabits dark closets. Wright, p. 198.

Tom Tit Tot. (Suffolk) The English Rumpelstiltzchen. See E. Clodd, Tom-Tit, a Tut or a Tut-Gut are Lincolnshire names for hobgoblins.

Trwtyn a Tratyn. The Welsh Tom Tit Tot. Rhys, p. 229.

Wag-at-the-Wa'. (Scottish Border) A grotesque but friendly hobgoblin. Henderson, p. 257.

Wee Willie Winkie. Scottish fairy of sleep, like Old Luk Oie in Denmark. Subject of well-known Nursery Rhyme.

Whuppity Stoorie. The Scottish Rumpelstiltzschen. Chambers, *Popular Rhymes of Scotland*, pp. 72–5.

Wilkie. A Shetland name for a fairy. *County Folk-Lore; Orkney and Shetland,* p. 47.

Will o' the Wisp. Commonest name of the *Ignis Fatuus.*

Wryneck. (Lancashire and Yorkshire) A malignant spirit. 'He caps wryneck, and wryneck caps the Dule.' Henderson, p. 254.

Yallery Brown. (Lincolnshire) The name of a small malignant fairy, so evil that it was dangerous to earn even his gratitude. Mrs. Balfour, *Legends of the Cars.*

Appendix II

EXTRACTS FROM FAIRY POEMS

A Medieval Fairy King. (From *The Romance of King Orfeo*, reproduced in *Fairy Tales, Legends and Romances Illustrating Shakespeare*, W. C. Hazlitt, 1875, pp. 87–8.) Meroudys (Eurydice) speaks:

> Whe(n) I gan my-selve awake,
> Ruly chere I gañ to make,
> Fore I saw a sembly syzt;
> To-werd me come a gentyll knyzt,
> Wele i-armyd at all ryzht,
> And bad I schuld upoñ hyzeng,
> Come speke with hys lord the kyng.
> I ansuerd hym with wordes bold;
> I seyd, I durst not ne not I wold.
> The knyzht azen he rode full fast,
> Than come ther kyng at the last,
> With an hundreth knyztes also,
> And an hundreth ladés and mo,
> All thei ryden on whyte stedes,
> Of mylke whyte was all ther wedes,
> I saw never, seth I was borne,
> So feyre creatours here be-forne.
> The kyng had a crouñe on hys hede,
> It was no sylver ne gold rede,
> It was all off presyous stone,
> Als bryzt as any soñ it schone!
> Also sone as he to me come,
> Whether I wold ore not, up he me name,

And made me with hym forto ryde
Upon a stede by hys syde;
He brovzt me to a feyre palas,
Wele tyred and rychly in all case;
He schewed me hys castellus and toures,
And hys hey haules and boures,
Forestes, ryvers, frutes and floures;
Hys grete stedes schewyd me ichone,
And sethyn he made me azene to gone
Into the sted where he me fette,
In that same sted ther he me sete,
And seyd, 'Madame, loke that thou be
To-morrow here under this tre,
And than schall thou with us go,
And lyve with us ever-more so;
Iff that thou make us any lete,
Where-ever thou be, thou schall be fete,
And to-torne thi lymys all,
No thyng helpe the ne schall!
And thoz thou be all to-torne,
Zit shall thou a-wey with us to be borne!'

The Fairy Queen in the Fifteenth Century. (From the **Romance of** *Thomas and the Fairy Queen*, op. cit., pp. 104–5, 107.)

Hir palfray was of dappulle gray,
　　Sike on se I never non,
As dose the sune on somers day,
　　The cumly lady hirselfe schone;
Hir sadille was of reuylle bone,
　　Semely was that sight to se,
Stifly sette with precious stone,
　　Compaste aboute with crapoté;
Stonys of oryons gret plenté, (orient)
　　Hir here aboute hir hede hit hong;
She rode out over that lovely le,
　　A-while she blew, a-while she song.
Hir garthes of nobulle silke thei were,
　　Hir boculs thei were of barys stone; (beryl)
Hir stirropis thei were of cristalle clere,
　　And alle with perry aboute be-gon;
Hir paytrelle was of a rialle fyne,
　　Hir cropur was of arafé,

233

> Hir bridulle was of golde fyne,
>   On every side hong bellis thre.
> She led iij grehoundis in a leesshe,
>   viij rachis be hir fete ran,
> To speke with hir wold I not seese,
>   Hir lire was white as any swan; (complexion)
> She bare a horn about hir halce, (neck)
>   And undur hir gyrdille mony flonne; (arrows)
> For sothe, lordynges, as I yow telle,
>   Thus was the lady fayre be-gon.

(After he had had intercourse with her she became frightful.)

> Thomas stondand in that sted,
>   And beheld that lady gay,
> Hir here that hong upon hir hed,
>   Hir een semyd out that were so gray;
> And alle hir clothis were away,
>   That here before saw in that stede,
> The to shanke was blak, the tother gray,
>   The body bloo as beton leed!
> Thomas seid, 'alas! alas!
>   In feith, this is a dolfulle sight!
> That thou art so fadut in the face,
>   That before shone as sunne bright!'
> 'Take thi leve, Thomas, at sune and mone,
>   And also at levys of eldryne tre:
> This twelmond shall thou with me gon,
>   That mydul-erth thou shalt not se.'

(In the first extract the letter *z* has various pronunciations; at the beginning of a word it is sounded as *y*, in the middle a gutteral. *ch* or *gh*, at the end *z*.)

These early nineteenth century fairies derive from the Shakespeare and Herrick tradition.

George Darley, *Sylvia: or The May Queen* (London, 1827), Act IV, sc. v, pp. 137–8.

> Hurrah! the bluff-cheek'd bugle band,
> Each with a loud reed in his hand!
> Hurrah! the pattering company,
> Each with a drum-bell at his knee!
> Hurrah! the sash-capt cymbal-swingers!
> Hurrah! the klingle-klangle ringers!

Hurrah! Hurrah! the elf-knights enter,
Each with his grasshopper at a canter!
His tough spear of a wild oat made,
His good sword of a grassy blade,
His buckram suit of shining laurel,
His shield of bark, emboss'd with coral;
See how the plumy champion keeps
His proud steed clambering on his hips,
With foaming jaw pinn'd to his breast,
Blood-rolling eyes, and arched crest;
Over his and his rider's head
A broad-sheet butterfly banner spread,
Swoops round the staff in varying form,
Flouts the soft breeze, but courts the storm.

From The Plea of the Midsummer Fairies. (The Works of Thomas Hood
edited by his Son and Daughter, 1871, Vol. V., pp. 213-51.)
Shakespeare speaks:

p. 243.   'Oh these be Fancy's revellers by night!
            Stealthy companions of the downy moth—
            Diana's motes, that flit in her pale light,
            Shunners of sunbeams in diurnal sloth;——
            These be the feasters on night's silver cloth;——
            The gnat with shrilly trump is their convener,
            Forth from their flowery chambers, nothing loth,
            With lulling tunes to charm the air serener,
            Or dance upon the grass to make it greener.

            'These be the pretty genii of the flow'rs,
            Daintily fed with honey and pure dew——
            Midsummer's phantoms in her dreaming hours,
            King Oberon, and all his merry crew,
            The darling puppets of Romance's view;
            Fairies, and sprites, and goblin elves we call them,
            Famous for patronage of lovers true;——
            No harm they act, neither shall harm befall them,
            So do not thus with crabbed frowns appal them.'

Puck describes himself.

p. 240.   'Alas!' quoth Puck, 'a little random elf,
            Born in the sport of nature, like a weed,

235

For simple sweet enjoyment of myself,
But for no other purpose, worth, or need;
And yet withal of a most happy breed;
And there is Robin Goodfellow besides,
My partner dear on many a prankish deed
To make dame Laughter hold her jolly sides,
Like merry mummers twain on holy tides.'

Tennyson's version of the Boggart who flitted with the family. *Walking to the Mail.* (*The Works of Alfred Lord Tennyson* (London, 1892), p. 81.)

But his house, for so they say,
Was haunted with a jolly ghost, that shook
The curtains, whined in lobbies, tapt at doors,
And rummaged like a rat: no servant stay'd:
The farmer vext packs up his beds and chairs,
And all his household stuff; and with his boy
Betwixt his knees, his wife upon the tilt,
Sets out and meets a friend who hails him, 'What!
You're flitting!' 'Yes, we're flitting,' says the ghost
(For they had packed the thing among the beds,)
'Oh well,' says, he, 'you flitting with us too—
Jack, turn the horses' heads and home again.'

SHORT-LIVED FAIRIES

C. M. Doughty made a strange use of Elves in that curious poetic drama, *The Cliffs*, published in 1909. It is full of inversions and archaisms, but is by no means wholly derivative. In Part IV, pages 188–9, Howt, the aged elf, describes with some pathos the short span of life allowed to them, compressed within three little fives of years.

He outlines the three ages of Elves, Bud, Greenleaf and Sereleaf,

'And when twice hundred, of the Moon's round years,
Are hardly, full of changes, o'er us passed;
Us rest few frozen days and weary nights.'

He describes the elvish funeral, the sons bearing out their father with their jerkins 'upsidown', and laying spells on swart moles and dank worms, that the ground be left untroubled. Then they call the dead elf's name thrice aloud, and go home to divide between them his tools and his homely store. This is out of the straight line of tradition, but has an earthy touch which commends it to the imagination. And indeed, though fairies are long-lived almost to immortality, we come across fairy funerals every now and then.

Appendix III

THE COTTINGLEY FAIRIES

At intervals the tale of the Cottingley Fairies is brought up again, and it certainly makes an impressive story.

In September of 1965 an article in *The Dalesman* recapitulated the affair briefly, and Edward L. Gardner dealt with it in more detail in a short book, *The Cottingley Photographs and their Sequel*, published in 1945 and republished in 1951. The story is as follows:

In 1917 Frances Griffiths, a child of ten from South Africa, was staying with a thirteen-year-old cousin, Elsie Wright and her parents, at Cottingley. They spent a good deal of time playing in a wooded glen by the beck near their house, and used to come back and tell Mr. and Mrs. Wright that they had seen fairies. The Wrights thought that they were romancing. Mr. Wright had recently been given a small camera, and Elsie asked him to let them take a photograph of the fairies to show that they were speaking the truth. After some pleading he lent them the camera with a single plate in it. It was a bright, sunny day; they went off and returned after an hour, saying that they had taken the fairies. In the evening Mr. Wright developed the plate, and in the negative saw Frances leaning on the bank with a group of gauzy fairies dancing in front of her. He was convinced that the girls must have used some cut-out paper figures, and went into the glen to find snippings of paper, and found nothing. A few days later he gave them a second plate, and this time Elsie was taken, with a winged gnome stepping on to her knee. The parents still thought that there was some deception, and there the matter rested for some time, except that Frances sent a print of one of the photographs to a friend in South Africa.

Three years later, in 1920, Mrs. Wright happened to attend a

238

lecture given by Dr. Gardner, in which he mentioned the possibility of spirit-photographs. She told him that her daughter had claimed to photograph the fairies, and hunted out the two negatives for him. He took them to a professional photographer, a Mr. Snelling of Harrow, who said that these were out-of-door photographs, single exposures, and that he was ready to declare that they were not fakes. Dr. Gardner took the negatives to Kodak, who were not prepared to certify that the effects could not be faked, but could find no evidence of faking. Shortly after this Sir Arthur Conan Doyle took up the matter, and wrote an article about it for the Christmas Number of the Strand Magazine. Before doing so, he asked Dr. Gardner to go up to Cottingley and see the Wrights. According to Dr. Gardner's account he had, up till then, been sceptical, but he was impressed by the Wrights as honest, straightforward people, and he found that the out-door setting of the photographs was genuine. He arranged for Frances to spend her summer holidays at Cottingley, and obtained some marked rolls of films from Illingworth, to ensure that the photographs were genuine. The weather happened to be very wet, and only three photographs were taken. One of them was said to be particularly difficult to fake. The next year Cottingley was visited by Mr. Geoffrey Hodson, who said that he saw a great many fairies there, but did not succeed in taking any photographs. His theory of the matter was that both girls were clairvoyantes and that Frances was a medium, with a quantity of loose ectoplasm out of which the fairies shaped bodies slightly more opaque than was natural to them. He regarded the fairies as nature spirits, mainly instinctive in their intelligence, whose function was the shaping and energizing of plant growth.

So far for the case. Against it any folklorist puts up a very strong aesthetic resistance; for these fairies seem the very model of the butterfly-winged, gauze-clad fairies of the children's magazine illustrations. They were dressed, too, in exactly the style of the period, particularly one bobbed-haired, short-skirted fairy who was offering a bouquet to Elsie in one of the 1920 snapshots. It is true that Kirk and later authorities say that the fairies commonly wear the costume of their own time and country; but as one looks at these photographs every feeling revolts against believing them to be genuine.

A further factor is the type of people who brought forward the case. E. L. Gardner, Geoffrey Hodson and Arthur Conan Doyle might all be described as cranks. Even Mrs. Wright herself was interested in theosophy. Of course, if one automatically sets down any believer in certain tenets as a crank it is difficult to know how he can prove his case. Against the possibility of wishful thinking on the part of those bringing forward the matter one must set the testimony of three separate photographic experts.

It seems as if the matter must wait for further evidence of the effect of mind upon mechanical devices.

A LIST OF BOOKS CITED AND
CONSULTED

I. POETRY AND DRAMA

ALLINGHAM, WILLIAM, *Rhymes for the Young Folk*. Cassell & Co., n.d.
— *Fairyland: A Series of Pictures from the Elf-World* by Richard Doyle with a Poem by William Allingham (London, 1870).
BARRIE, J. M., *The Plays* (Hodder and Stoughton, 1928).
BLAKE, WILLIAM, *Poetry and Prose*, ed. Geoffrey Keynes (Nonesuch Press, 1946).
CAMPION, THOMAS, *Works*, ed. A. H. Bullen (Chiswick Press, 1889).
COLLINS, WILLIAM, *The Poems of William Collins*, ed. Edmund Blunden (London, 1929).
DARLEY, GEORGE, *Sylvia; or The May Queen* (London, 1827).
DE LA MARE, WALTER, *Come Hither: A Collection of Rhymes and Poems for the Young of all ages* (Constable, 1923).
— *Crossings: A Fairy Play* (Collins, 1924).
— *Peacock Pie* (Constable, n.d., *c.* 1916).
DOUGHTY, C. M., *The Cliffs* (Duckworth, 1909).
DRAYTON, MICHAEL, *Works*, ed. J. W. Hebel, 5 vols. (Shakespeare Head, 1931).
Early English Lyrics, E. K. Chambers and F. Sidgwick (London, 1907).
HERRICK, ROBERT, *Poems*, ed. R. W. Moorman (Oxford University Press, 1925).
HEYWOOD, THOMAS, *The Hierarchie of the Blessed Angels* (1635).
HOGG, JAMES, *Selected Poems* (Oliver & Boyd, 1940).
HOOD, THOMAS, *The Works, edited by his Son and Daughter*, 10 vols. (1871).

241

The Jovial Crew, A Comic Opera (1731). (Adapted from *A Joviall Crew or The Merry Beggars*, by R. Rowe. Acted 1641.)

KEATS, JOHN, *The Poetical Works*, ed. R. Buxton Forman (Oxford University Press, 1910).

LEWIS, C. S., *Poems*, ed. Walter Hooper (Geoffrey Bles, 1964).

LEWIS, M. G. 'Alonso the Brave', from *The Monk*, 3 vols. (London, 1796).

Lyra Celtica, ed. E. A. Sharp and J. Mathay (John Grant, 1932).

MACLEOD, FIONA (William Sharp), *Poems and Dramas* (Heinemann, 1910).

MEW, CHARLOTTE (b. 1869, d. 1928), *Collected Poems* (Gerald Duckworth, 1953).

MILTON, JOHN, *Poems in English with Illustrations by William Blake*, ed. G. Keynes (Nonesuch Press, 1926).

MONTGOMERIE, ALEXANDER, *Poems, Supplementary Volume* (Scottish Text Society, Edinburgh, 1910).

NICHOLSON WILLIAM, *Poetical Works* (Castle Douglas, 1781).

POPE, ALEXANDER, *Poems*, edited by John Butt (Methuen, 1963).

The Romance of King Orfeo. In *Fairy Tales, Legends and Romances Illustrating Shakespeare*. W. C. Hazlitt (1875).

ROSSETTI, CHRISTINA, *The Poetical Works*, ed. W. M. Rossetti (Macmillan, 1904).

ROWLAND, S., *The Knave of Spades*, Hunterian Club No. 22. (1874).

SCOTT, WALTER, *The Poetical Works* (Author's Edition, Edinburgh, n.d.).

SHELLEY, P. B., *The Complete Works*, ed. R. I. (The Julian Edition, 1927).

TENNYSON, *The Works of Alfred Lord Tennyson* (London, 1892).

Thomas and the Fairy Queen. In *Fairy Tales, Legends and Romances Illustrating Shakespeare*, W. C. Hazlitt (1875).

TICKELL, THOMAS, *Kensington Gardens*. *The Works of the English Poets*, ed. Samuel Johnson, 1779, Vol. 26.

WALPOLE, HORACE, *Horace Walpole's Fugitive Verses*, ed. W. S. Lewis (Oxford, 1930).

WARNER, WILLIAM, *Albion's England, A Continuance* (London, 1606)

YEATS, W. B., *Collected Poems* (Macmillan, London, 1950).

II. FICTION AND CHILDREN'S BOOKS

ANDERSEN, HANS CHRISTIAN, *Fairy Tales*, ed. Svend Larsen, trans. R. P. Keigwin, 4 vols. (Edmund Ward, 1958).

ANSTEY, F., *The Good Little Girl*. In *Modern Fairy Tales*, ed. R. Lancelyn Green (Dent's Children's Illustrated Classics, 1955).

ARMFIELD, CONSTANCE, *Sylvia's Travels* (London, 1911).

B.B., *The Little Grey Men* (Eyre and Spottiswoode, 1942).

BALDWIN, MRS. ALFRED, *The Pedlar's Pack* (Chambers, Edinburgh, n.d.).

BARRIE, J. M., *Peter and Wendy* (London, 1911).

BENSON, STELLA, *Living Alone* (London, 1919).

BROOME, DORA, *Fairy Tales from the Isle of Man* (Puffin Books, 1951).

BROWNE, FRANCES, *Granny's Wonderful Chair* (First edition 1857) (Dent's Children's Illustrated Classics no. 55).

Le Cabinet des Fées, 41 vols. (Published in Amsterdam and Geneva, 1785 and 1789).

CARROLL, LEWIS, *Silvie and Bruno* (London, 1889).

— *Silvie and Bruno Concluded* (London, 1893).

CHISHOLM, LOUEY, *The Enchanted Land* (London, 1906).

CRUIKSHANK, GEORGE, *George Cruikshank's Fairy Library, Hop o' my Thumb, Cinderella, Jack and the Beanstalk* (n.d., circa 1853).

DANE, CLEMENCE, *The Moon is Feminine* (1937; reprinted in Evergreen Books, 1941).

DAY, THOMAS, *The History of Sandford and Merton* (4th edition, corrected 1787).

DE LA MARE, WALTER, *Broomsticks* (Faber, 1925).

DICKENSON, M. C., *Borrobil* (1944).

EWING, J. H. *The Brownies and Other Tales* (London, 1871).

FARJEON, ELEANOR, *The Little Bookroom* (Oxford, 1955).

HEWLETT, MAURICE, *The Lore of Proserpine* (London, 1913).

HOLLYBAND, C., *The French Schoolmaister* (1573).

HOUSMAN, LAURENCE, *Moonshine and Clover* (Faber, 1922).

INGELOW, JEAN, *Mopsa the Fairy* (First edition, 1869) (Dent's Children's Illustrated Classics no. 62).

JACOBS, J., *English Fairy Tales* (Nutt, 1890).

— *More English Fairy Tales* (1894).

KIPLING, RUDYARD, *Puck of Pook's Hill* (Illustrated by Arthur Rackham) (New York, 1906).

LEWIS, C. S., *The Lion, the Witch and the Wardrobe, Prince Caspian, The Voyage of the Dawn-Treader*, and four more books about *Narnia* (Geoffrey Bles. 1950–56).

MACDONALD, GEORGE, *Dealings with the Fairies* (London, 1867).

— *The Lost Princess, or The Wise Woman* (London, 1895).

— *Phantastes* (First published 1858). Reprinted in the Everyman Library.

— *The Princess and the Goblin* (First published 1872).

MILNE, A. A., *Once on a Time* (Hodder and Stoughton, circa 1916).

MONTGOMERIE, N. and W., *The Well at the World's End* (Hogarth Press, 1956).

Mother Goose's Nursery Rhymes and Fairy Tales (Routledge, n.d., *circa* 1880).

NESBIT, E., *Nine Unlikely Tales for Children* (London, 1901).

NORTON, MARY, *The Borrowers* (Dent, 1952).

PAIN, BARRY, *The One Before* (London, 1902).

PARRY, E. A., *Katawampus and The Second Book of Krab* (London, 1927).

SINCLAIR, CATHERINE, *Holiday House* (Edinburgh, 1831).

STEPHENS, JAMES, *In the Land of Youth* (Macmillan, 1924).

— *Irish Fairy Tales* (London, 1920).

THACKERAY, WILLIAM MAKEPEACE, *The Rose and the Ring; or the History of Prince Giglio and Prince Bulbo* (1855). *The Oxford Thackeray*, ed. George Saintsbury, Vol. X.

THIRKELL, A., *Wild Strawberries* (First published, 1934). Penguin Edition.

TOLKIEN, J. R., *The Hobbit* (Allen and Unwin, 1937).

— *The Lord of the Rings*, A Trilogy (Allen and Unwin, 1954–55).

WARNER, SYLVIA TOWNSEND, *Lolly Willowes* (London, 1926).

WHITE, T. H., *Mistress Masham's Repose* (Cape, 1947).

WILLIAMS-ELLIS, A., *Fairies and Enchanters* (Nelson).

YONGE, C. M., *The History of Sir Thomas Thumb* (London, 1855).

III. SOURCES AND AUTHORITIES

AARNE–THOMPSON, *The Types of the Folktale*. A Classification and Bibliography by Antti Aarne, translated and enlarged by Stith Thompson (Helsinki, 1961).

ADDY, S. O., *Household Tales with Other Traditional Remains* (Nutt, 1895).

ADLARD, JOHN, *Mr. Blake's Fairies*. Bulletin of the Modern Language Society, 2LXV (Helsinki, 1964).

ALLIES, JABEZ, *Ignis Fatuus, or Will o' the Wisp and the Fairies* (Worcester, 1846).

— *On the Ancient British, Roman and Saxon Antiquities and Folk-Lore of Worcestershire* (1840).

ANDREWS, E, *Ulster Folk-Lore* (1913).

ATKINSON, J. C., *Forty Years in a Moorland Parish* (1891).

AUBREY, JOHN, *Miscellanies* (London, 1890).

BALFOUR, M. C., *Legends of the Cars*. Folk-Lore II (1891).

— *County Folk-Lore IV: Northumberland*. (F.L.S., 1904).

BAROJA, JULIO CARO, *The World of Witches*, translated by Nigel Glendinning (Weidenfeld and Nicholson, 1954). (Published in Madrid, 1961.)

BARING GOULD, S., *The Vicar of Morwenstowe* (1876).

— *Lives of the Saints*, 16 vols. (Edinburgh, 1914).

BELL, S. H., *Erin's Orange Lily* (Belfast, 1956).

BENWELL, B. (See Waugh).

BERNERS, *The Boke of Duke Huon of Bordeaux, done into English by Sir John Bourchier, Lord Berners* (1601, first published 1548) (Early English Text Society, 1893–7).

BILLSON, CHARLES, *County Folk-Lore I: Leicestershire & Rutland* (F.L.S., 1895).

BLACK, G. F., *County Folk-Lore III: Orkney & Shetland Islands* (F.L.S., 1903).

BLAKEBOROUGH, R., *Wit, Character, Folklore and Customs of the North Riding of Yorkshire* (1898).

BONSER, W., *A Bibliography of Folklore* (F.L.S., 1961).

BOTTRELL, W., *Traditions and Hearthside Stories of West Cornwall*, Third Series (Penzance, 1870–80).

BOVET, RICHARD, *Pandaemonium, or the Devil's Cloyster* (1684).

BOWKER, JAMES, *Goblin Tales of Lancashire* (London, 1883).

BRANSTON, BRIAN, *The Lost Gods of England* (Thames and Hudson, 1957).

BRAY, A. E., *Traditions, Legends, Superstitions and Sketches of Devonshire on the Borders of the Tamar and the Tavy*, 2 vols. (London, 1838).

BRIGGS, K. M., *The Anatomy of Puck* (Routledge and Kegan Paul, 1959).

— *Pale Hecate's Team* (Routledge and Kegan Paul, 1962).

BRIGGS, K. M. and TONGUE, R. L., *The Folktales of England. Folktales of the World*, General Editor R. M. Dorson (1965).

BROWN, THEO, *The Black Dog*, Folklore, Vol. 69. (September, 1958).

BUCHAN, PETER, *Ancient Scottish Tales: an Unpublished Collection made by Peter Buchan* (Peterhead, 1908).

BURNE, C. and JACKSON, G., *Shropshire Folk-Lore* (1883).

CAMPBELL, ARCHIBALD, *Waifs and Strays of Celtic Tradition from Argyllshire*, Vol. I (Nutt, 1889).

CAMPBELL, J. F., *Popular Tales of the Western Highlands Orally Collected*, 4 vols. (1890).

CAMPBELL, J. G., *Clan Traditions and Popular Tales of the Highlands and Islands*. Waifs and Strays of Celtic Tradition, Vol V (1895).

— *The Fians*, Waifs and Strays of Popular Tradition, Vol. IV (1891).

CARMICHAEL, ALEXANDER, *Carmina Gadelica*, 4 vols. (1928–41).

CHAMBERS, R., *Popular Rhymes of Scotland* (Edinburgh, 1870).

CHESTERTON, G. K., *Autobiography* (Hutchinson, 1937).

CHILD, F. J., *The English and Scottish Popular Ballads,* 5 vols. (New York, 1957).

CLODD, EDWARD, *Tom Tit Tot* (London, 1898).

CONAN DOYLE, ARTHUR, *Photographs of Fairies, Strand Magazine,* Christmas Number (1920).

COOTE, H. C., *The Neo-Latin Fay,* Folk-Lore Vol. II (1879).

COPE, JOAN PENELOPE, *Bramshill* (Constable, 1938).

COUCH, QUILLER, *The History of Polperro* (Penzance, 1871).

COURTNEY, MARGARET, *Cornish Feasts and Folklore* (1890).

CROKER, T. CROFTON, *Fairy Legends and Traditions of the South of Ireland,* 3 vols. (London, 1826).

— *Legends of the Lakes,* 2 vols. (1829).

CROMEK, R. H., *Remains of Galloway and Nithsdale Song* (1812).

CROSSING, WILLIAM, *Tales of Dartmoor Pixies* (1890).

CUNNINGHAM, ALLAN, *Traditional Tales of the English and Scottish Peasantry* (1874).

CURTIN, JEREMIAH, *Irish Folk-Tales,* collected 1835–1906, ed. Seamus Ó Duilearga (Talbot Press, Dublin, 1960).

— *Myths and Folk-Lore of Ireland* (1890).

DASENT, G. W., *A Collection of Popular Tales from the Norse and North German* (First edition, 1859) (Norroena Society, 1906).

DAVIDSON, H. R. ELLIS, *Weland the Smith, Folklore,* Vol. 69 (September, 1958).

DELARUE, PAUL, *The Borzoi Book of French Folk Tales* (Koopf, New York, 1956).

DE LOYER, P., *A Treatise of Specters or Staunge Sights, Visions and Apparitions appearing sensibly unto Men* (1605).

Denham Tracts, 2 vols. (Folk-Lore Society, 1892).

DEWALD, E. T., *The Illustrations of the Utrecht Psalter* (Princeton University Press, Oxford University Press, 1933).

DICKENS, CHARLES, *Frauds on the Fairies,* in *Household Words,* Vol. III. No. 184, October 1st, pp. 97–100.

DOUGLAS, GEORGE, *Scottish Fairy and Other Folk Tales* (Scott Publishing Co., n.d.).

DOUGLAS, MONA, *Islanders* (Brown & Sons, Douglas, n.d.).

EVANS, A. J., *The Rollright Stones and their Folk-Lore, Folklore,* Vol. VI (1895). (See also Folk-Lore Record II, 1879, p. 176, *The Rollright Stones.*)

FROST, W. H., *Fairies and Folk of Ireland* (New York, 1900).

GARDNER, E. L., *Fairies: The Cottingley Photographs and their Sequel* (Theosophical Publishing Company, 1945; republished 1951).

Gervasius Tilburiensis (F. Liebrecht, Hanover, 1856).

GILL, W. W., *A Manx Scrapbook* (Arrowsmith, 1932).
— *A Second Manx Scrapbook* (Arrowsmith, 1932).
— *A Third Manx Scrapbook* (Arrowsmith, 1963).
GIRALDUS CAMBRENSIS, *The Historical Works*, ed. Thomas Wright (Bohn, 1863).
GOMME, ALICE, *A Dictionary of British Folk-Lore. Part I. Traditional Games*, 2 vols. (Nutt, 1898).
GOMME, G. L., *English Traditions and Foreign Customs* (Gentleman's Magazine Library).
GREGORY AUGUSTA, *Gods and Fighting Men* (Murray, 1910).
GRIMM BROTHERS, *Grimm's Fairy Tales* (Routledge, London, 1948).
GRIMM, J., *Teutonic Mythology*, trans. J. S. Stallybrass, 4 vols. (London, 1883).
GRIMM, *Brüder Grimm Gedenken*, ed. A. M. Greverus (Marburg, 1963).
GUTCH and PEACOCK, *County Folk-Lore V. Lincolnshire* (F.L.S., 1908).
GUTCH, E., *County Folk-Lore II. North Riding of Yorkshire* (F.L.S., 1901).
HALLIWELL-PHILLIPPS, J. O., *Nursery Rhymes and Nursery Tales* (Warne, n.d.).
HARLAND, J., and WILKINSON, T. T., *Lancashire Folk Lore* (London, 1882).
HARRISON, W., *Mona Miscellany* (Douglas, 1869).
HARTLAND, E. S., *English Fairy and Folk Tales* (Scott Publishing Library, n.d.).
— *County Folk-Lore I. Gloucestershire.* (F.L.S., 1895).
HAZLITT, W. C., *Fairy Tales, Legends and Romances Illustrating Shakespeare* (London, 1875).
HENDERSON, GEORGE, *Popular Rhymes of Berwickshire* (1856).
HENDERSON, GEORGE, *Survivals in Belief among the Celts* (MacLehose, 1911).
HENDERSON, WILLIAM, *Notes on the Folk-Lore of the Northern Counties of England and the Borders* (F.L.S., 1879).
HIROKO IKEDA, *The Introduction of Foreign Influence on Japanese Children's Literature through Grimm's Household Tales.* In *Brüder Grimm Gedenken* (1963).
HODSON, GEOFFREY, *Fairies at Work and Play* (Theosophical Publishing House, 1925).
HOLE, C., *English Folk Heroes* (Batsford, 1948).
HOPKINS, G. M., *Note-Books and Papers*, ed. H. House (1937).
HUNT, ROBERT, *Popular Romances of the West of England* (First edition, 1881) (Chatto and Windus, 1930).

HYDE, DOUGLAS, *Legends, Tales and Stories of Ireland* (Dublin, 1887).
— *Beside the Fire* (Nutt, 1890).

JERVISE, ANDREW, *The Land of the Lindsays*, re-edited by James Gammock (1882).

KEIGHTLEY, THOMAS, *Fairy Mythology* (First published 1850) (Bohn, 1900).

KENNEDY, PATRICK, *Legendary Fictions of the Irish Celts* (London, 1866).

KIRK, ROBERT, *The Secret Commonwealth of Elves, Fauns and Fairies* (1691) (Stirling, 1933). This edition is not a good one, but a definitive edition is shortly forthcoming, edited by Stewart F. Sanderson, which will be based on the original manuscript and contain full notes.

KITTREDGE, G. L., *Friar's Lantern*. Publications of the Modern Language Association of America, Vol. XV. pp. 415–41.

Lancelot of Denmark, trans. from the Middle Dutch by Dr. P. Geyl (The Hague, 1924).

LEATHER, E. M., *Folk-Lore of Herefordshire* (1913).

The Mabinogian, trans. from the *White Book of Rhydderch* and the *Red Book of Hergest* by Gwyn Jones and Thomas Jones (London, 1948).

MACDOUGALL and CALDER, *Folk Tales and Fairy Lore* (Edinburgh, 1910).

MACGREGOR, A. A., *The Peat-Fire Flame* (Ettrick Press, 1937).

MACKENZIE, DONALD, *Scottish Folk-Lore and Folk Life* (Blackie, 1935).

MACKENZIE, OSGOOD, *A Hundred Years in the Highlands* (Bles, 1956).

MACMANUS, D. A., *The Middle Kingdom* (Max Parrish, 1959).

MACNEILL, MARION, *The Silver Bough*, Vol. I (Maclellan, 1957).

MACPHERSON, J. M., *Primitive Beliefs in the North-East of Scotland* (London, 1929).

MS Sloane 1727, British Museum. A seventeenth century magical manuscript.

MAP, WALTER, *De Nugis Curialium*, trans. Tupper and Ogle (Chatto and Windus, 1924).

MARIE DE FRANCE, *Poésies de Marie de France*, ed. B. de Roquefort (Paris, 1820).

MASSINGHAM, H. J., *Fee, Fi, Fo, Fum: The Giants in England* (Kegan Paul, 1920).

MILLER, HUGH, *Old Red Sandstone* (1887).
— *Scenes and Legends of the North of Scotland* (Edinburgh, 1857).

MOORE, A. W., *Manx Folklore* (Douglas, 1899).

MOORE and MORRISON, *A Vocabulary of the Anglo-Manx Dialect* (Oxford, 1924).

MORRISON, SOPHIA, *Manx Fairy Tales* (1911).

MUIR, PERCY, *English Children's Books* (Batsford, 1954).

Old Cornwall, Vol. II (1931–36).

Ordericus Vitalis, Historiae Normanorum Scriptores (Paris, 1619).

PARKINSON, THOMAS, *Yorkshire Legends and Traditions*, 2 vols. (1888 and 1889).

PATON, LUCY ALLEN, *Sir Lancelot of the Lake* (Routledge, 1929).

PERRAULT, *Popular Tales*, ed. Andrew Lang (Oxford, 1888).

PITCAIRN, ROBERT, *Ancient Criminal Trials in Scotland*, 4 vols. (Edinburgh, 1833).

POURRAT, HENRI, *A Treasury of French Tales* (Allen & Unwin, 1953).

Ralph of Coggeshall, ed. Joseph Stevenson, Rolls Series 66.

RHYS, JOHN, *Celtic Folklore: Welsh and Manx*, 2 vols. (Oxford, 1901).

RITSON, JOSEPH, *Fairy Tales, now First Collected* (London, 1931).

ROBERTSON, R. MACDONALD, *Selected Highland Folktales* (Oliver and Boyd, 1961).

— *More Highland Folktales* (Oliver and Boyd, 1964).

Robin Goodfellow, His Pranks and Merry Jests. Reproduced in *Fairy Tales Illustrating Shakespeare* by W. Carew Hazlitt.

ROBY, JOHN, *Traditions of Lancashire*, 2 vols. (1829).

Round About our Coal Fire, Chap-book (1740). (Reprinted 1883.)

RUDKIN, ETHEL, *The Black Dog*. Folk-Lore, Vol. 49 (1938).

ST. JOHN, JUDITH, *The Osborne Collection of Children's Books* (Toronto, 1958).

SCHIFF, GERT, *Johan Heinrich Füssli, Ein Sommernachtstraum* (Stuttgart, 1961).

SCOT, REGINALD, *The Discoverie of Witchcraft* (1584).

SCOTT, WALTER, *Letters on Demonology and Witchcraft* (1830).

— *Minstrelsy of the Scottish Border* (First edition, 1801), ed. T. F. Henderson, 4 vols. (Edinburgh, 1932).

SIKES, WIRT, *British Goblins* (London, 1880).

SIMPKINS, J. E., *County Folk-Lore VII: Fife* (F.L.S., 1914).

SIMPSON, E. B., *Folk Lore in Lowland Scotland*. (Letchworth Press, 1908).

SINCLAIR, JOHN, *The Statistical Account of Scotland*, 21 vols. (Edinburgh, 1799).

The New Statistical Account of Scotland, 15 vols. (Edinburgh, 1845).

SMITH, C. C., *Fairies at Ilkely Wells*, Folk-Lore Record I (1878).

SPENCE, JOHN, *Shetland Folk-Lore* (Lerwick, 1899).

SPENCE, LEWIS, *British Fairy Origins* (London, 1946).

— *The Fairy Tradition in Britain* (London, 1948).

STEELE, RICHARD, *The Lucubrations of Isaac Bickerstaff Esq. The Tatler*, No. 95 (1709, November, 15th and 17th.)

STEWART, R. GRANT, *The Popular Superstitions of the Highlands* (1823).

O'SUILLEABHAIN, SEAN, *A Handbook of Irish Folklore* (Pennsylvania and London, 1963).

THOMPSON, STITH, *Motif-Index of Folk-Literature*, 6 vols. (Copenhagen, 1955).

THORPE, B., *Yuletide Stories* (Bell, 1884).

TONGUE, R. L., *Somerset Folklore: County Series VIII*, (F.L.S., 1965).

UDAL, J. S., *Dorsetshire Folklore* (Hertford, 1922).

WALDRON, GEORGE, *The History and Description of the Isle of Man* (London, 1744).

WAUGH, A. and BENWELL, B., *Sea Enchantress* (London, 1961).

WENTZ, EVANS, *The Fairy Faith in Celtic Countries* (Oxford University Press, 1911).

WESTON, J. L., *The Legend of Sir Lancelot du Lac* (Nutt, 1901).

WILDE, F. S., *Ancient Legends, Mystic Charms and Superstitions of Ireland*, 2 vols. (London, 1887).

WILLIAM OF NEWBURGH, *Guilielmi Neubrigensis Historia sive Chronica Rerum Anglicarum* (Oxon, 1719).

WILSON, WILLIAM, *Folk Lore and Genealogies of Uppermost Nithsdale* (Dumfries, 1904).

WRIGHT, E. M., *Rustic Speech and Folk-Lore* (Oxford University Press, 1913).

WOOD-MARTIN, W. G., *Traces of the Elder Faiths of Ireland*, 2 vols. (London, 1902).

YEATS, W. B., *The Celtic Twilight* (London, 1893).

— *Irish Fairy and Folk Tales* (Scott Publishing Library, n.d.).

INDEX

251